Bullying and Cyberbullying

Bullying and Cyberbullying

What Every Educator Needs to Know

———

ELIZABETH KANDEL ENGLANDER

Harvard Education Press
Cambridge, Massachusetts

Library of Congress Control Number 2013939175

Paperback ISBN 978-1-61250-599-2
Library Edition ISBN 978-1-61250-600-5

Published by Harvard Education Press,
an imprint of the Harvard Education Publishing Group

Harvard Education Press
8 Story Street
Cambridge, MA 02138

Cover Design: Ciano Design
Cover Photo: Julie Lavelle/Flickr Open/Getty Images
The typefaces used in this book are ITC Stone Serif, ITC Stone Sans, and Filosofia

Contents

The Bullying Enigma

Just hit him back, and he'll leave you alone.

Hit him back, and you'll be suspended for hitting.

We want kids to always report to us when bullying is happening.

But don't tattle.

Adults must always intervene in bullying cases.

Why can't kids learn to deal with any of these problems by themselves?

This may not be the first book about bullying that you've picked up. Perhaps you've dipped into many articles or books, but like many educators, you still feel frustrated with a problem that seems to stubbornly defy a tsunami of opinions, discussions, stories, and proposed solutions. Anyone working in schools knows very well how serious bullying can be; on the other hand, it's not uncommon to hear even mild slights characterized as bullying. We want to help children who are being targeted, but we also know that there's no way to *require* children to like each other. We know that children can be cruel online, but realistically, how can educators address problems that are happening off campus and in cyberspace?

Everyone seems to agree that bullying has always existed. That fact alone can make it hard to understand why this problem sometimes feels as though it's spinning out of control. It's always been here—yet now it's also different. We know that referring to everything and anything as bullying *isn't* correct; but it's hard to say what bullying *is*, exactly. A teacher told me once that he felt like he was trying to clutch Jell-O. The problem is real—and serious—but we're having trouble getting a grip on it.

My purpose in this book is to help educators sort through the thorny issues that complicate our efforts to understand bullying and cyberbullying, and to suggest practical and realistic ways to address these behaviors effectively. Despite the plethora of publications in this field—many of which offer valuable insights according to their different areas of emphasis—I've been struck by how unusual it is to find approaches that are both concrete and genuine but that also cover the entire spectrum of online and offline bullying behaviors. I don't think these social problems between children can be addressed without a solid understanding of child development, how children actually bully today, what goes on in schools, and how digital behaviors emerge during childhood and interrelate with (and sometimes determine) in-school socializing. Bullying is a complex puzzle because solving it needs *all* of these pieces. And that's exactly the perspective that I present in this book.

Let me introduce myself by saying I'm not a college professor, *or* a professional trainer in bullying prevention, *or* a researcher in bullying and cyberbullying, *or* a parent of three kids (two teens), *or* a teacher. I'm all of those things. And each role I play adds an important skill and dimension to the mix. First and foremost, I'm a professor of psychology at a state university in Massachusetts. At that university, I run a center (the Massachusetts Aggression Reduction Center, or MARC) where I (with my colleagues and students) conduct research into bullying and cyberbullying, including a statewide survey of more than twenty-one thousand children in grades 3 through 12, and an annual regional survey of college freshmen (in 2010–2011, we studied 617 freshman; during 2011–2012, we studied another 616; to date this year, we've studied 293 more).[1] We study some typical issues, such as how many kids report being bullied, and some unusual problems, such as kids who cyberbully themselves (yes, they do attack themselves), children who try to report bullying only to be told not to tattle, and the types of bullying that adults don't react to. I'll talk a lot more about the findings of this research program later in the book. (Appendix A gives methodological details about the research cited in this book. Appendix B provides more information about MARC.)

But it's important that I don't only conduct research. I also do a great deal of work in the field with teachers, children, parents, administrators, and community members. MARC delivers programs, trainings, and services to teachers, students, and parents in hundreds of schools each year (during the 2010–2011 school year, we visited about 250 schools). Along with other MARC faculty, I deliver, or supervise the delivery of, virtually every one of those services. I've written and tested two evidence-based curricula (a third is in progress), as well as the training materials for the college students we train to work with kids in dozens of schools every year. (You'd be amazed at what school-age kids will discuss with college students, whom they generally revere—it gives us wonderful insights.) I've also trained tens of thousands of teachers, administrators, and staff in hundreds of schools. Finally, I've spoken to and worked with parents' organizations in hundreds of communities. I think it's being heavily involved in *both* research and fieldwork that makes my perspective particularly useful. And because parents are such an important part of this mix, my additional perspective as a parent of three children makes my approach to the whole issue more realistic and grounded.

In addition to this combination of experiences, I'm something of a rare bird in that I'm interested in both child development and digital communications. I've been studying child development and aggression, and the difficulties that occur during childhood that result in violence or abuse, for more than twenty-five years. But my second area of interest—which, until about 2005, had absolutely nothing to do with my first—has always been the impact of technology on human beings and communications. These interests remained entirely separate until, a few years into the twenty-first century, digital communications began to consistently emerge as the newest and most insidious form of aggression on the planet (and a growing problem among children). Virtually overnight, my two areas of study merged.

Let me also introduce a few caveats. I'm not an attorney or a licensed therapist, and so won't be dispensing legal, clinical, or therapeutic advice in this book. Thank goodness.

THE AGENDA

The first thing I do, in chapter 1, is to summarize some of my research findings about patterns of behavior among bullies—in particular the emergence of "gateway behaviors" that are particularly difficult to monitor and assess at school. The chapter provides guidelines for assessing ambiguous behaviors and discusses why the dynamics of bullying become more fluid in the context of cyberspace.

Chapter 2 sorts through the wildly varying estimates of the prevalence of bullying. How common are these behaviors, really? Which children are most at risk? And what strategies can educators use to reduce risk and enhance resilience?

In chapter 3, we'll take a close look at the bullies themselves. In the past, bullies have tended to be children with low status and poor social skills, but today there is evidence that even popular children engage in bullying. The chapter discusses the impact of electronic devices on the development of children's social skills, and traces the plume of influence from electronic communications that colors so many social interactions between young people today.

In chapter 4, the focus shifts to cyberbullying and how online behaviors influence (and typically exacerbate) in-person conflicts. We'll talk about some of the distinctive—and confounding—features of cyberbullying, and why it creates such a powerful sense of anxiety and helplessness among victims. In this chapter, I also outline some of the challenges in addressing online behaviors with tech-savvy kids.

In chapter 5, I go over new research findings about some of the unique problems that digital communications have brought us: sexting, self-cyberbullying, and other risky online behaviors from elementary school through high school.

Last but definitely not least, in chapters 6 through 8 I employ all these points to develop practical ways to address these issues—an area that is no less fraught than looking at the incidence and causes of bullying. What do we actually do in the moment, when we see these problems? Chapter 6 discusses the "9-second response" and other formal and informal approaches educators can use to address various kinds of bullying behavior. Chapter 7 draws on student surveys to suggest ways educators can empower bystanders and other peers to encourage prosocial behaviors and a positive environment. Finally, chapter 8 uses survey findings from parents to decipher their perspectives on bullying and cyberbullying, and uses that data to suggest tips for working effectively with parents.

FRAMING THE ISSUES

Before we start, let's discuss a few key points that are often not well understood, but can really help clarify everything that follows.

- First, the chronic overuse of the term *bullying* produces a set of problems that actually impede our prevention efforts.
- Second, bullying is an abuse behavior and needs to be understood as such.

- Third, bullying is not always so easy to recognize; teachers and administrators today sometimes struggle because they need better information about what to look for.
- Fourth, bullying in school is not separate from what happens on the Internet; we may tend to think of bullying and cyberbullying as distinct and unrelated events, but in actuality, they're neither.
- Fifth, bullying is also not a problem that adults alone should fix; children *do* need to learn how to address meanness, all on their own.
- Finally, when it comes to educating children about their own social lives, we may need to rethink how we convey these messages.

Overuse of the Word Bullying

Bullying is a term that's being, well, bullied. It's been rendered essentially powerless by being constantly kicked around. The term is often used to describe any type of nastiness, or, even more commonly, virtually any situation that involves a mean-spirited attack or hurt feelings. Accidents, fights, assaults, quarrels, malice, and differences of opinion are all mistakenly called "bullying" at times. The criterion for bullying isn't simply *anything that hurts another person*, although it's often confused for exactly that. Precisely defined, *bullying* is calculated, ongoing abuse that is aimed at a less powerful target.[2] Certainly, a single incident of cruelty between two children can develop into bullying or abuse by becoming repetitive. Problems that happen between children of relatively equal power can also change and develop into a situation where one child predominates. What we should not do, however, is be too quick to label every one-time incident, and every equal-power fight, as bullying.

Why focus on the overuse of the term? Calling every sniffle a "cold" has no real impact; however, calling every hurt "bullying" harms not only the targets and the bullies, but ultimately, all of the people and the entire psychological climate in a school.

Children can avoid responsibility

One of the ways that bullying can be distinguished from other conflicts is that it's largely a one-way street when it comes to responsibility. The first problem with the overuse of the term, then, is that by permitting children to blithely frame many interpersonal difficulties as bullying, we're encouraging (or at least allowing) them to abandon any consideration of personal responsibility in situations where they may bear some. A child who has been fighting or victimizing others, and knows that he or she will get some or all of the blame, may be strongly tempted to assume the role of a victim of bullying and thereby avoid the penalty.

Let me emphasize (for those preparing to send me nasty e-mails) that I am absolutely *not* saying that children who are targets of bullies should take responsibility for their own victimization.[3] What I am suggesting is that it's prudent to ask a few questions to help determine if a child is truly a victim of bullying before accepting that an abusive situation is happening. The desire to avoid responsibility for misbehaviors is completely normal, and trying to avoid punishment is one of the more understandable motivations for lying among children—who some experts estimate tell (on average) approximately one lie every ninety minutes by the age of six.[4] But adults, eager to be advocates for a child's well-being, may hear the word *bullying* and abandon any meaningful investigation. Their emotional response (often predicated on their own childhood experiences) kicks them immediately into protective overdrive, in which gear few or no questions are asked.

One could argue that children won't be motivated to call a situation bullying when it's not, because being a victim of bullying is a stigma. That may be true with peers, but when it comes to adults, using the term can actually be advantageous—it gets everyone's attention. Sometimes what they're really saying, as your blood pressure rises, is "I need you to sit up and take notice of what I'm telling you. This is important!"

If everyone's a victim, then no one's a victim
The second problem with overuse of the term is that by calling everything bullying, we greatly water down the very real and occasionally extreme distress that victims and targets of bullying experience. As a teacher, you've probably had your share of students and parents who pointedly identified even mild issues as bullying. But bullying isn't any old meanness that saunters down the sidewalk. Students who are subjected to bullying in school or online are not just living with perpetual fear; they feel unable to defend themselves, they endure wound after wound, yet they live in a world that doesn't defend them (or worse—doesn't even care to try). It's not just that the bully doesn't care—bullying can leave a victim with the sense that the world doesn't care.

It shouldn't be too much of a stretch, therefore, to realize that bullying can lead to learned helplessness, loss of motivation to try to learn, and loss of friends and support systems. For children who are vulnerable, the unremitting nature of this cruelty can contribute to depression and violence.[5]

Bullying appears, in some cases, to be a contributor to children committing suicide and homicide (particularly when children have other psychiatric risk factors).[6] Such extreme consequences don't occur in most cases; but predicting which few children will react more severely is difficult and tricky.

The more commonplace (and less visible) reactions that victims experience in response to bullying are still important, yet risk being ignored when the term is used in situations characterized by little or no impact. Even when there is no outward manifestation of harm, being deliberately isolated and laughed at cruelly *every single day* can be devastating socially and academically, because the target must both endure the present and constantly dread the future, hovering like Damocles' sword. It's this unrelenting cruelty and the callous nature of such an environment that is watered down when we include every social slight or quarrel under the bullying rubric.

Even worse, the weakening of the term can mean that children themselves take bullying much less seriously. Watering down the seriousness of bullying is exactly the opposite of what we want—but we contribute to that diminution when we allow the overuse of the word.

Bullying Is an Abuse Behavior

Probably the single most common confusion I see in the field is the mix-up between bullying and fighting. Fighting or quarreling is an equal-power conflict. Bullying is an abuse behavior that, like all abuse behaviors, occurs between a powerful aggressor and a target who lacks the power to fight back.[7] In fact, some researchers have argued that what we call "bullying" would be better described as "peer abuse."[8] Like all abuse victims, targets of bullying can behave in some very characteristic ways—for example, they may outwardly minimize bullying and refuse adult help, because their primary fear is retaliation. Few police officers today, if called to a domestic abuse situation, would accept a beaten wife's reassurance that she is "just fine" and simply turn around and leave. We understand that an abused wife fears retaliation and so minimizes her distress; we understand that she's not saying that it's just fine to be beaten. Targets of bullying who tell adults "we're just goofing around" or "I don't mind, we're friends" may likewise be trying to minimize their own victimization. When adults attempt to mediate situations characterized by an imbalance of power, bullies and abusers who are succeeding in their dominance over their victim also show characteristic behaviors. They have a strong incentive to feign cooperation during a mediation, but this doesn't always mean that once out of sight, they'll truly comply. Understanding that bullying is an abuse behavior can be key in interpreting these reactions correctly.

We Lack Information About Identification and Responses

Many, if not most, of us saw or experienced bullying as a child, and it's natural that as adults we should be on the lookout for the kind of overt, often physical bullying behaviors that we saw when young. But a glance at newer data shows us that bullying today, in the majority of cases, does not involve any physical contact.[9] My own studies, along with a number of others, show the overwhelming tendency to now use psychological methods, including those I call *gateway behaviors* (more on this in chapter 2). The sensationalized cases we see on the news that involve physical torment are now the exception, not the rule. This mistaken focus on physical bullying sometimes causes us to miss the forest for the trees. We need to know much more accurately what to look for, and what to respond to.

Related to the issue of what to look for is the profound impact of the digital revolution upon the lives of children today. This constant digital communication is juxtaposed with what is actually a pretty low level of knowledge (and sometimes, maturity). Children may easily learn which buttons to push, but they often fail to understand the *impact* of electronic communications—despite their myriad and apparently effortless use of electronic devices. The fact is that digital devices change *how* we communicate, not just how often we communicate. I'll talk about this in the second half of the book in much more detail. For now, I'll content myself with pointing out that children easily absorb cognitive patterns that help them effortlessly use new technology; yet at the same time, they are less conscious of what information is missing in digital communications, and how the thinness of that interaction can contribute to social problems that are manifested both online and in school.

I think it's safe to say that both the growth in nonphysical bullying techniques and the proliferation of electronic communications have had an enormous impact on children and their bullying behaviors. The bad news is that we are only now—after more than a decade of ravenous digital consumption—beginning to understand these issues. But there is also good news. The data is clear and consistent about the kind of behaviors we need to look for in school. In addition, the struggle that children appear to be having with technology is *not* a technological issue per se. What children need from us is help in understanding how to send and interpret accurate communications. Estimating the impact of what you write (or post) is a skill related to *life experience*—happily, it's not a technical skill.

Formal discipline cannot be the only response

You can't respond to bullying if you don't know what to look for. We all know how to respond to the more obvious, "old-fashioned" type of bullying: if we see children in a physical altercation, we pull them apart, investigate, and discipline accordingly. But what if the problem isn't so apparent? So far, the emphasis in bullying prevention has largely been on formal discipline. It's absolutely true that formal discipline plays a key role in responding to bullying.[10] But how effective is it in *preventing* it? And if bullying isn't obvious, what role can discipline play? What kind of impact can formal school discipline have on cyberbullying? What actions can parents and educators take if they are not invoking formal discipline? Simply put, formal discipline alone is *not enough of an answer.* We cannot depend on it to address every need. In addition to discipline, we need to know what should precede it to help prevent both bullying and cyberbullying.

Bullying and Cyberbullying—Neither Separate Nor Equal

Because of the obvious ways that cyberbullying is separate from bullying, it can be challenging to see how they impact each other. But while adults tend to regard bullying and cyberbullying as two different and unrelated types of bullying, I found that they both occur as early as elementary school—and that they frequently become inextricably bound together by the time kids are in high school.[11] To appreciate the interaction, though, it can be helpful to begin with the many ways that digital communication changes how we communicate and thus, in turn, changes the social interactions that ensue both online and offline. Kids don't see the school hallways and cyberspace as separate; for them, text messaging is just another way of talking, and the Internet is just another place where they see their friends. The profound impact that using technology has on cognitions and emotions is an area of knowledge that we're only just beginning to mine.

Teaching Children to Address These Issues on Their Own

Deciding when to react, and how not to overreact, to children's interactions—in person or online—can definitely be another challenge. On the one hand, it's clear that bullying and cyberbullying are behaviors we must address with children. On the other hand, it's an indisputable fact that occasional and mild mean behaviors are an inevitable part of life, and every child must learn to cope with such problems successfully. Actually, uncomfortable as it is, we *want* children to be exposed to mild meanness, because they must have practice in dealing with unpleasant people. We can always help children learn to cope with cruelty, but how can they do this if adults intervene in every incident, no matter how minor? If we accept that some things should be left to the kids to resolve, then what should trigger adult intervention? Every hurt feeling? Surely not. Seriously hurt feelings? Probably, but the nature of our intervention may depend on the circumstances. Repetitively hurt feelings? More likely. How can children learn to control these behaviors between themselves, if adults shoulder the entire responsibility for prevention? When mean behaviors are relatively mild, do we address the target, the aggressor, both, or neither? It's clear that adults have to correct antisocial behaviors, protect children from egregious harm, and help children cope emotionally when a peer is mean. But it can't just be about what we, the adults, need to do. We need to think about ways to empower kids to be coleaders in addressing bullying and cyberbullying—and part of that strength must come from being an active part of the solution.

Both the Message and the Messenger Matter

Information doesn't occur in a vacuum, of course. The context of the message and the messenger help determine the relative impact of a communication. When issues are viewed by children as being of concern only to adults, and not to peers, the "gag factor" may enter into play (i.e., it may be more socially advantageous for children to disparage the message rather than to agree with it). Choosing a messenger with high status (i.e., one whose message is socially advantageous to adopt) can definitely increase effectiveness. Put more plainly, a high-status peer can influence values about social interactions better than the vast majority of adults.[12]

Kids and the gag factor

Many bullying prevention programs are probably more effective than children give them credit for; even programs that middle schoolers contemptuously dismiss may be planting seeds that bloom at some later point. But it's still true that the most effective anti-bullying messages are those that genuinely reflect children's and teens' perspectives and experiences. That's the reason that programs led by kids, for kids, are among the most successful.[13] At the Massachusetts Aggression Reduction Center, we train graduate and undergraduate students to work with kids in grades K–12 under the assumption that a message they bring will be more genuine and more powerful than that from any older adult—even the "coolest." However it's done, though, it's important to try to get past students' sense that adults do not understand, and cannot speak to, their life experiences.

There's no area where this is more important than when discussing digital life with kids. A cringe-worthy example is a well-intended, adult-led discussion about misusing e-mail (which most kids don't use with peers) or expressing puzzlement about the appeal of social networking. You might as well wear a blinking neon sign that reads, *I Don't Get It.* Even when adults do "get it," having high-status peers deliver the message can endow it with more oomph.

Misleading slogans

Of course, ultimately the message matters as much (if not more) than the messenger. Most educators today have heard (and probably repeated) the mantra, "Tell an adult." I realize that this slogan is intended to be helpful, and sometimes it probably is; but I also see a number of significant problems with it. First, the word *tell* is a loaded word for children, with all of its implications of tattling. The slogan itself utterly fails to acknowledge the serious difficulty of violating one of the core tenets of childhood: *never snitch.* Another problem with this mantra is that it's been overused past the point of saturation. "If I hear 'tell an adult' one more time," an especially articulate seventh-grade boy once told me, "I'm going to throw up on the shoes of the self-righteous grown-up who says it."

Widely used slogans like this aren't just ineffective; if they simply didn't work, I wouldn't mind them so much. But their shorthand, catchall use can actually undermine more important prevention messages. Instead of asking children who witness bullying, "How can you help?" the "tell an adult" mantra, used in isolation, says to all bystanders, "Never mind helping. You can abdicate all responsibility here. Just pass the buck to the adults." The incredibly important role of other children may thus be actually *undermined* by the widespread adoption of such brief but catchy slogans. If we emphasize to students that adults are the answer, and that children themselves are not, and perhaps should not, be involved in addressing bullying, then we've essentially told children that we don't expect them to hold much responsibility in their own community.

Finally, a third (pretty major) problem is that, used in isolation, the "tell an adult" mantra implies that telling an adult is a strategy that will succeed. According to recent research, that isn't necessarily true (more on this in chapter 7).[14] It's painful to think, and to write, but I've seen too many cases of bullying to imagine that adults can always solve these problems for kids. I don't like feeling helpless. But honesty compels me to conclude that adults probably cannot always guarantee a resolution when children face such situations, and that makes me careful not to recommend *only* "telling an adult."

A similarly ubiquitous slogan is to "involve bystanders." But not all bullying episodes include bystanders. And when they do, are they the only peers who matter? What about the children who may not have actually witnessed bullying, but who knew about it, or who befriended (and thus empowered) a bully? What about the target's friends, or other friendly allies? The focus on *bystanders* doesn't always include them.

Of course, the idea that those who are physically present could actually stop or intervene in the bullying and report to adults is an appealing one. But although we tend to assume those strategies are helpful, recent hard data has made researchers question their actual success. This suggests to me that we may lack traction with this problem because we need to better understand the circumstances in which either intervening or reporting to adults actually helps with bullying situations. Although a great deal of the discussion about bullying prevention does emphasize just intervening or telling an adult, I think we need to understand more before we can truly and effectively empower those bystanders and peers.

WHAT CAN THIS BOOK DO FOR YOU?

This book is different because it needs to be. Let me begin by telling you what it *won't* do. It won't show you instant solutions, or one simple step that will always work. It won't turn you into an expert in social media. It can't make all adults—or all children— behave themselves. What this book *will* do, however, is be *directly useful*—offering perspectives that are concrete, grounded in research, up to date, practical, and realistic.[15]

One of the paradoxes I've discovered in working with educators is that our own childhood experiences with social cruelty can cause us to misdirect our responses to the bullying we see between students. Painful memories of being bullied may spur adults to seek simple, immediate solutions—but such a complex problem defies simplicity and takes time to solve. While I'm not going to review each and every potential theory, overall, the book should give the reader a good grasp on the complexity of the issue. With so many different facets, laying the entire problem at the door of a single factor can be tempting, but such an approach isn't likely to result in an effective response.

The pain of bullying is real, and pain always impels us to seek a rapid response. But changing a school climate isn't typically a fast operation, and social factors may work against us. For example, one type of bully today is a student who is popular and socially powerful. This fact often leaves students with the (sometimes correct) impression that being cruel is one way to increase social status. Because of the ingrained nature of this belief among kids, and because living with abusiveness leads to the general expectation that abusiveness and aggression are normal life circumstances, truly changing a school's psychological and social climate is, by necessity, something of a journey. I don't have any magic tricks to reveal, but the knowledge and behaviors that educators need to make a real difference can be found here. Expecting rapid, easy transformation is rarely if ever in the cards.

Ultimately, we can and should still expect to teach children that general civility is a centrally important social behavior. We hear a lot about respect, but I would argue that respect can be viewed as a positive sense of another person's value, a feeling you have inside of you for someone else. I don't see how we can require children to *feel* certain things. I do know, though, that we can require them to *behave* respectfully; that is, to adopt certain social manners that facilitate peaceful interactions and arrest hurtful behaviors. Requiring children to behave civilly, even if they don't like someone, does not mean that we don't care how they feel. It means that we're teaching them to care how *other* people feel.

But to teach kids successfully, we need to know what to look for; how to respond to it in a way that prevents both bullying and cyberbullying; how and when to wield formal discipline; and how to encourage appropriate assertiveness and self-efficacy in children while at the same time promoting those positive emotional connections with adults and peers that are so protective.

During the last twenty-five years, I've studied children, their social lives, their abusiveness toward each other, and the intersection between their face-to-face contact and their digital interactions. In making these studies, both anecdotally and in research, I've begun to better understand how to help others understand the phenomena that we call bullying and cyberbullying. The goal of this book is to help *you* understand it too. Read on.

CHAPTER 1

The New Face of Bullying

Understanding "Gateway Behaviors"

Bullying can be a single incident (laws in New Jersey, New Hampshire, and Australia).

Bullying is not generally considered a random act or a single incident.[1]

IDENTIFYING BULLYING—SIMPLE ON PAPER, DIFFICULT IN REAL LIFE

You may already have run across one or another of the classic definitions of bullying, most of which refer to three characteristics that are generally agreed upon as present in bullying cases.[2] These three characteristics, in and of themselves, aren't so complex.

- *Power imbalance*: The child who is the bully wields greater power—usually as a result of high social status.[3]
- *Repeated occurrence*: Bullying happens repeatedly—it's not a one-time encounter, even a one-time cruel encounter.
- *Intentionality*: Bullying is not an accident or an incident misinterpreted as an act of cruelty. Bullying is a dysfunctional relationship between two children. These children may or may not "know" each other in the traditional sense, but they do interact repeatedly.

Power imbalance. Intentional. Repetitive. In theory, once you know these three characteristics, you should be able to identify bullying immediately. But there's a limit to the usefulness of this abstract approach. None of these elements are actually so clear and simple in the field, although all three are often presented as though they were. *Intention* is an internal process, not outwardly visible, and different children interpret the intentions of others differently. *Repetition* is easy if you see bullying repeatedly, but if you see it once, how do you know whether it's the first time or the hundred-and-first time? There are clues that can help reveal a *power imbalance*, if you know what to look for (more on that later). But it's also true that before even trying to judge intention, repetition, and power imbalance, you first have to recognize that a behavior could be bullying. It was easier to spot the overt physical manhandling that used to characterize bullying; today, students are safer physically, but recognizing the new behaviors is more challenging.

IT'S NOT THE BULLYING OF TWENTY YEARS AGO, PART I: GATEWAY BEHAVIORS

In decades past, kids who bullied tended to be physically large, relatively weak academically, and not particularly admired by other kids in school.[4] Bullying frequently involved overt physical altercations during child-only interactions that happened away from the purview of adults. But the world has changed, and while today's adults may have grown up in a world where most bullying involved a blatant, physical behavior, their children live in an environment where they are more closely supervised, and where unconcealed physical threats or attacks are much less likely to be tolerated. Bullying today has evolved predominantly into forms of psychological, social cruelty, which as an attack method has the advantage of requiring neither a large physique, personal physical risk, nor child-only privacy away from adults.

The difficulty is that many adults still look for the physical bullying of yesteryear and subsequently miss what's happening right in front of them—dismissing it, despite the best of intentions, as something much less serious. When the overt behavior lacks drama, it's understandable to assume it has little impact. Adults may fail to realize that contemporary bullies tend to perfect understated methods for demonstrating dominance and contempt for their target *without* drawing obvious attention from adults by breaking concrete rules. Old-fashioned bullying is risky today. Threatening someone with a fist will almost certainly bring detection and punishment, and the reduced time spent away from adult supervision means fewer opportunities to jostle others. However, bullies can still reliably put targets in their place in full view of peers and adults by using such subtle behaviors as whispering about them right in front of them, snickering as they walk by, or rolling their eyes when they voice an opinion in class. These rude, socially malicious behaviors are definitely *not* always indicators of bullying (only when they're intentionally and repetitively targeted at a less powerful peer), but regardless of their purpose, they can be done anywhere. In my study of twenty-seven thousand schoolchildren in grades 3 through 12, the classroom tied for *first place* with hallways for the location where bullying was reported as most likely to happen by high schoolers and middle schoolers. (Yes, you read that right!) Davis and Nixon's subjects also reported that the classroom was a frequent location for bullying.[5] The more that gateway behaviors move into the mainstream rooms and hallways of schools, the more normal they feel to the children and adults who occupy those spaces.

Today's increased supervision of children, despite being well intentioned and probably keeping children safer in many ways, may have unwittingly contributed to the normalization of bullying behaviors by requiring bullies to adopt methods that can be used in more public areas. These changes also mean that adult advice on handling bullies may be not only outdated but actually counterproductive. A generation ago, it wasn't unusual to advise children to hit a bully, to demonstrate that one wasn't an easy target. Hitting a bully back may have been a viable option in 1975, but today, a target who hits back is liable to immediately land in hot water, and could then occupy the unenviable position of being in trouble with both the bully *and* the adults.

Rates of Gateway Behaviors Versus Physical Bullying

I call these psychologically contemptuous, rude behaviors *gateway behaviors*, since they're used as "beginning" or low-level, low-risk ways of asserting power or expressing contempt. Left unchecked, bullying behaviors can escalate, both in frequency and in quality.[6] The research findings agree with fieldwork observations—today, gateway behaviors are used substantially more often than other, more obvious types of bullying behaviors. In my 2011 study of college freshmen, subjects were much less likely to report being victimized by a physical bully than they were by a bully using gateway behaviors.[7] In fact, only 12 percent of victims reported being physically bullied; the rest (88 percent) were victimized through psychological weaponry. (Remember that this isn't a measure of all psychologically mean behaviors—for gateway behaviors to be counted as bullying, they had to meet the three criteria and also be rated as significantly upsetting.)

This data is consistent year to year. In 2012, only 6 percent of subjects reported being victims of physical bullying while in high school, but 34 percent reported being victims of distressing rumors or lies and 32 percent reported being victimized through pointed, public exclusion.[8] Other recent studies have found similar proportions of physical versus nonphysical bullying.[9] One study of changes in bullying over the past few years found that reductions in physical bullying far outpaced any reductions in psychological bullying.[10] The Youth Voice Project found that psychological bullying was much more common than physical bullying in a sample of thirteen thousand students.[11] More than a decade ago, Craig reported that physical bullying was more frequent on the playground, but psychological bullying was more common in the classroom.[12]

In my research, bullies themselves also reported using gateway behaviors most frequently, but only 19 percent reported that they were ever disciplined for these actions.[13] That's interesting, but not totally surprising. Given the low-key nature of gateway behaviors, it's easy to make mistakes when considering them as a form of potential bullying.

Taken individually, gateway behaviors seem common and innocuous; it's certainly true that having teachers fill out a three-page bullying report form every time a seventh-grade girl rolls her eyes would bring every middle school in America to a screeching halt. *Gateway behaviors in and of themselves don't constitute bullying.* Infrequent use of such behaviors in a nonsystematic way is just evidence of the periodic meanness between children that everyone has to learn to deal with. But it's the *continually repeated* and *targeted* use by powerful peers, with the intent to demean and harass, that truly creates bullying victims. Being targeted frequently and repeatedly was, in fact, the factor most strongly associated with being particularly vulnerable to bullying in the 2012 freshman study. Anecdotally, more than a few teens have told me that they'd rather just be hit. "At least that way you get it over with," one teenage boy pointed out to me, "but this just goes on and on. It never stops and no one notices it and you have to feel like c**p every single day."

All freshman subjects in the 2012 study were asked which type of bullying they felt was the most serious. It's interesting that subjects who had never been victims rated physical and psychological bullying as having a similar impact (or physical bullying as more serious); but subjects who had been targets rated psychological bullying as far more severe. Similarly, to the adult eye, gateway behaviors may appear mild and even insignificant, but they're clearly quite significant when continuously aimed at a much less socially powerful peer.

This evolution toward the use of gateway behaviors as preferred bullying tactics didn't come out of nowhere. As noted earlier, it's not just that adult expectations around supervision and aggression have changed; children are also raised notably differently today, with two particularly important changes. One is the reduction in child-directed playtime spent only among other children and away from the direct coaching of adults; the other, the obvious influence of digital communications. It's possible that the changes in the way that children are being raised have impacted their social skills, including their willingness to be socially cruel.[14]

How Do I Tell if It's Bullying?

As I pointed out above, it's vanishingly unlikely that every gateway behavior used in your school is a manifestation of bullying. Much of the time, these behaviors are used to be mean in passing or even just to tease. So, how do you know when you're seeing true bullying? I'll tip my hand by saying that, first, you don't always need to know if something is actually bullying; and second, there are no hard-and-fast rules that will allow everyone to reliably detect intention, repetition, and a power imbalance. My point is that it's easy to list *abstract* characteristics of bullying, but when we're looking at actual people, such a list is not terribly useful. You may see a cruel act without knowing if it's the first time it's happened or the hundredth, or whether the behavior is the result of carelessness or deliberate intent.

Candidly acknowledging the limitations inherent in the formal, abstract definition does not imply theoretical weaknesses; but it does reveal the need to operationalize the concept and make it much more useful in real life. As I'll discuss next, while it's difficult to judge an internal process like intention, there are clues that can help detect other characteristics, such as repetition and power imbalance.

Assessing power imbalance

As previously noted, it used to be that seeing a physically large child manhandling a smaller classmate was a pretty obvious indication of bullying. But because most children's power today is derived from social status (not physical size), what's important now is considering any known differences in social power (popularity and social status) between the children involved.[15]

In my research, subjects who reported that they were able to exploit bullying successfully for their own social gain rated themselves as significantly more popular than other children.[16] Thus the first possible red flag is the existence of social differences between the two students: either one student is much more popular than the other, or the alleged target may belong to a socially vulnerable group. Popular kids and groups vary from school to school, but there's more consistency when identifying vulnerable categories of kids. For example, special needs children who are mainstreamed are often very vulnerable, with low social power.[17] Among older children, it's common for students who identify (or who are identified, accurately or not) as gay, lesbian, bisexual, or transgender (LGBT) to be socially vulnerable and subjected disproportionately to bullying.[18] Consistent with other research, LGBT subjects in my 2012 freshman study were about 50 percent more likely to report being victims of bullying, compared with students who did not identify themselves as LGBT (although due to low numbers, that difference wasn't statistically significant).[19] In the same study, half (49 percent) of the subjects reported that the most common reason for bullying during high school was "when one bully targets someone because of *something about that person*" (e.g., how they looked, if they were gay, if they belonged to a clique, had a parent who drank, etc.). The second most common answer (at a much lower 17 percent) was that bullying usually happens because "someone was targeted when they were disliked."

Another red flag that reveals a possible power imbalance is the way a target responds to adult offers of help. Bullying targets, like other abuse victims, tend to respond in characteristic ways.[20] You might expect that a child who is being targeted by a bully would gratefully welcome adult offers to help with the situation. But children who are being bullied, similar to adults who are being abused, may simply fail to respond at all when approached by adults (even with offers of support); they may minimize a situation ("we were only goofing around") or even defend the bully by begging a teacher, "don't get [the bully] in trouble." Adults are often reassured (sometimes falsely) by these responses, and accept them as proof that bullying isn't occurring, instead of seeing them as a possible indicator that the target does not feel free to speak candidly, especially in front of a bully. Probably the most powerful tip-off here is when the adult has a strong sense that bullying is going on—perhaps he or she saw something actually happen, or knows that these two kids aren't really friends, and that one is much more socially powerful than the other—but both students deny there's a problem. A suspicious denial doesn't necessarily mean that there is a problem. Similarly, though, it doesn't always mean that there *isn't* a problem. In an unequal-power conflict, one student is much too fearful to blame the more powerful peer.

Power imbalances may sometimes reveal themselves, but intention is a purely internal process, and thus isn't likely to be apparent. When children are being mean, they use visible behaviors to hurt others (such as a cutting remark or snarky laughter). The difficulty is that they also use similar behaviors in much less insidious circumstances—when they're teasing, or being mean just once. It's thus often hard to tell when someone is bullying, because a bully may use the *same behaviors* as someone who's just teasing or being occasionally mean. The differences are internal (the student's intent to wage a repeated campaign). So when adults see cruelty, such as gateway behaviors, how can we assess intent, and thus know that it's bullying?

Assessing intention

Intention, because it's an internal process, is probably the most difficult element to judge from overt behavior. Even if there were some way to literally view an aggressor's intention, the perceptual differences between targets could result in one interpreting a behavior as intentional meanness, and another experiencing the identical behavior as benign. I vividly recall a little girl telling me that a boy in her tennis class was being deliberately mean. "How do you know he was trying to be mean?" I asked. "He was lobbing a ball at me when we played," she replied. She was interpreting lobbing as intentional spite. Other children might only see it as reflecting their opponent's lack of skill.

Consistent with these field observations, my research also noted that assessing intention in a strictly objective manner is probably impossible. In the lab, I found that different people attributed different intentions to the exact same behavior. In my 2012 freshman study, I showed subjects a picture of two girls laughing. Only 12 percent of nonvictims felt that the girls were probably bullying someone; but 22 percent of the victims in the study attributed the laughing to bullying. Of course, it's not only that students might attribute a mean intent to a neutral action; the other side of that coin is that some children fail to register cruelty even when it is intentionally directed at them. Either way, judging intention from external behavior seems, at best, an iffy business.

Assessing repetition

Perhaps you've decided that there are indeed red flags that merit further investigation into a situation, or maybe it's just your sixth sense that's tingling, and you want to explore a student's circumstances further. Perhaps parents, or others, have reported a situation to you and your job is to figure out if it is, indeed, bullying. The logical next step is to consider whether the situation has occurred only once, or is repeated.[21] As I've noted, most researchers studying bullying regard "true" bullying as an ongoing, abusive relationship between children.[22] This is a frequent source of confusion, especially for parents, who may label any hurtful behavior as bullying. While one-time actions aren't technically bullying, they can be a first step toward a new bullying campaign; and parents have a legitimate need for reassurance that any hurtful act should, and will, be taken seriously. For these reasons, author Stan Davis has argued that whether or not an incident is bullying shouldn't be a primary consideration in formulating a response, particularly an initial response.[23]

It's also important to distinguish, when possible, between problems that are ongoing but detected only for the first time, and problems that are genuinely one-time incidents. Just because an incident is the first time a child has *reported* bullying doesn't mean that it's the first time it has happened. The bottom line is, the child may know things that he hasn't disclosed to you, and he may be the only source likely or able to divulge that information. The only way to tap that vein is to develop enough of a connection with the student that he is likely to tell you the entire history. If you suspect that a child may be experiencing repeated episodes of cruelty, but you're not sure whether the child would divulge such information to you personally, the most responsible course of action is probably locating an adult who can be comfortably confided in. That person may or may not be you. (Don't misinterpret this as a criticism. The chemistry that unfolds between you and the children you teach is not entirely in your control.)

Dealing with Gateway Behaviors

Combining the predominance of gateway behaviors with our general inability to know internal characteristics of bullying (like intention) reveals the difficulty of knowing when you're seeing bullying. True, gateway behaviors are used to bully, but they're also used to tease, and to be mean just once; so how can an adult tell the difference? It's those covert factors (repetition, power imbalance, and intention) that differ between teasing and bullying situations—not the overt behaviors. If you see a student being denied a seat at a cafeteria table, you probably won't be able to tell whether it's the first time this has happened. Similarly, you may not know if the kids are simply mad at each other that day, or if an ongoing campaign is being waged. Sometimes there are clues about a power imbalance, and sometimes you may see repetition. But much of the time no such clues are in evidence. If you ask the child who was denied the seat, she's likely to say that it's OK with her, or not a big deal. Ask the kids at the table, and they're apt to deny the whole thing. Report the incident as "bullying," and you'll be asked for evidence of repetition, intention, and power imbalance—evidence you likely can't produce. The fact is, you simply saw a mean act; categorizing it on that basis alone is almost impossible.

Even though you may not be able to definitively label a situation as bullying, teasing, or just being mean, the good news is that you can still respond effectively. The solution is to focus on what you can see—the behaviors—instead of what you can't see—the internal motives and feelings. When the outward behaviors that you notice are breaking a school rule, you know what to do: follow the school's protocols (e.g., send them to the principal's office). So far, so good. Gateway behaviors are trickier precisely because they *don't* break school rules. In those cases, the student is obeying the letter of the law but is still behaving in a *socially inappropriate* way—and it's the inappropriateness of that behavior that calls for a brief but effective response. Consider: it's fine (even nice) for kids to laugh along with peers, but it's socially inappropriate to laugh pointedly *at* someone. My argument here is that because of the strong connection between social behaviors and social climates, socially cruel behaviors absolutely require a response, *regardless* of intent. Yet it's still true that exclusion and eye-rolls, by themselves, are small transgressions. So even if they're sometimes used to bully, why focus on them?

The best analogy I can think of is littering. If you saw a student toss a wad of paper on the ground, you wouldn't have an internal debate over whether or not the littering was intentional; you would just respond, presumably by telling the student to pick up the paper and throw it in a trash can. Gateway behaviors are the litter of the social climate. Regardless of intent or purpose, they shouldn't be happening, because they make the psychological landscape dirty and unpleasant. In chapter 6, I talk about exactly what you need to do when responding, and why educators need to respond even to behaviors that don't overtly break any rules.

One final point about the deceptively "minor" nature of gateway behaviors. While an action may look like "no big deal" to an outsider, from the perspective of a targeted child who knows that it is a bullying situation, any adult's lack of response can feel like a callous emotional betrayal. And the difference in perspective between students and educators isn't confined to physical encounters. What happens in a digital environment can, similarly, feel incredibly hurtful to children, while barely registering for many adults.

IT'S NOT THE BULLYING OF TWENTY YEARS AGO, PART II: CYBERBULLYING

Almost two-thirds (65 percent) of the subjects in the freshman study told us that during their time in high school, no adult even asked about the possibility of cyberbullying when discussing a bullying situation with them. The role that cyberbullying plays is easily misunderstood, especially to the generation whose most memorable interaction between electronics and real life was fighting over the remote control. Of course, many younger teachers today grew up taking the TV remote for granted, but they still typically lack the intensely cyber-immersed childhoods of today's students. For anybody over twenty-five (as of this writing), perceiving how much face-to-face behaviors can intersect with those perpetrated with a keyboard or touchscreen may not be intuitive. Adults often ask me to speak on bullying *or* cyberbullying, as though these were two completely separate and different events. Even though interacting in person obviously isn't the same as typing messages to someone or posting a comment on a website, one type of communication can affect the other. But the question isn't only whether bullying and cyberbullying are disconnected from each other. In addition, let's think about how digital environments change how we communicate, and how those digital communications feed, interact, and interplay with in-school encounters.

Gateway Behaviors in Digital Environments

Obviously there is no direct physical bullying online or through texting, but there can still be serious threats that contrast markedly with a general plethora of mildly nasty or thoughtless remarks. For example, a cyberbully could threaten to hurt the target or someone close to the target (a family member, or a friend) or get someone into serious trouble (e.g., reporting the target for a crime he or she didn't commit). Comparing serious and milder threats online in the freshman study shows the same pattern that's seen in face-to-face events: fully 82 percent of boys and 89 percent of girls reported that they had never received a *serious* threat online (either in middle or high school), and explicit online threats of physical violence were reported by only 6 percent of boys and 5 percent of girls. In contrast, relatively milder actions such as name calling, mean comments, or embarrassing photos posted online were reported by 24 percent of boys and 34 percent of girls. Like bullying in school, cyberbullying appears to be dominated by incidents that, taken individually, represent less extreme but still hurtful behaviors. And also like more traditional bullying, it may be the accumulation of individually small actions that cause some of the more serious harm.

How Do I Tell if It's Cyberbullying?

When you see a situation unfold in front of you, in school, there are clues that can help alert you to a power imbalance between two children. Furthermore, children's social status—and thus their social power—in school tends to be a relatively stable characteristic. This helps us detect and assess power imbalances in general. But in a digital environment, the power imbalance between actors is rarely stable, and thus is often challenging to pin down. What's not always simple in person is often even more complicated online.

One of the fascinating things about digital environments is how much online power is fluid and changeable. As I pointed out above, social power in school tends to be a stable quality; popular first-graders usually grow into popular fifth-graders and popular tenth-graders.[24] But in cyberspace, power differentials can shift quickly and dramatically.

One commonly cited digital power grab is when an online attacker remains anonymous. Anonymity is frequently cited as a preferred mechanism for gaining power over one's victim, and it's true that an anonymous cyberbully can cause a lot of distress. But it may actually be a relatively unusual way for bullies to gain power, at least during adolescence. In my study of twenty-seven thousand schoolchildren, I found that by high school, three-quarters (74 percent) of cyberbullying victims *knew* the identity of their cyberbully; anonymity may be theoretically desirable as a power mechanism from a bully's point of view, but in practice, it seems to be unusual between teens.[25]

The migration of bullying online introduces a reasonable probability that even if a situation at school seems to involve a stable power imbalance, the roles can change once the students go digital. Almost half of the subjects (46 percent) in 2011 reported that once bullying went digital, the incident shifted to a more equal-power fight.[26] Online, students were more apt to use tactics they might have felt too timid to use in person, such as seeking revenge, fighting back, getting their friends to help them, or simply "deciding that the bully didn't really have any power over me." Because that online change in power can, in turn, impact what's happening at school, adults need to be conscious of these situations, which means routinely inquiring whether a problem between students has migrated into cyberspace. The older your students are, the more likely their answer will be yes.

Is Cyberbullying Actually Bullying?

Before we continue, it's important to note that the harassment that occurs online may often not fit our traditional three criteria for bullying (repetition, intent, and power imbalance).[27] It's not only that power imbalances can shift unpredictably online; the difficulty is also that while the target may *experience* those three criteria, an alleged cyberbully may never have *intended* them. To illustrate what I'm talking about, imagine a more traditional—in-person—bullying scenario. A boy is bullying a target in a school hallway; he does this every day just before recess. The three elements of bullying can be identified here: the interaction is repeated; the bully knows and sees that there's an audience, which enables him to demonstrate his superior power; and clearly he's not being cruel by accident. His victim would be likely to completely agree with this assessment.

At times, digital behaviors closely resemble in-school bullying in that aggressor and target largely agree on intention and outcomes. Imagine, for example, a student who sets up a webpage committed to "The Group Who Hates Sally Smith." That aggressor clearly intends to be hurtful; the webpage is updated regularly with new content, so she intends the hurt to be repetitive, and because she invites others to become "members" of the group or webpage, she's clearly looking for the audience to admire her power. But many other times, what the so-called cyberbully actually intends is much less clear, and the target may experience the harassment completely differently. Suppose a student posts a maliciously funny image on Facebook about another student. In this case, the aggressor, who's trying to be funny, sends the image to two of his buddies. They think it's hilarious and forward it on to dozens of other students. You could certainly argue that the creator of the meme *should* have realized that his snarky picture could get sent to many others, but this action still probably wouldn't meet the criteria for bullying. The creator's intention wasn't to demonstrate his power or dominance, and although the picture was forwarded repetitively, he sent it out only once. He may not have even intended it to hurt the target, if he believed that the target would never know. However, the subject of that image might indeed experience what happened as bullying—the humiliating picture was sent and seen repeatedly and was certainly sent on purpose. The object of the "joke" is likely to feel markedly powerless as well, since once out on the Internet, that image is essentially uncontrollable.

The point here is that when we talk about assessing power, repetition, and intent in a digital environment, there are two perspectives—the alleged bully's, and the target's—and they may be very different. What counts more—the intention of the *bully*, or the subjective experience of the *victim*? As I've noted, sometimes this is hard to tease apart even in face-to-face incidents; the difference between these two perspectives can be magnified when the interactions are digital.

Because the intent to hurt or bully can be absent or not apparent in a digital environment, the essential lesson is that it's critically important for children to understand the dynamics of communication in that type of environment—and how easily casual digital actions can escalate out of their control. From our perspective as adults, and as part of our attempts to understand bullying and cyberbullying behaviors, it behooves us to realize that the intent and effect of behaviors we call cyberbullying may be out of sync between the alleged bully and the target. Cyberbullying may have an impact on the victim that's similar to bullying because it may be experienced similarly; but the cyberbully and the bully may be two very different animals. Assessing for cyberbullying, therefore, relies heavily on the subjective experience of the target—and we need to keep in mind that the *existence of a cyberbullying victim won't always imply the coexistence of an intentional cyberbully.*

WHAT COMPLICATES OUR ABILITY
TO ELIMINATE BULLYING

Having laid out the process for detecting and discussing bullying and cyberbullying, I need to offer a caveat. In spite of our desire to make everything right for children, the truth is that certain factors limit our power to address abusive behaviors between them. Children interact both with and without adults present; our grown-up perspectives and judgments aren't always spot on; and the hard fact is that children need to experience some small degree of meanness to learn to cope with it. The reality of these limitations means that it's important to understand where the lines are drawn, what we can and cannot promise, and how to be genuine about those limits when we talk to children.

The Child-Only World

To completely understand the dynamics of bullying, adults would need full knowledge of 100 percent of the behaviors that happen between children. That's clearly unrealistic. As we've seen, even in closely supervised environments, many behaviors occur that adults may not recognize as bullying. Children also interact with each other in a child-only world, where adults don't rule and are often unaware of what happens. That child-only world isn't a place, so much as a sort of alternative plane. Vivian Seltzer at the University of Pennsylvania has referred to it as the *peer arena*.[28] These child-only peer interactions are *influenced* by adult values and rules (children do carry their internalized beliefs with them between both worlds) but they are not entirely governed by them.

Children know that regardless of what happens in the adult world, they will still have to deal with interactions in the child-only world by themselves, without adult protection. We can supervise—to a point— when children are in the "adult" world. We can tell a child to stop bullying another child; we can watch and listen and supervise. But inevitably those children will at times interact without our supervision. They'll pass each in the hallways; they'll sit within view of each other in the same classroom; they'll interact on the playground, and on school grounds after school; they'll see each other as they walk home, or on the bus, or online. Even if the children are kept physically distant from each other, their friends and cohorts, and online interactions, may well form a link between the two players.

Bottom line: it's always possible that what appears, in our world, to be a one-time, unintentional event can actually be part of a pattern of intentional cruelty, the majority of which occurs in the child-only world where adult detection is unlikely. It's also theoretically possible to stop bullying where *we* live, while doing little more than slowing it down (if that) in the child-only world. It's true that children today spend less time there than did previous generations; one typical study found that mothers estimated they had more than twice as much unsupervised play time as their own children.[29] In 1969, 42 percent of American children walked or biked to school alone and unsupervised by adults; today, only 16 percent do.[30] Despite reductions, though, the child-only world is still there; every child knows it, and every adult should be sensitive to it.

The Issue of Perspective

Apart from child-only interactions, there's another complication in detecting bullying: the difference between child and adult perspectives. Adults may see a single incident of teasing as benign, not realizing it is part of an extremely hurtful pattern. Conversely, adults may perceive as "mean" behaviors that are regarded with indifference by their subjects. For example, about two years ago, I was analyzing some data on online bullying with students and noticed that the boys were reporting situations that appeared to be cyberbullying at the astounding rate of *98 percent*. Recognizing what was obviously some sort of mistake, I explored the issue with a group of male students. They readily acknowledged regularly encountering what appear to be quite callous and cruel comments during online game play. The interesting twist here was how they interpreted that type of chatter: instead of viewing it as bullying, they saw it as a type of game-related trash-talking, similar to the remarks often flung across basketball courts and in football lineups. Research I conducted on this in the following year, as well as studies done by other researchers, found that 75 percent of subjects reported that trash-talking definitely happens during online game play, but isn't a personal attack akin to bullying.[31] Rather, it's a game-playing strategy, and would happen to *anyone* the person was playing against.

This example brought home to me that there is sometimes a huge difference between what adults and kids perceive as bullying. However, the issue of perspective can be tricky. The circumstances may indeed not feel mean at all to the child, as in the gaming scenario. But a child who is a target may deny the problem for a variety of other reasons, which are not all simply a matter of perspective: they may fail to interpret the meanness correctly; at times targets (e.g., special needs children) fail to recognize that the behaviors aimed at them are actually abusive. Or they may downplay the seriousness of the situation and, like other abuse victims, may even side with the bully—not because the situation isn't serious, but because they greatly fear retaliation. These latter situations are clearly different from the gaming example. Sometimes "it's OK" means that it's truly all right; but at other times a reassurance might just reflect a lack of understanding or the possibility of retribution. The point is that if it appears alarming to you, a student's assurance that it's all fine doesn't completely rule out a problem.

This fact can render these situations very confusing. Generally speaking, the first priority in responding is to be sensitive to the tendency of targets to downplay bullying situations in their efforts to protect themselves. But at the same time, keep a corner of your mind open to the possibility— especially in gaming situations—that what appears awful to the adult eye might not be experienced as abusive by the students. The trick, it would seem, is to utilize your rapport with the student to separate *false* minimization because of fear of retaliation, from minimization because of true lack of impact, either from genuine indifference or from a failure to appreciate the situation. Look for hints and consider histories that will allow you to decide if a lack of impact is real or feigned. The absence of factors such as strong self-confidence, a myriad of other support systems, or even special needs that affect social skills may suggest that a false minimization is happening and intervention is called for.

Learning to Navigate Social Challenges

We may wish we could ensure safety 100 percent of the time, including in that child-only world, but it's a wish we would probably regret if it were granted. Difficult as it is to acknowledge, child-only interactions have value as well as risk for most children. In the adult world, children are essentially powerless; it's in that child-only world where they get to flex their muscles and practice coping with explicit power differentials. It's true that someone has to be on the losing end of that interaction, and completely understandably, no one wants to see a child suffer. But if children were to grow up with literally no experience of meanness (either in themselves or in other peers), they might never develop the social coping skills needed to successfully navigate around it. These more challenging social exchanges probably help many children develop better skills for coping with social encounters. It is even theoretically possible that children's extreme reluctance to report to adults what happens in child-only exchanges essentially compels them to learn advantageous social skills.

What's so emotionally painful is that not all children benefit from the same kinds of life lessons. For example, children who have been previously abused may learn, from an episode of peer abuse, not to cope effectively but rather just to assume their role as victim. For some children, a typical peer interaction isn't going to be the setting in which they learn how to cope. For many others, it will be.

UNDERSTANDING THE BEHAVIORS ISN'T ENOUGH: WE NEED TO UNDERSTAND THE PLAYERS

When you throw a baseball, you throw a round white ball, and the catcher receives a round white ball. Every ball is white and round; and every pitcher and every catcher deals with the same thing. But when it comes to social behaviors, the pitcher can throw one thing and the catcher can catch something entirely different. What a target experiences from a bully depends both on what's actually being thrown and how the catcher interprets it. One boy may construe a spoken "Hi!" as friendly; another may see it as mocking. One girl may laugh along if others laugh at her; other girls might glower or become upset at precisely the same behavior.

Everyone knows that different people interpret or experience social behaviors differently. So, as this chapter has shown, when it comes to understanding bullying and cyberbullying, the recipient's perspective matters a great deal. We may know what the ball looks like now (gateway behaviors; cyber behaviors), but how often are these behaviors used to bully, and how often do intentional slings and arrows really hit their mark? Some targets become victims, just as a bully has intended; others are much more resilient. In the next chapter the focus shifts from the ball itself (the actual behaviors) to the catcher. We need to look at not just what percentage of kids are bullied, but also at how many of those kids are resilient, and what makes them that way. Meanness will always be with us, to some degree. We can't construct a world where every child, no matter how vulnerable, is spared that. But we can try to construct children who are more resilient. In the real world, empowerment of targets is probably our most formidable defense.

CHAPTER 2

How Common Are Bullying and Cyberbullying, Anyway?

Parsing the Numbers to
Identify—and Help—Children at Risk

"The scope and effects of bullying are underestimated."[1]

"Bullying is more common than previously thought."[2]

"The level of playground bullying is being exaggerated."[3]

In 2006, an article in a medical journal discussed a concept known as "disease mongering."[4] The trouble emerges, the authors wrote, when a disease becomes widely covered in popular media, and competing estimates about its frequency can lead to an exaggerated sense of danger. Although they were writing about a different problem, bullying might be a victim of the same syndrome. Contributing to the possibility that some dangers may be underplayed while others are overestimated is the wide variety of estimates produced by different studies.

Examples of apparently contradictory findings include the following studies:

- In 2011, the StageOfLife.com website hosted a bullying survey; any interested teens could respond. An amazing 91 percent of teenagers responding reported that they had been bullied.[5]
- My own research in 2011 looked at rates across all four years of high school and found that 31 percent of subjects reported being victims of bullying, and 41 percent reported being victims of cyberbullying.[6]
- A survey by the National Crime Prevention Council that sampled 824 nationally representative thirteen- to seventeen-year-olds found that

43 percent of students reported being victims of cyberbullying in the last year.[7]

- A 2008 survey of more than twenty thousand teens in Massachusetts found that 32 percent reported being bullied and 5 percent reported being cyberbullied in the last year.[8]
- The 2009 National Crime Victimization Survey (a national survey conducted annually) found that 28 percent of students reported being a victim of bullying and 6 percent were cyberbullied in the last year.[9]
- An analysis of the 2009 Massachusetts Youth Health Survey (a survey conducted on several thousand students around the state using a random cluster technique) found that 23 percent of high school students reported being victims of bullying within the last year.[10]
- A 2010 study examining data from 2008 found that between 22 and 37 percent of subjects were bullied.[11] Most of this was emotional bullying.
- A review of three different surveys about Internet use found that 11 percent of subjects reported being the victim of "cyber harassment" during 2005.[12]
- In another sample of 4,441 students in 2010, 7.5 percent reported being victims of cyberbullying in the last thirty days and 21 percent were victims during their lifetime.[13]
- In a 2011 survey of three thousand Wisconsin children, 17 percent reported being victims of cyberbullying.[14]

It's definitely enough to make one's head spin, but let's put it through the juicer.

HOW OFTEN ARE KIDS ACTUALLY BULLIED IN PERSON?

Victimization rates for traditional bullying aren't really all that disparate. With the exception of the 91 percent, which should be discarded since the survey used a self-selected group of subjects, the percentages reported above range from 23 percent to 32 percent over one year and 31 percent for the four-year period. There is some variation here, but not really a great deal. I feel pretty confident in concluding that, for any given year, 25 to 30 percent of students are bullied in person. Not all of these incidents are serious, of course, but this type of statistic typically doesn't differentiate severity of the bullying.

Notably lacking are statistics on bullying at very early ages. In my own research of grade-school students, I didn't examine K–2 children largely because their lack of literacy skills means that interviews are the only reliable method for measurements, and such interviews require more resources than were available. I do, however, have data from a pool of 1,940 parents, measured during 2011.[15] In that survey, 6 percent of kindergarten parents, 7 percent of first-grade parents, and 19 percent of second-grade parents reported that they were aware their child was being, or had been, bullied at school or online (and as we'll see, cyberbullying can indeed start this early). Although I prefer to emphasize statistics that come directly from the subjects, in this case, parent reports may be a reasonable approximation of the truth. The youngest children are actually the most likely to report everything to their parents, so parents of very young children may have, relatively speaking, the most accurate knowledge about their child's victimization.[16]

HOW OFTEN ARE KIDS ACTUALLY CYBERBULLIED?

Recall that my definition of *cyberbullying* is characterized by a subjective perception of being cruelly targeted through electronic means, because although the target's experience may definitely feel abusive, the originating incident may lack the intention, repetition, and/or power imbalance that traditionally define in-person bullying. Unlike bullying rates, reported cyberbullying rates tend to vary wildly. The frequencies listed above fluctuate between 5 and 6 percent at the low end to 41 and 43 percent at the higher end. Some researchers asked students about cyberbullying that happened in the past year; others asked about the child's entire lifetime; my own research asked about the last four years (the duration of high school). Most studies focused on older children; I found lower rates among elementary-age kids, similar to other findings that include younger age groups. What's challenging is to organize all of these different numbers into a rational conclusion about whether or not we as adults need to be worried about this issue, or whether the problem of cyberbullying could be an invention of popular society or the media.

But I think there are good reasons for the different percentages, and once we grasp those reasons, the numbers begin to make sense. Sometimes researchers simply ask, "Were you cyberbullied?" That question probably results in the lowest rates, since some children may not identify online incidents as cyberbullying.[17] Other researchers list a few specific types of cyber behaviors, such as "texting cruel remarks" or "posting mean comments." The more types of cyber behaviors you list, the higher the percentage of subjects who endorse one or more of them. The studies finding 21 percent asked about posting mean comments, rumors, threats, posing as the target, and posting mean or hurtful pictures. My own research (which found 41 percent victimization rates, similar to the NCPC study) added to this list pressured or coerced sexting, posting false stories or lies, dissemination of personal data that the target didn't want revealed, and being stalked electronically. I think it stands to reason that the more types of cyberbullying a survey includes, the higher the likelihood that the subject will say "yes" to at least one of them. The tricky part is being aware of different types of cyberbullying, as children rarely discuss these with adults. Since our knowledge of cyberbullying is only developing, and the potential types of cyberbullying are changing constantly, it's particularly difficult to keep track of different ways that a subject might have been victimized. It is through MARC's exposure to children both in the field and through research that we have been able to pick up on so many different types, and thus to include them in our research.

Another obvious reason for such disparate findings, as I pointed out above, is that different researchers study different ages or different time periods. The most common time frame considered is a single year, but some study the preceding thirty days, while others may follow the entire span of high school. Not surprisingly, the longer time periods tend to reflect higher numbers. Also not surprisingly, the younger children in these studies all report lower numbers than do their adolescent peers.

Bottom line: studies that ask briefer and more general questions, that include younger children, and that study shorter periods of time are the most likely to have the lowest estimates of cyberbullying.

But It's Really Not Just One or the Other

Statistics such as these may reflect a prevailing tendency to view bullying and cyberbullying as separate; but other data (including some of mine) suggests that these behaviors tend to be fundamentally interactive and related. Especially for teens, bullying and cyberbullying often happen in tandem, and kids seem to view the digital world as just another place where they see their friends. If we compare the incidence of these two types of bullying in the same sample, the data shows that the older children become, the more bullying and cyberbullying interact. In my study, most elementary school bullying happened only in school; but reports of in-school-only incidents reduced steadily across the grades until, by high school, only 8 percent of teens reported them.[18] All other victims reported being bullied either online, or both online *and* in school. And the trend associating increased age with higher proportions of bullying online appears to continue into college; when I looked at the nature of bullying in college, I didn't find even one case that occurred only in person. Although the study of the interplay between in-person and online bullying may be relatively new, other researchers in the past have similarly noted that as children grow, their bullying utilizes increasingly more psychological attacks.[19] All cyberbullying is, of course, psychological in nature.

Most High School Bullying and Cyberbullying Happens in Ninth and Tenth Grades

Even if the records of bullying frequency were more consistent, the figures themselves wouldn't necessarily paint a very useful picture. In other words, rather than just knowing the one-size-fits-all number, it can be more interesting—and useful—to know how bullying *progresses and develops, waxes and wanes* as children travel through their school years. Isn't it likely that the social lives of ninth graders are very different from the social lives of twelfth graders? Suppose a student *is* being bullied or cyberbullied in ninth grade—is that bullying likely to persist, or is it more likely to dwindle by tenth grade? When working with a student who admitted to being bullied, I was interested in knowing how unusual that student's experience was (relative to his or her peers), and what that student could reasonably expect in the near future. So that's one of the issues I studied among students reporting on their high school years.[20]

In a nutshell, my study found that bullying and cyberbullying usually do not persist across all four years of high school.[21] In fact, only 4 percent of the subjects in my study reported being victimized across all four years. Therefore, a student who reports being bullied throughout high school is much more unusual, and may be struggling much more, than one who reports being targeted during one year only. Being targeted at some point during only one year was actually the most common type of victimization, and that year was most likely to be ninth grade. Among the students who are targeted in ninth grade, about half will be targeted only in that year; the other half will be targeted in both ninth and tenth grade. If they are targeted in tenth grade, it's very unlikely that it will continue into eleventh grade. As students progress through high school, it becomes less and less likely that any bullying victimization will be sustained.

What all this really suggests is that asking students if they've been targeted in the previous twelve months is likely to elicit a fairly wide spread of answers, depending on the respondent's grade. A more meaningful analysis of that type of data would include per-grade and across-grade breakdowns.

Let's sum up so far. Probably between a quarter and a third of children report being targeted by bullies in a given year. It's harder to know how common cyberbullying is; the more specific and numerous the data about cyberbullying, the more frequently events will be reported. It does appear clear that as children grow, digital bullying occupies an increasingly larger proportion of all bullying incidents. Among high schoolers, incidents of bullying and cyberbullying seem to occur predominantly in ninth grade, and for 50 percent of the targets, they continue into tenth grade. After that, incidents are reported much less frequently, and students who report ongoing bullying during high school may be at much greater risk.

DISTINGUISHING THE ACTION FROM THE IMPACT

When my oldest child was about three years old, he was diagnosed with a type of disability that affected his ability to pronounce some words. This persisted through childhood, and he was occasionally mocked for his mispronunciations, but at least some of the time he was (luckily) unaware of the teasing. Is bullying really bullying if the subject doesn't understand, or doesn't care, what's going on? In the vast majority of studies, statistics on bullying and cyberbullying never take into account the impact—or lack of it—on the target.

Taking impact into account can be useful for a few different reasons. First, it's interesting to compare children who correctly perceive and are *very* impacted by bullying with those who similarly perceive it but who aren't particularly troubled. Second, while we know that bullying increases the risk of a host of bad outcomes for the target (e.g., depression, academic trouble, social problems), we also know that it doesn't increase those risks equally for every target. Put simply, bullying impacts different children differently. It's not enough just to know how many kids bully or are bullied. We also need to know which bullies and which targets are at risk for escalating difficulties, and how some children develop resiliency in the face of cruelty. Ultimately, since we can't make the world a uniformly kind place, we want all children to be able to withstand at least some of the minor cruelties that life will inevitably throw their way.

Resiliency and Vulnerability

I think any educator who's considered it readily perceives that bullying doesn't impact all children equally. In psychology, we conceptualize these differences as *resiliency* and *vulnerability*.[22] In this context, I'm using the term *vulnerable* to refer to children who are more severely impacted by bullying. (*Note:* This is distinct from an alternative use that refers to character-istics that make certain individuals more likely to be bullied, such as having special needs, or a different sexual orientation.[23]) In contrast, Langevin de-scribes *resilient* children as those who are bullied, but do not internalize that bullying.[24] Bowes et al. define it as when children do better than we might expect, given their bullying victimization.[25] Why are more resilient children able to "shrug off" peers who try to abuse them, while others feel so devastated?

There are different ways of measuring and considering vulnerability or resiliency. One method is to compare *bully/victims* (students who are bullies at times and targets at other times) with those who are identified as only victims or only bullies. There's little doubt that bully/victims are vulnerable children. They are at significantly higher risk for anxiety and depression, and are also likely to be at higher risk for aggressive, homicidal, and sui-cidal behaviors; they have more problems with externalizing (blaming oth-ers or circumstances inappropriately) and internalizing (blaming oneself even when not responsible).[26]

A second method (probably a better one) is to compare targets of bully-ing who report being the most upset with targets who feel very differently. In the freshman study, subjects who reported that they were targeted were asked how much it bothered or upset them on a scale of 1 to 10 (with 10 being "extremely upset and bothered," and 1 being "not bothered or upset at all").[27]

Almost half (47 percent) of targets (24 percent of all subjects) rated their "upsetness" as 1, 2, or 3; I labeled those victims as *resilient*. Interest-ingly, a similar proportion (46 percent of targets, and 23 percent of all sub-jects) were *vulnerable* (ratings of 8, 9, or 10). The remaining 7 percent of targets were *moderates*. Although this dearth of moderates was a little sur-prising, other studies have reported similar findings. A 2007 survey by the National Crime Prevention Council also classified about half of bullying targets as resilient and half as vulnerable.[28] A study measuring children's responses to a variety of potentially abusive home situations noted that a similar proportion (about half) were resilient.[29]

Targets were further separated into those who were just victims, just bullies, and finally, bully/victims. About 13 percent of subjects reported being bully/victims in high school; 17 percent of students reported being only bullies, and another 18 percent were only victims. Again, other re-search has found similar proportions.[30] Being vulnerable was clearly as-sociated with being a bully/victim. Of all the vulnerable targets, almost half (48 percent) were bully/victims. In contrast, only 9 percent of resilient targets were bully/victims.

Identifying Victims Who Are Most at Risk When Bullied

What does identifying *vulnerable* or *resilient* children, or vulnerable bully/victims, have to do with measuring the frequency of bullying and cyberbullying? It's really a matter of economies. Ultimately, the answer to bullying is to address the entire broader community; but we also need to channel special resources toward the children who are most at risk for serious difficulties. We may know that from 13 to 24 percent of students may be at higher risk of more severe problems, like violence and mental illness, if they are bullied. So how can we identify these vulnerable children, and accord them some extra attention and care?

Do different kinds of bullying result in resiliency or vulnerability?

Some types of bullying and cyberbullying have been found to be much more common than others. In general, for example, gateway behaviors (both in person and online) were much more frequent than physical bullying in a variety of studies.[31] The question remains, however: are some specific types of bullying not only more *frequent* but also more *upsetting*? We know that some kids were more upset by the bullying they experienced— they were vulnerable, in other words. But were they more upset because they experienced particular types of bullying?

If type of bullying determines vulnerability or resiliency, then we would expect to see a pattern whereby, for example, vulnerable targets were more likely to experience "bullying type 1" but resilient targets were more likely to experience "bullying type 2." Intuitively, this makes some sense. Indeed, some compelling research has found that *bias-based* bullying (bullying that focuses on the target's race, ethnic group, sexual orientation, etc.) is more closely linked with serious psychiatric outcomes (such as suicidality).[32] Overall, however, that's not the pattern that emerged from the freshman study data. Instead, vulnerable and resilient subjects alike reported being on the receiving end of the same types of bullying behaviors. For example, both groups reported that the most common types of behaviors used to bully them were "name calling" and "eye rolling." Both vulnerable and resilient targets agreed, moreover, that the most distressing types of bullying they experienced were "name calling" and "rumors or lies spread about you." It may be that some students who are repeatedly subjected to bias-based harassment respond both to the content of the harassment and to its repetitive nature.

Is vulnerability related to more frequent bullying?

Perhaps what makes vulnerable subjects feel less able to shrug off bullying isn't being victimized in a specific way, but simply being victimized more frequently. All bullying, by definition, is repeated, but there's repeated and then there's incessant (in other words, the frequency of events still varies). In fact, frequency of being bullied *did* emerge as important in determining vulnerability versus resiliency. Upsetness scores were strongly correlated with number of times being bullied, for bullying both in school and online.[33] Resilient subjects were more likely to report being bullied once or twice, but vulnerable subjects were more likely to report being bullied more than twice. If the subject was both bullied frequently *and* targeted by both friends and nonfriends, they were overwhelmingly characterized as vulnerable (see more about being bullied by friends below). Bottom line: it seems to be the frequency of bullying, rather than the type of specific bullying behavior, that distinguishes vulnerable from resilient children. These vulnerable children are, perhaps, simply being worn down by frequently repeated abuse.

Ways We Can Help Children Be More Resilient and Less Vulnerable

Some things you can influence and others you can't. For example, boys were more likely to rate themselves as resilient in the face of bullying, but obviously girls cannot be taught to be boys (although further study may reveal male attitudes or perspectives that females can possibly learn to adopt). Nevertheless, there are other differences between vulnerable and resilient targets that we can capitalize on.

1: Talk about the issue of bullying between friends

We talk to kids a lot about bullying these days, but how frequently do we bring up the issue of bullying specifically as it pertains to friendship? Although it's always a reprehensible behavior, bullying takes on added emotional significance and impact when it happens between people who are supposed to be able to trust each other. Friendships are supposed to be the port in a storm—not the storm itself. Indeed, Hodges's and Boulton et al.'s data showed that even one good friendship that does not involve bullying (particularly a "best" friend) can be deeply protective against being bullied by others, and other studies have concurred.[34] In the field, I often run across adults who assume that their students don't need to talk specifically about bullying and friends because students (particularly teens) presumably understand that friendship carries with it certain obligations of loyalty and kindness. But that assumption may not always be correct. The data in my freshman study showed that many kids revealed being bullied by a "friend"—but there were real differences in the type of friend. Children who were resilient were more likely to be bullied by a friend who was *not* a close friend (e.g., either an acquaintance from school or a more casual friend who was not part of their closest circle of friends). Children who were vulnerable, in contrast, were more likely to be bullied by a close friend. If, by directly addressing bullying by friends, we could reduce its incidence, we might also reduce the proportion of vulnerable targets.

2: Be sensitive to signs of emotional distress or struggle

Not surprisingly, vulnerable children in this study were more likely to report that during high school they struggled with anxiety or depression. Certainly, many teens experience anxiety or depression, but resilient children were closer to the norm on these variables. Vulnerable subjects were significantly more likely than resilient targets to have problems with anxiety, depression, or controlling their temper during high school. What we don't know, however, is whether the anxiety and depression made vulnerable children feel the impact of bullying more deeply; if the more frequent and impactful bullying resulted in these emotional difficulties; or if some other factor caused both to occur together (for example, perhaps having fewer friends caused both the depression/anxiety and the more impactful bullying among vulnerable targets). The data on percentages, unfortunately, doesn't permit us to draw conclusions about which factor caused which.

Other research can offer guidance here, but still no firm conclusions about causation. Several studies have found an association between being bullied and anxiety and depression, and it seems plausible that emotionally compromised children are disproportionately targeted.[35] But other research has found that, at least sometimes, third factors may determine if bullying causes emotional distress. For example, in 2010, researchers compared children with different genotypes (genetic patterns) and found that only children with a certain genotype had an increased risk of developing emotional distress following bullying.[36] That study found that, among those with the vulnerable genotypes, bullying clearly caused emotional problems, rather than vice versa.

In the end, though, whether bullying causes anxiety or depression or vice versa probably isn't the most important question. Likely both are causal, but regardless of which causes which, the association suggests that the risk of depression is elevated among both bullies and targets.[37] If adults notice behaviors that suggest a student might be feeling excessively anxious or depressed, and then refers that student for evaluation to the psychological staff at school or to his or her pediatrician, their intervention could help reduce the vulnerability of that child to bullying.

3: Be on the lookout for signs of dating or family violence

One of the great injustices of life is that once you're a victim of abuse, you're statistically more likely to be revictimized. A large research literature has documented this phenomenon, noting that once a victim has been abused, the probability of future abuse rises.[38] There are several theories about the reasons for this association, including PTSD and learned helplessness.[39] Perhaps people who conclude that they're powerless (i.e., are convinced that abuse cannot be stopped or helped) become more attractive victims to future bullies.

I studied two types of possible prior victimization: bullying by siblings, and threats or aggression in prior dating relationships. Bullying by siblings appears to be more common. Across all subjects, I found that 20 percent reported that they had a sibling who sometimes or often bullied them. The more vulnerable bully/victims were the most likely to report this (29 percent), relative to either bullies (23 percent) or victims (21 percent) alone.[40]

Previous victimization in a relationship (threatened or real domestic or dating violence) largely followed the same pattern as sibling bullying. Compared with victims, bully/victims were more than twice as likely to report being bullied by a date (15 percent versus 6 percent) or by someone they were trying to break up with (14 percent versus 2 percent). Vulnerable victims in general reported prior victimization in greater numbers, but bully/victims were more strongly associated with these problems than other types of victims. In any case, being on the lookout for signs of prior abuse or bullying could be useful in getting targets the support they need to decrease their future or present vulnerability to bullying and cyberbullying.

4: Don't dismiss "tattlers" by refusing to hear them out

One mantra about bullying that I frequently hear is "tell an adult." Unfortunately, society's strong disapproval of "tattling" may make this directive problematic, and possibly even detrimental to a child. If an adult decides that telling is "tattling," the child who alerts an adult to a bullying situation may be dismissed as reporting false or insignificant information, or possibly exploiting a valid complaint to further a third agenda (e.g., to get someone in trouble because they are mad at them, or to make themselves look good in adult eyes). Children may thus become bewildered, hurt, and distrustful when an adult turns around and reprimands them for doing precisely what they've repeatedly been urged to do.

Another difficulty is that adults may not be particularly good at judging what is tattling and what isn't. In the 2010 Youth Voice Project, Davis and Nixon reported data that revealed that adults do not use the "don't tattle" admonition as fairly and objectively as they believe they do.[41] For example, in that study, students of color and special needs students were more likely to be told not to tattle, when compared with white and typical (i.e., not special needs) students. (One could conceivably argue that special needs students might be more likely to "tattle" because of cognitive or social skills limitations, but clearly no such argument could be made because of a child's racial or ethnic background.)

In our study, I found that both resilient and vulnerable children were told "don't tattle" at similar rates in elementary school, but by middle and high school, vulnerable children were being told not to tattle at much higher rates. It may be that vulnerable teens are less able to effectively communicate their concerns, or perhaps the more frequently bullied, vulnerable children also report more frequently, so that adults are less likely to regard any single report as significant. In any case, I think it's safe to conclude that using "don't tattle" is a questionable teaching mechanism. Certainly, some issues can and should be put off for a more convenient time, but students who seek to report should ultimately get a hearing—especially since they're relentlessly encouraged to do so. Nevertheless, it's indisputably true that children don't always report with the purest of motives, and we do need a better mechanism for detecting and responding to such behaviors.

5: Give children who report attention and reassurance

Although resilient and vulnerable children reported to adults at similar rates, resilient subjects were more likely to characterize reporting as an activity that made them feel better. This effect may be due in part to characteristics in the reporter, but the Youth Voice Project did find that adult behaviors impacted a child's experience during reporting. In that study, Davis and Nixon found that adults who made children feel better listened to their report closely without jumping to conclusions or rushing the interview, and also reassured children that they were worthwhile.[42] My own research has similarly found that listening to and following up with children who report was most effective, in the victim's view, even in cases when the adult could not entirely "fix" the problem.[43]

6: Advocate for children who need help developing stronger social skills

The development of social skills, with its significant impact on learning and development, is an area of learning that education can no longer afford to ignore.[44] Not surprisingly, popularity and strong social skills also appear to help children shrug off bullying to a considerable extent. It may also be true that being able to brush off bullying increases one's popularity. In any case, resilient subjects rated themselves as significantly more popular than those who were vulnerable.[45] Resilient subjects rated themselves, on average, a 6.7 out of a possible 10 in popularity; vulnerable subjects rated themselves almost a full point lower, 5.8 out of 10.

Although many victims gave the impression of having weaker social skills, an analysis of the data showed real differences between bully/victims and other victims. The bully/victims evidenced the weakest social skills, as measured by a reliable scale (Chronbach's alpha [standardized items] = .972) that included items such as, "Do you have one or a few close friends you feel you can count on?" and "Did you have small problems with friends that frequently 'blew up' into large fights (and that were not resolved successfully)?" The strongest social skills were noted in those who were uninvolved in bullying or cyberbullying (i.e., they were neither victims nor bullies). Among bullies and victims, the strongest social skills were, in order, bullies, then victims, and finally (with the weakest skills), bully/victims. Bully/victims were least likely to prefer face-to-face communication; bullies and victims preferred it more, and uninvolved subjects preferred it most often. More than half (60 percent) of male bully/victims reported feeling "different" in high school, versus only 31 percent of bullies and 35 percent of victims. Almost half (47 percent) of female bully/victims were bullied by a friend, compared to only 28 percent of victims.

As I reported above, both vulnerable and resilient subjects reported that they were, at times, bullied by friends; but resilient subjects were more likely to be bullied by someone who was *not* a close friend, whereas vulnerable subjects were more likely to be bullied by close friends or by both close and not-close friends.

7: Pay more attention to students who are less strong cognitively and academically
Research conducted decades ago noted that bullies in general were children with weak academic skills.[46] Today, either the population of children who bully has changed, or researchers have become more skilled at identifying a broader range of students who engage in these behaviors. Bullies today may be anywhere on the spectrum of academic achievement. But because so many adults (parents or educators) continue to associate bullying with poor grades, they may reject out of hand any suggestion that a high-achieving student could also be a bully. In an effort to more clearly describe which bullies are higher achievers and which tend to struggle

academically, I undertook to compare more resilient bullies and more vulnerable bully/victims on measures of academic skills. Because this sample was composed of students attending a moderately competitive college, their high school performance wasn't highly variable (i.e., the sample didn't include students who did very poorly in high school or (for the most part) students who excelled). A second measure—the presence or absence of an Individualized Education Plan (or IEP)—proved a better way to study academic ease or struggle. (All special needs students are put on an IEP; thus being on an IEP is a good measure of having a documented disability or other special needs.) In studying this issue, I took something of a unique approach. Although plenty of other studies have found correlations between being a special needs student and vulnerability to bullying and cyberbullying, I assessed both whether or not students were on an IEP during their K–12 years, and if so, *when*.[47] Using this data, it was possible to identify three types of IEP patterns. Subjects who remained on an IEP for all grades between kindergarten and high school were classified as type 1; those on an IEP in elementary school, but not in middle or high school, were type 2; and subjects who reported being on an IEP only in middle and high school were designated type 3.

Generally, both resilient and vulnerable targets reported similar rates of being on type 1 and type 2 IEPs. Resilient subjects were slightly more likely to be on a type 1 or 2 IEP, but the difference was not great. More interestingly, only 8 percent of resilient targets were on a type 3 IEP, compared to 31 percent of vulnerable students. It's hard to say exactly what cognitive vulnerability a type 3 IEP suggests, but because this IEP begins during preadolescence or adolescence, it may reflect previously undetected cognitive or learning difficulties, or emotional and/or behavioral problems that emerge at adolescence. A type 3 should potentially be considered a risk factor for other coexisting vulnerabilities, including a particular vulnerability to bullying and an inability to regard bullying as an unimportant or insignificant event.

Like other vulnerable subjects, male bully/victims were far more likely to be on IEPs, and especially on type 3 IEPs (23 percent) compared to bullies (9 percent) or victims (6 percent). This pattern wasn't true for girls, but other research on both girls and boys has found higher academic achievement among bullies who had higher status, which is the group consistent with our bullies here (see above, regarding popularity and vulnerability).[48]

Cognitive patterns seen in vulnerable children can extend beyond academic skills. For example, bully/victims also appear to interpret and perceive their school environments differently. In my research, bully/victims consistently rated their school environments as more hostile. They were least likely to characterize the adults at their school as consistently caring about bullying, and they were least likely to say that the adults at their school were responsive when they saw obvious bullying. They were most likely to state that they were bullied "continuously" during high school, and found reporting to adults during high school a more negative experience. Almost a quarter of bully/victims (22 percent) felt that reporting to adults actually made a bullying situation worse; in contrast, only 2 percent of victims felt that way. Vulnerable bully/victims were least likely of all subjects to say that reporting will "usually" help a bullying situation. Bully/victims were by far the most likely group to say that their school's climate actually *encouraged* bullying (36 percent versus 17 percent of victims and 13 percent of bullies), and they were slightly more likely to believe that bullies are kids whom adults "tend to like" (37 percent versus 26 percent of bullies and 28 percent of victims).

We still can't point definitively to cause and effect. Perhaps more vulnerable victims attended schools with more negative social climates. Or, perhaps their schools weren't actually different, but these victims may have had a stronger tendency to perceive their ambiguous school climate as more negative. Either conclusion is possible, but the latter explanation is probably more plausible. Hostile interpretations of ambiguous situations have long been noted in aggressive children, although it is fascinating to ask why some aggressive children (in our study, the bullies) do not appear to show those cognitive misinterpretations as widely.[49]

Risk Factors Beyond Direct Influence

Although the preceding list shows that there's a lot we can do to detect and influence risk situations, there are some differences between resilient and vulnerable children that we may not be able to directly influence. But it's good to know about them anyway. Though we may not be able to change these factors, knowing them can help us evaluate risks and thus intervene appropriately.

8: Public bullying might impact targets more

Subjects who were vulnerable were more likely to report that other peers were aware of their victimization (presumably, either by having seen the bullying directly or by being told about it). Among resilient targets, about half said peers were aware of their harassment; for the more vulnerable targets, this figure was about 75 percent. This could be due to vulnerable students being subjected to more public bullying, but it's also true that vulnerable targets were more likely to actually tell peers what was happening. (Vulnerable children reported more often to peers, although both vulnerable and resilient children reported to adults at very similar rates.) It's possible that public bullying is more humiliating, and could increase targets' sense that the bullying is damaging their general social reputation and status. This could remain true even if the victim is the person who actually reveals the bullying to others.

9: Boys are generally more resilient

In the freshman study sample, girls were significantly more likely than boys to report feeling vulnerable—a result consistent with findings from the grades 3–12 study in schools and with other research.[50] More than half of the girls (54 percent) scored as vulnerable, compared with only 26 percent of the boys. Previous studies have found that girls are more vulnerable to bullying and cyberbullying victimization in general, possibly because of their more frequent use of technologies that may increase the frequency of being bullied.[51] And as we saw earlier, higher frequencies mean more vulnerability. Girls also have an elevated tendency to bully friends, in comparison to boys—another factor that may increase their vulnerability.[52]

10: Less-stressed families = greater resilience

I did find a slight (but not strong) effect for family size and vulnerability to bullying. Parental stress is linked to a host of behavioral issues in children, and bullying and cyberbullying may not be exceptions. In this sample, vulnerable children were slightly more likely to come from larger families, where parents have more children to attend to and less attention and energy to devote to each child. Resilient targets were also more likely to have been raised in suburban (versus urban or rural) settings, which tend to be more affluent, with more resources for children.

SHIFTING OUR FOCUS TO THE BULLY

So what have we learned here? That bullying is neither a rampant epidemic nor a rare event, but that whether it's more or less common is not the only important question; rather, asking what helps targets be more resilient can be key in developing skills needed to deal with cruel social behaviors. Even if we were to successfully reduce bullying to a much rarer event, we would still want to know why some children are able to cope successfully and others aren't. But we're still missing one piece of the puzzle.

In the last chapter, I used the analogy of a pitcher throwing a baseball to a catcher to describe how, when we examine social behaviors, a ball isn't always a ball. That chapter discussed the nature of the baseball and what it looks like (gateway behaviors; cruel behaviors online); in this chapter, we begin to get the idea that targets (the catchers) may have certain characteristics that influence how they interpret the ball. That is, children have cognitive and emotional styles and experiences that affect how they deconstruct the social behaviors lobbed at them by peers. But the bullies (the pitchers) also merit some examination. What are their motivations? What kind of pitch will they throw? Is bullying the result of profound changes in our society? Are children today being raised differently? And what does the research done on bullies themselves reveal about their motives? You may be surprised to read how bullies themselves view their intentions. Read on.

CHAPTER 3

Why Do Children Bully
and Cyberbully?

The Impact of Digital Technology on Social Behavior

So, why *do* children bully and cyberbully? The question invokes impassioned debate, probably because the causes of antisocial behaviors—including bullying—aren't simply of academic interest; the answers have broader social and political implications. For those who believe that certain children simply choose to bully, the response is obvious: reward positive behaviors and deter them from that negative choice, often through punishment. Yet those who believe that children who bully are at the mercy of their genes or their dysfunctional environments may feel that punishment is inappropriate—even unjust.

Complicating this tangle of opinion is the fact that bullying has always been around, yet has also indisputably changed. Bullying is more common and more varied today than ever. So the question might better be put: Why has bullying changed from a marginal behavior to a more pervasive problem? If you read enough, you'll run across a number of opinions:

- *Nothing has actually changed*: Proponents claim that the entire problem has not really changed but has been blown out of proportion into an "epidemic" by theorists, the media, and overprotective parents; or that cyberbullying is just another type of bullying, with no unique features; or that bullying behaviors and frequency have not really changed.
- *Children today are more troubled*: Actually, by many measures, adolescents are doing quite well in our society. Sex offenses, suicide, high school drop-out rates, juvenile offending, and other such measures generally show decreasing, not increasing, trends.[1]
- *Changes in society are the root cause*: This perspective generally focuses on social changes such as mothers working outside the home, drug abuse, or supposedly eroded values. These problems might be related

to bullying, but they're probably not primarily responsible, having emerged on the scene decades before the current situation. (I'll return to these issues a bit later.)

- *Teachers are apathetic or unprepared*: This argument is difficult to sustain; teachers today go through more training and more effort to achieve their positions than ever before.
- *The Internet has promoted irresponsibility and maliciousness in children*: Internet communications and social websites are of course partly responsible for a change in bullying patterns. But remember that while cyberbullying may be a real problem, its more traditional first cousin is still very much in the picture.

When it comes to how and why bullying has changed, I'm not going to pretend to have all the answers; but one glaring difference is that in past decades, bullying appeared to be a behavior usually engaged in by "at-risk" children. Studies from more than thirty years ago found a pattern of strong associations between bullying, academic problems, and social difficulties.[2] More recent data paints a different picture. The freshman study and other research reveal the emergence of two types of children who bully. One type, the bully/victims (bullies who are also victims), resemble the more "traditional" at-risk kids; but another type, the "just" bullies (who are *not* also victims), appear to be children who evidence fewer risk factors in general.

These two groups seem to be different socially and academically. As noted in chapter 2, bullies rate themselves as significantly more popular than bully/victims, and they have stronger social skills. They're more likely to prefer face-to-face communication (36 percent versus 23 percent for bully/victims) over digital communications. Bully/victims, in contrast, are more likely to be on an IEP (35 percent versus just 14 percent for bullies). Bully/victims see adults as less responsive to, and less caring about, bullying and cyberbullying. The long-term outcomes for these two groups of bullies are different as well. While in college, 45 percent of bully/victims were targets of bullying, but only 12 percent of bullies experienced college victimization. Of these, 22 percent of bully/victims, but only 6 percent of bullies, were vulnerable (significantly impacted by the college bullying). In short, with their higher likelihood of academic and social problems, bully/victims appear to resemble the group of "at-risk" students who have long been studied as bullies. In contrast, those who are simply bullies, with their popularity, higher social skills, and better functioning with adults, seem to resemble more closely the students who, in the past, would have been less likely to be bullies in the first place.

Or would they? Although I've suggested that two significant changes may be in play here—that bullying is more likely to involve psychological methods, and that the better-functioning "just bullies" weren't involved in bullying several decades ago—other interpretations are definitely possible. Maybe in the older studies, high-functioning bullies were actually around and operating, perhaps using these psychological bullying methods regularly, but simply went unnoticed. Perhaps adults weren't able to see them as stereotypical "bullies" because of their better social functioning, and assumed that bullying happened only through physical behaviors. I tend to shy away from this interpretation, simply because it's hard for me to imagine that parents, educators, and researchers universally failed to observe that psychological bullying was present and being wielded by higher-functioning kids.[3] It seems more likely to me that both high-functioning bullies and psychological bullying were present forty years ago, but were simply the exceptions and not the rule (whereas today the opposite appears to be true). In the end, though, we can't definitively say if *how kids bully* and *who bullies* has changed today, or if it's just that we're finally noticing these elements. I would estimate the answer is a little of both.

In either case, it is a matter for concern that abusive behaviors are currently being committed by children and teens who should, by any reasonable measure, be capable of internalizing our values about aggression and abuse, but are rejecting everyday opportunities to behave prosocially. One of the uncomfortable things about today's bullying is the sense that even when we provide children with every privilege, they may still opt to engage in destructive antisocial behaviors. As an unsettling case in point, consider the maelstrom surrounding the suicide of Rutgers University freshman Tyler Clementi. His alleged cyberbully was no misfit; rather, he was a privileged child coming from an apparently happy home life, of sound mental health, and enjoying many advantages in life. He had no obvious reason or rationale for allegedly attempting to either spy on or publicly humiliate his roommate. In any single case, we may wonder if the bully had a pathological personality; but that doesn't wash off when you're considering a problem that happens as frequently as this one. They can't *all* be sociopaths.

DO STUDENTS BULLY BECAUSE OF CHANGES IN SOCIETY?

If behaviors used to be one way, and now they are different, then something causal must have changed. As noted above, a host of reasons have been offered. Could toxins in our water and air contribute to some kind of problem with central nervous system development that makes kids more susceptible to aggression or abusiveness? Has the development of the Internet and electronics fundamentally changed how children grow up today? Could people be worse parents than they used to be? Could this generation of children be more bombarded with violent media?

Some factors in society have indisputably changed. More families need two working parents to stay in the middle class, and more children attend daycare at a younger age; but research on family factors and bullying suggests that such social changes are less important than both the style and methods of parenting, and sibling relationships and bullying.[4] Further, many of these social changes predate the changes in bullying that we've observed. It's not that something that's been around for more than forty years *couldn't* be involved, but to be a credible and central cause, such shifts would probably need to be combined with a more recent development. It's also been observed that social factors, taken by themselves, often can't entirely explain behaviors. Consider, as an example, violent media. We have particularly seen an increase in violent video games, and a large body of research has associated violent media with an increase in aggression, at least among some children. These findings have led to the theory that an increase in aggression and bullying could be due solely or primarily to the increasingly aggressive games children play. Yet this theory, placed beside the reality we see among children, cannot satisfy by itself. Many boys who play violent video games are not aggressive, and furthermore, a great deal of the bullying and cyberbullying problems seen today occur between girls, who are much less likely to play such games.

In short, simple, single-cause answers often don't entirely fit. As with any complex problem, there are multiple causes, and for different children, different types of influences will prove important. One child may be affected strongly by his parents' divorce; another child (perhaps even a sibling) may be much less affected. One child may strongly benefit from a stay-at-home parent; another child may benefit more from the peer socialization advantage of daycare programs.

So let's try to improve the question. Not, What causes bullying? but, What new or changed factors are *contributing* to the new and different bullying and cyberbullying that we see today? Are there significant changes in the last decade that could account for why psychological bullying may be the preferred method, and why higher-functioning children may be becoming more involved in bullying and cyberbullying?

Electronics' Impact on How Children Grow Up

Plenty of parents today (myself included) grew up addicted to their favorite TV show. But there are many legitimate differences between children's television viewing habits during past decades and those of today, not to mention the many different screens they now use. These differences may be a real factor in altering how children are growing up and how their social environments are changing.

New devices: It's not just the TV anymore

In the 1970s, the average home had one television set (perhaps two) showing three or four channels. Today, the average American household has three televisions receiving 130 channels (and newer televisions connect directly to the Internet). In addition, American households now have an average of four *additional* Internet-connected devices (computers, laptops, tablets, cell phones, smartphones, iPods, music players, e-readers, gaming systems, etc.). Thirty to forty years ago, the family likely watched their one TV set together; today, family members scatter, each to his or her own screen. Nielsen statistics gathered in late 2011 and early 2012 suggest that for the first time, the "other" screens are actually displacing television time in American families.[5]

The interactive nature of screen-watching

But screens aren't only more numerous; they are also increasingly focused on interactive technology. I grew up as a television consumer, subject to mass media campaigns in the form of television commercials; I remember singing along to their familiar jingles. But television was one-way. I couldn't alter or affect what was shown. Commercials weren't aimed at my personal interests or shopping patterns, and I contributed none of the content that we all watched. Today, many of the most popular Internet sites and electronic activities are basically infrastructures into which the user pours his or her own content, often for the amusement or interest of others.[6]

The number of hours spent screen-watching

In the 1970s, Americans spent (on average) 2.9 hours per day watching their TV screens. This average increased slightly to 3.1 hours by the 1980s and then skyrocketed to 6.3 hours by 2004. Although TV watching actually decreased thereafter, the total time watching screens kept increasing, to 7.6 hours by 2010.[7] Any activity engaged in for this amount of time every day is unlikely to leave no mark.

But the issue with screen-watching today isn't only the time spent; it's also the type of screen encounter. Some screens show images (television, video online, photo-sharing applications, or video phone calls), while others show only or use primarily text (messaging, blogging). Some screens are passive (YouTube, television) while others are interactive (gaming, sharing and posting content, social networking websites). It seems reasonable to assume that these different digital experiences have, in turn, different impacts.

And of course, children of different ages are impacted differently, both by type of screen exposure and by time exposure. Preteens and young teenagers rack up more than eleven hours a day, including one and a half hours spent in texting activities. However, this number really isn't a fair comparison; in the 1970s, one wrote on paper, and although teens couldn't post or text-message, they did spend hours on the telephone. In 2012, we read, write, and chat on a screen, but it's hard to know what category all of those screen hours belong in. If a fifteen-year-old is reading a newspaper article on the Internet, how could that screen activity possibly equate to playing a video game? Does reading on a tablet differ in any fundamental way from reading on paper? Some activities may not have substantially changed, even though the vehicle has.

Displacement of more direct person-to-person contact

Some things are learned through the medium of the screen; other things are *not* being learned, as we forgo other activities to be with our beloved screens. Time spent with digital electronics is time that children don't spend playing or interacting with others face-to-face. Popular communications such as messaging, online gaming, posting text, and blogging deprive users of opportunities to practice reading nonverbal cues and body language; at least one study has found that kids who engage in less media time have healthier social relationships.[8] Face-to-face contact also promotes the development of social skills by requiring people to confront and cope with socially awkward situations. These situations range from mildly embarrassing (e.g., introducing yourself to someone you want to date) to truly challenging (e.g., defusing a playmate who's becoming increasingly frustrated and angry). While these uncomfortable moments can also occur online, a digital encounter doesn't give you the chance to study complex body language or facial cues to see if, for example, your social strategy is working (even common video chatting, such as through Skype or Facetime, doesn't typically have the quality and detail needed to pick up nuances).

To visualize how being deprived of in-person interactions might impact coping skills, imagine a situation where one girl says something mean to another girl. The target here might decide to cope by arranging with a friend to grin and whisper together immediately after the comment, thus making the mean girl feel discomfited and uneasy. That strategy probably couldn't be conceived, carried out, or evaluated in a digital environment. But forming an effective strategy in dealing with a "small" awkward situation like that can pave the way for the ability to deal with more serious social problems. Perhaps a year or two later, the grinning-and-whispering strategy will be used again by one of the participants to deal with something more serious, like bullying. But without the chance to practice (in person), kids may never master such a skill, and feel less able to cope if bullying does happen.

Of course, digital communications can (advantageously) permit us to smooth over some of life's socially awkward moments. If you want to have some fun with this concept, tell your students how uncomfortable it *used* to be to ask someone out on a date; how you discussed it ad nauseam with your friends, debated tactics, prepared scripts, and so on. This will strike them as hilarious—that you couldn't just shoot off a casual text. But avoiding awkward moments has a cost, too. The awful clumsiness of asking people out on a date is one of those situations that forces us to cultivate our social skills. Absent those uneasy but important social moments, children today may find themselves with many fewer opportunities to smooth off their rough social edges. Most teachers I encounter in the field feel that children today have significantly less-developed social skills, relative to their counterparts a decade or so ago.

Modeling of bullying and snarkiness is rampant in prime-time TV

In 2009, Elizabeth Mills, a graduate student in MARC, began a project designed to count the number of snarky, rude put-downs occurring on the most popular sitcoms.[9] Five episodes each of the four highest-rated sitcoms were analyzed over an eight-week period in 2009. Instances of verbal aggression were coded, including the role of the aggressor and others, the type of aggression, and the show's depiction of the aggressive act as being either rewarded (e.g., increase in the aggressor's social status or power) or punished (e.g., bystander stood up for the target, against the aggressor). These shows averaged between 8.4 and 10.4 antisocial acts per episode. The show's *supporting* character(s) often had the role of aggressor, and utilized mainly gateway behaviors such as posting secrets online, eye rolling, contemptuous looks, and sarcastic insults (females were more likely to use relational aggression). Almost two-thirds of the time, these behaviors were rewarded by use of a laugh track; 34 percent of the time there were other rewards as well. Only 8 percent of these antisocial actions met with a punishment, and the most common punishment was a bystander standing up for a target in opposition to the aggressor.

Could the increased exposure to such hostile behaviors on TV be fueling an increase in rude and cruel behaviors, both in person and online? Apart from obvious mechanisms, like modeling, one study suggests that there may be a biological mechanism linking viewing with action. Coyne and her colleagues found that increasing exposure to verbal and relational bullying on a screen is likely to increase the adolescent watchers' tendencies to be socially cruel themselves, by actually "priming" the brain for such behavior.[10]

Electronics' Impact on Bullies' Methods and Motives

It's easy, in the middle of all the bad news, to forget that many kids don't particularly want to bully; they don't want to be cruel, are too timid, or feel that bullying is fundamentally wrong. Still others probably view cruel behavior as occasionally justified, but don't see themselves as "bullies" per se. The point is that it's not as though some children simply wake up one day and decide to become bullies. Rather, given the right set of circumstances, some children who wouldn't otherwise bully might be drawn into it.[11] And the digital world does, sometimes, provide the "right set" of circumstances. How does the emergence of online and digital communications make bullying easier?

The more obvious stuff: It's quicker and easier

It's far easier to send a message to many people at once electronically than it ever was with paper and pen—obviously. It's a cinch to forward embarrassing messages or photos, and it's the work of a moment to post or share anything you receive or read. This makes it easy to send communications but it also makes rumors—even casual ones—potentially more widespread, and thus more damaging. Subjects I studied in 2011 often reported feeling anxious about not being connected via their cell phone (even for one hour), and the number-one issue that caused this anxiety was the possibility that they would miss a rumor spread via text message.[12] Whether they are *catastrophizing*—that is, imagining rumor-mongering dangers where none or few exist—or whether an errant rumor could genuinely get around all too easily is still up for study. At the time of this writing, I am currently studying a new group of subjects (355 have been examined so far). Of these, 39 percent opined that a hypothetical rumor, begun electronically, will spread to about one hundred students in *fewer than 15 minutes*, and 64 percent felt it would spread to a hundred students in less than one hour. Only 10 percent of subjects felt that ignoring the rumor was the best way to squash it, and 48 percent felt that a quick response would result in the least social damage. This data seems to suggest that the anxiety kids feel about the extremely rapid spread of damaging rumors may actually be justified.

Lack of visual and auditory cues that normally suppress aggression

Digital environments may, at times, unwittingly promote "negligent" cyberbullying. In person, a series of interpersonal cues generally functions to discourage people from being too hurtful, especially when they're just being careless. For example, seeing the wounded look on a friend's face after thoughtlessly blurting out how ugly their sweatshirt is will usually cause the careless speaker to stop what they're saying. In a digital environment, however, those cues are absent, and someone being thoughtlessly cruel is liable to continue nattering on, oblivious. Does careless cruelty constitute "intent"? In a way, yes (the remarks aren't true accidents) and in a way, no (seriously hurting the recipient's feelings is probably not the primary goal). Perhaps we can christen a new type of digital abuse: *negligent cyberbullying*. This type doesn't reflect the essential personality of the child involved; it just represents an environment where that person isn't getting the feedback he or she would normally receive, and which would normally serve to stop the casual cruelty.

It's important to note that the lack of immediate visual cues can also embolden digital users in a positive way. Online, where discouraging feedback cues (e.g., scowls, disapproving or disgusted looks) are absent, users may be able to express important, sensitive thoughts or feelings that they otherwise feel too intimidated or fearful to discuss. In that type of situation, the lack of negative feedback cues can be powerful and positive. In my relentless focus on the problems with digital environments, it's easy to forget how much good they can do, and how empowering they are, for so many people.

Lack of tone: It's easier to misunderstand what's being said

Although the lack of punctuation and grammar in messaging is usually bemoaned by educators as evidence of the destruction of the English language, there's another problem with this writing style. Punctuation and complete sentences aren't just academic exercises; they're part of the way that writing conveys tone, and thus meaning. For example, consider the phrase: "I'm *soooooo* going to kill you." Most readers would conclude that the person who wrote that is emphatically saying that they're not, actually, going to kill you. But if you write the phrase without emphasis or punctuation, like this:

im so going to kill you

then it's much harder to know if the writer is being threatening or humorous.

The difficulty with conveying tone in brief digital messages hasn't gone unnoticed. Scott E. Fahlman is a computer scientist at Carnegie Mellon University who claims to have invented the sideways "smiley" emoticon (which looks like this :) or this: ☺).[13] He thought up the emoticon to compensate for the difficulty in conveying tone in digital communications that couldn't otherwise be identified as sarcastic, friendly, and so on. The widespread use of emoticons suggests that many users perceive how difficult it can be to convey tone in an electronic environment.

That suggests, in turn, that it's fairly easy to misunderstand a digital communication and inadvertently start the preteen equivalent of World War III. Imagine a scenario where a twelve-year-old girl receives this message from her friend: "omg I cant believe he dissed u like u wr so ugly." (Translation: "Oh my god I can't believe he disrespected you like you were so ugly.") Assuming the friend was trying to be supportive, you could take the message "like you were so ugly" to mean, sarcastically, "Of course you weren't ugly!" But if the indignant, supportive sarcasm doesn't come across clearly in the message, the recipient might well conclude that her friend was literally calling her ugly. And thus the battle is engaged, and all because the brief nature of messages doesn't promote a clear transmission of tone.

Social networking provides lots of information and, sometimes,
more fuel for the fire

The final way that kids who aren't likely to bully in person might become engaged in it online is simply through increased opportunity. Among elementary-age children, simply owning a mobile digital device (especially a smartphone) increases the probability that they will be either a bully or a victim online, presumably because ownership increases their digital opportunities.[14] Why does owning a smartphone increase the odds of trouble with peers online? Perhaps it increases the use of social networks, and a 2010 study found that people who regularly visit social networking sites post more about themselves, and they post it more often.[15] This means there's more information and more data to read about someone, and increases the likelihood that a reader might run across some fact or thought that they feel inclined to challenge, negate, or even use in an attack.

The Disappearance of Children's Play

Milteer has argued that the role of play in children's lives is so central that play should be an integral part of the very definition of childhood.[16] Despite this, the role of play in early childhood education has changed dramatically in the last decade or so, with the emergence of a trend toward formal academic structure over more traditional, play-based preschool and kindergarten.[17] While most proponents of academic early education do acknowledge the more obvious benefits of play (healthy exercise, creativity), the conclusion that play is also linked to both academic and social success is somewhat more controversial, at least among policy makers. Evidence suggests, however, that formal academically oriented early education does not appear to increase academic outcomes in the long run and, in fact, may damage both social and academic development. Almon studied twenty-three-year-olds who, while in preschool, had taken part in an experiment where they were separated into two different groups: one preschool group was taught using more formal academic techniques, while two other preschool groups participated in a play-based program.[18] Although academic achievement didn't ultimately differ between the two groups, by adulthood, the academic group had a much higher rate of social and emotional problems, such as a lack of personal relationships, higher arrest rates, a need for special education services while in school, and problems at work. Almon argued that such evidence suggests that replacing preschool play with formal education not only lacks benefits—it is actively harmful.

But *how* is play (during preschool, kindergarten, or after school) related to bullying? Apart from its link to social skills (higher social skills mean more friends, more self-confidence, higher status, etc.), imaginative play promotes a child's sense of power and control, which is critical for resiliency.[19] Researchers have noted further that one important purpose of play is to teach children skills that are useful in more challenging social situations, such as bullying.[20] These *social coping skills* may be positive (such as trying to befriend someone who is being mean) or negative (such as using lies to distract or displace the attention of a bully). Although bullying-prevention programs typically don't promote negative tactics (adults usually view them as socially undesirable), in the real world, learning tactics such as dismissal, trickery, and deception can be powerful strategies, and targets can and do use them to defend themselves. Indeed, learning to run social minefields is a critical element in play, and any strategy (short of cruelty or violence) that empowers a victim or prevents bullying should probably not be dismissed out of hand without due consideration.[21]

Changes in the Nature of Friendship

The changes in the way children grow up today may also be impacting their ability to form positive, enduring, and protective relationships. We know that good friendships during school years protect children against bullying.[22] Could deterioration of the ability to form friendships—meaningful, intimate relationships—be increasingly common and thus account for some of the bullying and cyberbullying problem?

As discussed earlier, several factors, including higher use of digital communications and paucity of playtime in early childhood, are associated with social skills problems and sometimes with negative and unfriendly social behaviors.[23] Social skills difficulties, in turn, are related to a lack of stable and positive friendships during childhood and beyond.[24]

An ongoing thread of research has found that friendships are protective and particularly important for girls. Traditionally, research studying gender and friendships has found that girls' friendships are more intimate, more intense, and more emotionally supportive than boys'.[25] This tendency toward greater intimacy and support in friendships has been found to extend through the lifetime of females.[26] But despite these well-documented tendencies, the girls in the freshman study reported that, if they bullied others, they were far more likely to victimize their friends. In contrast, boys reported that they were most likely to victimize acquaintances, rather than their closest friends. In the field and in the lab, one intriguing (and common) mechanism for the between-friends bullying has really stood out. Girls seek support from each other when they're upset with someone and, today, when seeking such support from friends, will often text-message them repeatedly.[27] Although it's normal, and actually desirable, to seek support when upset, doing so *through texting* exposes the upset girl to repeated written messages about her hurt or angry feelings. One effect of reading these repetitious messages seems to be to "prime" users to feel the negative emotions increasingly intensely.[28] Thus the effect is called *cognitive priming*.

What cognitive priming implies is that if upset individuals access friends' emotional support by *talking* with them, their feelings may be calmed; but if they gain that emotional support by repeatedly text-messaging their friends, doing so may actually *escalate* or inflate their feelings. A teen may be a little upset with a friend who stains a borrowed sweater; but after reading and re-reading messages about her frustration, she may find that her feelings have escalated into much more intense anger. In the freshman study, girls were more likely than boys to report that they went online or texted friends when they felt upset about something (90 percent versus 71 percent). When upset, girls were much more likely to prefer sending and receiving text messages (83 percent versus 53 percent of boys).

I discuss the cognitive priming effect more in chapter 4, but for now, my point is that while texting may make girls feel better able to access support when they want it, its written, repetitive nature may also serve to artificially heighten their negative feelings and thus cause more conflict in their friendships. That anger and conflict, in turn, can trigger bullying and cyberbullying episodes between friends. Bullies frequently cite anger as an important motive for pursuing a campaign against a peer (see next section). Conflicted friendships can also leave girls without the deep emotional connections that can be so protective. When asked about their friendships in high school, both boys and girls in my research similarly described their friends as fun and able to talk about personal things, but boys were much more likely to describe their closest friends as very loyal, always friendly, and able to work out problems or fights. It's possible that cognitive priming has impacted at least some girls' friendships, but if so, it's an issue that could probably be mitigated, at least partially, through simple education and awareness.

WHAT DO BULLIES THEMSELVES TELL US ABOUT THEIR MOTIVES?

In studying how subjects perceive the motives for bullying, I separated two distinct types of motive. First, subjects were asked about the motive for bullying in general. Is the bully usually angry? Seeking power? Trying to look popular? Second, I asked about the "trigger," or the *immediate* motive, a bully had for choosing that target. Was the bully angry at the target or in a fight with them? Was target choice motivated by the target's characteristics?

In the Abstract, They See Power as the Ultimate Motive

When asked about the overall motive for bullying, most subjects (73 percent) reported that bullying is not about anger; it's about power and control, and demonstrating to targets, bystanders, and others that they have that power and control. This helps explain why the *power imbalance* discussed earlier is so central to the concept of bullying. This finding aligns very well with other research, which has similarly found that children in general see bullying as an expression of the power dynamic.[29] A minority of the subjects felt that bullying was fundamentally about anger.

The trigger for the bullying they saw—the rationale for victim choice—was usually seen as a characteristic ("something about") the target. Slightly less than half of the subjects felt that was the most important immediate reason. Smaller groups of subjects fielded different explanations. About a sixth felt that the bully usually disliked the target (possibly because of some characteristics, but this was not explored explicitly), and another fifth felt that most bullies select a target because they're in a "minor" fight that has escalated out of control. Although opinions weren't universal, the trend favored the pursuit of social power as the primary rationale for bullying.

In Their Own Situations, They See Anger as the Primary Motive

Although in the abstract, subjects viewed bullying as a confirmation of power over targets with vulnerable characteristics, when bullies were asked about their own motives for bullying, most described the cause as their anger at the target or, less often, "showing the target that I didn't like them." This was true for both male and female bullies, who viewed their bullying more as an exchange between them and someone they were mad at or pointedly disliked, rather then as a move for power and status. They usually didn't see the target as having certain characteristics that provoked an attack.

A lot of the aggression and meanness expressed in the freshman study sample was about being "mad." Both one-time cruelties and repetitious bullying situations were attributed to anger about 70 percent of the time, and bully/victims were only slightly more likely to blame being mad, in comparison with bullies. Interestingly, anger was cited much less often by cyberbullies; only 51 percent of cyberbullies said their motive was anger, in comparison with 75 percent of in-person bullies. Demonstrating popularity was among the *least* cited reasons given by both bullies and bully/victims as their primary motive for bullying.

These findings appear to contrast strongly with the general views about bullying expressed by the study sample, but other studies have also associated bullying with anger.[30] Moreover, anger has been statistically associated in a host of studies looking at other types of abuse (e.g., spouse and child).[31] It's been fingered as a contributing cause in psychological dating abuse (a behavior I consider closely related to bullying).[32] Although in my research anger was less often associated with cyberbullying than bullying, it was still the top reason cited by both types of bullies, and other research has yielded similar results.[33] But how do we reconcile the widespread perception that bullying is really all about power, with the findings that anger is also involved?

Do Bullies Really Feel Anger as a Motive?

Bullies report anger as the motive for their behavior, but it's hard to know, frankly, if that answer is straightforward. Bullies may genuinely feel anger toward their targets, but they could also be faking or exaggerating their anger. The loosening of self-control typically experienced when angry could be a convenient justification for their behaviors; rather than struggle to control their anger, bullies might welcome it as an opportunity. So I perceive two uncertain dimensions: Is the anger genuine? Or is it being used as an excuse for bullying?

It does seem likely that at least some bullies and aggressors genuinely feel anger, even when it's unwarranted. Many social encounters are unclear, requiring some type of judgment on the part of the participants (e.g., interpreting the meaning of others' social behaviors), and researchers have noted across many studies that children who tend toward bullying and aggression sometimes exhibit markedly hostile and angry interpretations when faced with ambiguous situations.[34] These overly hostile perceptions have even been noted in aggressive children *prior* to the development of any aggression, suggesting that they are a genuine cognitive problem and not a justification, at least for some children.[35] In other words, there's solid evidence to suggest that some aggressors may see justifications for anger where most of us see none, and that this tendency appears to have its origins in cognition (not in emotions per se).

The second dimension is the possibility that bullies may be conveniently using their anger (real or faked) to justify their abusive behaviors. While bullying behaviors may increase status, bullies may also encounter the attitude (among adults and children) that it's socially unacceptable to bully someone for their characteristics. Citing anger avoids that problem.

I explored this issue by asking eighteen-year-old subjects to look back on any cruel behaviors they had engaged in during high school and to justify or explain them. Subjects could characterize their behavior as either essentially excusable or, alternatively, as wrong or thoughtless. I hypothesized that a subject who sees his behavior as excusable would view it as provoked or appropriate under the circumstances. What I found pretty much fit the theory that repeat bullies are more likely to view bullying behaviors as appropriate, given their perception of the circumstances. Those who were mean once (not repeat bullies) were more likely to say that they "weren't thinking" or what they did "wasn't ideal." Repeat bullies, on the other hand, were more likely to characterize their behavior as "understandable and justified" or to feel that they had "no other options." Bullies may sincerely view their own behaviors as more justified by circumstances, relative to other observers.

Anger in other types of abusers has been viewed as a tool that the abuser exploits as a rationalization. Therapists who work with batterers have noted that once anger-management therapy has been completed, some abusers will simply shift to another justification.[36] Another study found that some child abusers used the circumstance that caused their anger as a justification, even if it was a hostile interpretation.[37] It's difficult to say whether feigned or genuine anger is more likely to be associated with severe abuse or bullying.[38]

This issue seems most important when we're considering how to intervene with bullies themselves. Genuine anger problems are very different from a cynical tendency to exploit anger as a rationale. And there's no reason to assume that anger is static. Perhaps some bullying situations begin as anger but continue for other, less impulsive reasons (or just fizzle), while sustained bullying situations are more about status. When I asked bullies why they stopped bullying someone, 59 percent said that they "stopped being mad." But the role of anger in bullying is *there*, in some form, and it does have broader implications. If our prevention efforts don't address the possibility that anger is sometimes the motive, then children who are angry may be inclined to see what they do as definitely *not* bullying. If we present bullying as only about power, that may confirm for some that the issue of bullying doesn't apply to them. It's still key, of course, to help children develop values that emphasize diversity and tolerance, rather than inequality and the power some people hold over others; but we need to recognize that children who bully, and possibly their friends and closest cohorts, view their bullying situations more like equal-power fights—and so might not think that the messages of tolerance and respect apply to *their* situations. In their own minds, they're not picking on someone because of that person's inferior appearance, ethnic group, or sexual orientation; they're attacking someone because they're legitimately angry.

Bottom line: anger has something to do with bullying, at least part of the time. It may be an issue only for the kids who are already prone to anger, or it may be the spark that lit the fire, or it may be used as a justification for bad behavior. Whichever it is, we'd better start studying it and addressing it in our discussions with students.

UNDERSTANDING AGGRESSION

All children have the capacity to hurt others. As preschoolers, children not only begin to understand that aggression hurts others, but they also begin to form intent, which is the basic underpinning of interpersonal violence. It's during early childhood that the capacities for both prosocial behavior and aggression increase dramatically.

Parenting Problems Generally Linked to Aggression in Children

Attachment refers to the emotional bond between child and caregiver, and can be critically important. It's vital to note that attachment problems are not rare (estimates of insecurely attached infants can be as high as 40 percent of all infants), and can happen between babies and responsible, educated, and conscientious parents. Attachment problems aren't inevitably the result of poor parenting, but can result from stressful experiences (such as a difficult pregnancy or financial problems) that interfere with a parent's ability to feel positively about his or her infant. Attachment is one of the most important processes in a child's life (arguably the most important) and is almost certainly strongly related to a child's tendency to be either prosocial or aggressive. Secure attachment to parents predicts a high level of prosocial behavior, and infant attachment problems sometimes lead to hostile or aggressive behavior during the preschool years. Attachment is also related to social competence as discussed next.

Parenting style during middle childhood and adolescence also has a significant impact on aggressive behavior. The research strongly bears out the relationships between attachment, parenting style, and aggression. One typical study found that parents who maintained a secure attachment and had a positive influence on their young teens had children with more prosocial behavior.[39] In contrast, another study found that parents who exercised a high degree of physical control had adolescents with significantly more behavior problems.[40] Of course, this relationship is never quite so simple and is always a two-way street; different types of children provoke different types of parenting. Parents who feel a need to strictly control one child may not feel that need with other children. The complexity of these relationships reminds us that pointing the finger at parents may not be productive (especially in any individual case); but when we're considering why bullying sometimes occurs, it's important to consider attachment and parenting circumstances.

It's also important to remember that environmental factors don't always increase aggression; these influences work both ways. Mother Nature may have provided for processes that increase the potential for aggression, but there are also mechanisms that work against it.

Normal Processes That Repress Aggression

Within the first few years of life, the critical process called *socialization* begins, and toddlers start to acquire the rules and values of their society. Although at first young children obey rules because they're afraid of being punished, or because they want to please others, after a while they internalize them; that is, they begin to believe that these rules are correct. Ultimately, socialization is the heart of most law-abiding and peaceful behavior.

Social competence is an ability seen in a child who plays regularly with peers and is liked by them, and is related to behavior in preschool years. Children with adequate social competence are able to play in a friendly manner with other children. Such play is critical, because it enables them to learn about many different issues, including the acceptability (or unacceptability) of aggression and violence. Children with high social competence are better able than children with poor social competence to absorb peer lessons about prosocial and aggressive behavior.

CYBER ISSUES: THE CURVEBALL THAT COMPLICATES EVERYTHING

We've got the nature of the baseball (gateway behaviors; cruel cyber behaviors); we see the differences in the catcher (vulnerable or resilient); and we're beginning to get a grip on the pitcher (sometimes angry; sometimes seeking to justify; less play, more screens; worse social skills). Now it's time to extend the analogy. Imagine that as the ball is flying through the air, a bizarre wind shifts violently and skews the ball to the right or left—or even right back at the pitcher. An unpredictable element has been introduced into what was before a fairly predictable pastime.

This unpredictable element is, of course, what happens in cyberspace. That's what's new, and it's affecting the entire game. Some of it is expected but a great deal of it is decidedly not. Students themselves certainly don't always understand these factors. How many adults really do, and how can we teach the children, if we don't fully grasp these issues ourselves? So in the next chapter we're going to consider two important issues: first, how does social behavior shift or skew in digital environments, and second, what kinds of new problems are uniquely associated with the use of electronic communication devices and computers?

CHAPTER 4

How Bullying and Cyberbullying Interact

The Amplification of Conflict in Cyberspace

"Cyberbullying is no different from any other forms of bullying."[1]

"Cyberbullying is different. Without the need for physical confrontation, cyberbullies can strike anytime, anywhere."[2]

You might chuckle if a student told you that his or her cell phone was as essential as food and water, but that's precisely what 34 percent of college students told Cisco's researchers in their recent study.[3] The central role that connectivity plays in the lives of today's children and teens means it's unlikely that any—even those being cyberbullied—will give up their technology entirely. Children (and probably most adults) see technology as a rubicon from which there is no going back. The necessity and, yes, the advisability of using technology remains strong despite any problems with the medium. When I asked subjects how they would feel if they had to give up their cell phone for *one hour*, "bored" and "anxious" were the most common answers given, apart from a fear of not hearing about an emergency.[4]

Of course, digital life begins long before adolescence, and extensive online experience today is the norm, not the exception. In 2011, I found that over 90 percent of eight-year-olds were already interacting with peers online.[5] Cell phone ownership in fifth graders (ten to eleven years old) increased from 40 percent in 2010 to 52 percent in 2012, in my survey of 11,700 elementary school students.[6] Almost all (98 percent) eighteen-year-olds reported to us that they had accounts on social networking websites. Digital participation during childhood isn't just common—it's essentially *universal*.

Some of the activities children and teens engage in online promote bad feelings between peers; but most do not, and many even promote wonderful insight, involvement, communication, and empowerment. But, good or bad outcomes, we can't ignore what happens online. And one thing that happens, as recent news coverage has made clear, is cyberbullying. So the first question to ask here is, Is cyberbullying really different from bullying and if so, how? That's what this chapter is about—exploring what's singular about cyberbullying and cyber behaviors.

BULLYING AND CYBERBULLYING ARE NOT THE SAME, BUT THEY DO INFLUENCE EACH OTHER

By now, most adults who work with children readily perceive the enormous influence of their digital interactions on their everyday lives. But there are still niches where the interaction between online and offline hasn't really penetrated. For example, it can be difficult to see how cyber knowledge is relevant in elementary school. "This really isn't my problem," a second-grade teacher once said to me, nervously eyeing a lesson plan about cyber-skills. "Can't they just talk about it in computer class?" But children view these venues as substantially related; for them, the online world is just another place where they see their friends.[7] Indeed, my study of thirty-three thousand students in grades 3–12 found that as children grow, the odds that a bullying incident will occur *only* in school become smaller and smaller; by high school, more than 90 percent of reported bullying happened both online and in school—or only online. Ybarra's research found, similarly, that there was a substantial overlap between school and online bullying, even among middle schoolers.[8] A longitudinal study in Australia and Washington found somewhat less overlap, but still found that engaging in in-person bullying at a younger age predicted whether or not a child would cyberbully.[9] In the three-legged race of social life, in-school and online interactions appear to have their feet firmly tied together.

Yet despite their interconnectedness, it remains true that in a digital environment, interpersonal dynamics, perceptions, and communications substantially change. And bullying behaviors are affected as much as any other type of behavior.

Cyberbullying: Distinctive? Or Distinctively Similar?

Journalist and pundit Larry Magid has argued that distinguishing cyberbullying from bullying is essentially as pointless as calling bullying with a fist, "fist-bullying" to draw a distinction between it and "regular" bullying.[10] He has a valid point. Separating every mechanical method by which children might abuse one another is unnecessary and renders the entire situation needlessly complex. But although there's probably little reason for distinguishing "laughing-at-someone-bullying" and "telling-rumors-bullying," distinguishing bullying that happens *in an electronic environment* from *in-person* bullying might have some utility and does have some basis in research.

By definition, all bullying shares some characteristics. It's more common when adults are not present or not paying attention; it's generally accomplished in front of an audience and with a power-seeking motive; and its goal is cruel dominance (although even these widely held assumptions are sometimes off-base; more on that later).[11] But cyberbullying is also different from bullying, and not only because cyberbullying occurs while people are using a keyboard instead of speaking. Some of the differences seem to be largely due to the way that online communications change how we communicate in general.[12] Tripping someone in a hallway versus spitting on them may not differ much in motivation, interpretation, and consequences; but typing language into a digital environment versus speaking it aloud does have real differences, regardless of whether praise or abuse is being communicated. Cyberbullying is not equivalent with all digital communication, but being a type of digital communication, it shares the more general category's characteristics. Thus, these real differences are worth a look.

DIGITAL COMMUNICATIONS DIFFER FROM NONDIGITAL FORMS

One could take the position that digital communication is just a type of written communication—like writing a note on paper. But that perspective won't take you far. There are radical differences between the written word on paper and in cyberspace.

Ease of Use and Dissemination

Let's begin with the obvious. Using digital communications—text messaging, instant messaging, writing and posting communications online— is so much faster and easier than writing on paper that it's rapidly become the standard mode of communication for many adults and children. Writing by hand was always somewhat cumbersome and slow, and hastily began to succumb to modernity as soon as the telephone became commonplace. Writing by hand requires a lot of equipment (paper, pens, typewriters, envelopes, postage stamps); a lot of thought (a good letter requires a knowledge of grammar and spelling, if not elegance of expression); and a lot of time (in the writing, if you stop to choose the right words or rewrite, and in the mailing, as a letter can take days to reach its recipient—in prior centuries it could take weeks or months). Digital devices have relieved us from all of these constraints—there's a single device, and delivery is almost instantaneous, which in turn allows us to shoot off one line if we're not up to a whole letter, and lets tone and reflection fall by the wayside. (This is not to suggest that digital letter writing is better in every way. Many still enjoy paper letter writing—remember how exciting it was to receive a handwritten letter? Also, think of all we know about past generations from the physical letters they left behind. Without tangible correspondence, it's harder to see how future generations will learn about our inner workings.)

Even more salient than ease of use, though, is the different potential for dissemination. One need only compare the trouble and bother of copying and handing out paper notes about, say, the state of your vegetable garden with the click-a-button convenience of posting on Facebook or texting your friends, to see why the broad dissemination of routine information, once a rarity, is now commonplace. We are swimming (perhaps drowning) in a sea of data and information.

But human cognitive processes struggle, unfortunately, to digest and process this extraordinary potential for wide dissemination. Humans have evolved with conversation that most often occurs between two people or a small group of people, and for which wide dissemination is limited and difficult. If you're chatting by the lockers, you're not scanning every potential word with hypervigilance, knowing that any nugget of content might make the evening news as the viral quote of the week. Instead, you just talk. You enjoy the emotional connection you're experiencing with your friends and the topic you're discussing. Faithful and accurate replication of your words and mannerisms would be challenging (short of surreptitiously recording you), and even if replication were done well, it would be difficult (without digital media) to spread what you said beyond a few concentric circles of your acquaintanceship.

The trouble is that just as we relax and enjoy our offline chats, so do we relax and enjoy our online chats and postings without the vigilance and filter we sometimes need to apply to information that could easily be widely disseminated. Think of Brett Favre, Anthony Weiner, Christopher Lee, Larry Johnson, Gilbert Gottfried—and these are just a few of the famous cases of unintended fame. Posting or sending something that eventually goes mega-public (even though you don't intend it to) is the common cold of today's social faux pas.

Hopefully we'll learn, as a society, to adjust our attention when engaging in digital talk. But for now we generally don't watch what we say electronically, and the exposure of pictures and text that are embarrassing and even serious is a preferred method for cyberbullying. In my 2011 study of college freshmen, 22 percent of girls said that someone else had revealed a private fact or photo of them that they didn't want disclosed.[13] This potential for wide dissemination is one way that electronic communications differ dramatically from just talking, and one important way that using cyber communication contributes significantly to bullying.

False Sense of Privacy, Anonymity, Disinhibition, and Casual Cruelty

Digital communications can *feel* deceptively private. This is related to the dissemination issue—that is, the feeling that this conversation isn't going further than you and me—but other elements can add to a false sense of privacy. Writing to someone in the safety and privacy of home, enclosed by four walls, can make the exchange feel like it's happening at home and not on the World Wide Web. But while a cozy home may contribute, you don't even need walls to feel that a digital give-and-take is just between you two. Just tapping out a message on your cell phone can feel private, even if you're standing in Grand Central Station in New York City during rush hour. If you spoke aloud on the phone, the people milling around you would be able to hear at least half of the conversation, and you might well rein in what you'd say as a result. For example, instead of announcing "I'm pregnant!" you might cryptically impart, in a low voice, "The test was positive." But a written text message feels more private because none of the people physically surrounding you can see the small screen, so they don't have any idea about the content of the message. You can type anything at all. This sense of insulation can, in turn, contribute to disinhibition about what you reveal, and sometimes, to the thoughtless production of casual cruelty.

Anonymity

Much has been made about anonymity and its role in promoting cyberbullying. Many writers cite first and foremost the ability of cyberbullies to be anonymous.[14] It's notable, however, that not all research supports the assumption that cyberbullies typically believe themselves to be anonymous.

My study of grades 3–12 found that, by high school, about 74 percent of cybervictims *knew* the identity of the cyberbully. Anonymity online was much more common in the elementary years.[15] As the children got older, their online interactions more and more closely reflected and influenced their peer relationships in school.

Disinhibition and lack of nonverbal cues

Communicating electronically makes people less inhibited about both content and tone. People say and do things when online or texting that they wouldn't say or do otherwise.[16] This isn't really news, at least according to the students I study. They clearly grasp this phenomenon, since 90 percent of girls and 75 percent of boys agreed that digital environments lead to disinhibited tone and disclosures.[17]

It appears that the perceived privacy of the interaction and the lack of face-to-face cues generate this disinhibition. The fact that your discussant isn't right there in front of you is an important difference between electronic communications and talking. When physical presence is removed, so too is a host of verbal and nonverbal social communication cues, including body language, tone of voice, and facial expressions. As an example of how such cues usually influence our responses, consider the interesting fact that research has actually correlated the scheduling of a school exam with a sudden crisis in the health and, yes, the very *life* of students' grandparents.[18] The result is that almost all teachers have had students pitch to them an improbable "grandparent" excuse for a late assignment or for missing an exam. While we listen respectfully to the story of a grandmother's hospitalization, we usually manage to convey our skepticism through our body language—arms crossed, face attentive but skeptical. Students who watch and note these nonverbal cues often quickly decide to backpedal. Without those feedback cues, however, they remain uninhibited by and unaware of their excuse's implausibility, and may simply charge ahead blindly with the sales pitch.

In the case of cyberbullying, the lack of feedback cues in front of us means that correspondingly, we don't always know when something is hurting another person's feelings. Let's turn the tables on our example. If a student really *does* have a sick grandparent, his visible distress can lead the teacher to accommodate a family crisis. But if the student has simply e-mailed a note about the situation, the teacher lacks the nonverbal feedback cues that signal distress, and might not accept the explanation. Similarly, any exchange that lacks all the detailed and rich nonverbal data could result in a lack of understanding, "negligent" cyberbullying, or nasty remarks that reach far beyond their original intent.

There is evidence that body and language cues, in person, can reduce aggression. One study of sixty-four male undergraduates in Canada found that seeing a victim's pain cues reduced aggression in most situations.[19] Bullies who are more interested in third-factor goals (e.g., enhancing their social status) or who underestimate the impact of what they do can be made so uncomfortable by the social cues of in-person events that they reduce or even stop aggression. In my research, a substantial proportion of bullies reported were *dabblers*; they only bullied once (that is, they engaged in one cluster of repetitive attacks on a less powerful person). The most common reason for stopping (38 percent) was because "I started to feel bad about the whole thing" (perhaps these subjects were taken aback by the impact of their cruelty and concluded that it wasn't worth it).[20]

While in-person pain cues may serve to put the brakes on, in a digital environment there is a *lack* of nonverbal cues, which may contribute to online bullying by those who typically wouldn't bully in person.[21] A meta-analysis of forty-nine studies looking at the intersections between aggression and social cues revealed that online bullies tend to reduce their focus on the target (who is, after all, not physically present) and increase their self-focus, which could explain an increase in the propensity to be aggressive by reducing any focus on the victim's suffering.[22]

Sometimes third factors—for example, alcohol use—interact with a digital environment to increase disinhibition even further. That's hardly surprising; alcohol use is related to disinhibition of aggression generally. My own research has found that problems with alcohol are reported more often among subjects who admit to being bullies or bully/victims, both in person and online.[23] Slightly more than a quarter (26 percent) of the subjects in this study said that for them, using substances made them more likely to cyberbully specifically, suggesting that factors that disinhibit people generally may do so electronically as well. [24]

Inflation/Escalation of Emotions

One of the most fascinating characteristics of digital communications is how it can alter your feelings in a way that paper writing generally doesn't. As I mentioned in chapter 3, even prior to the widespread use of electronic communication technology, psychologists had noted that repetitive exposure to emotional materials sometimes "primed" subjects and made them feel emotions more intensely.[25] Once digital technology came into play, it greatly increased the repetitive exposure of individuals to emotion-laden content. Consider a semifictional exchange between teens (not word for word, but based on a real conversation):

TEEN 1: M so mad at C. She wrecked my swter [sent to multiple friends via text message]
TEEN 2: dnt blame u she did same 2 me [reply]
TEEN 3: I no u r mad [reply]
TEEN 4: im mad at hr 2

And so on. The point is that each reply text reiterates the emotion (anger), and thus primes and increases the initial sender's feelings. On paper, such a message might go out to only one or two people, who would take days (or longer) to reply. The time lapse would undoubtedly blunt the priming effects, especially in the case of mild emotions like irritation. But through the medium of text messaging, the original sender might receive back literally dozens of reiterations of his or her feelings, in writing, within a few minutes or hours. Reading over and over about these feelings is thus likely to artificially inflate and escalate them.

This can theoretically occur for any type of emotion, positive or negative. Like a boy a little bit before noon? By the evening, you're in love. Are you annoyed with your friend? By the time school lets out, you may be furious. And of course, the kids involved aren't saying to themselves, "Gee, I'm feeling substantially more angry than I did this morning over such a little thing. That's crazy!" Instead, they simply think, "I am *really* mad at her." The more their feelings are primed and reiterated by their support group of friends, the stronger their feelings are and the more justified they feel in experiencing them.

It's ironic that this kind of false emotional escalation can happen when kids are doing what should be a healthy reaction to any distressing emotion, even mild ones. The difficulty is that students (more often girls) are seeking this support in a digital arena, where the dynamics change. I tried to replicate this effect in the lab by introducing freshman subjects to a mildly annoying scenario. After reading about the scenario, half the subjects read one text message from a sympathetic friend, while the second half (randomly assigned) read five text messages from friends sympathetically reiterating the subject's annoyance. Subjects who received one text message rated themselves as less annoyed than subjects who received five text messages, although the presented scenarios were identical.[26] As I noted in chapter 3, girls seem to be more likely than boys to experience this phe-

nomenon—a pattern consistent with the fieldwork we do at the Massachusetts Aggression Reduction Center, where we often speak with teenage girls
about this type of difficulty in their friendships.

Another way to study this is through the examination of mild social
problems that escalate into serious ones. In the 2011–12 freshman study, I
asked subjects about this type of problem with friends during high school.
Girls were more likely than boys to say that a minor disagreement with a
friend had blown up into a big one. Further, more than half (52 percent) of
the girls said that during the blow-up they had been texting many friends.
Only 27 percent of boys texted friends in similar circumstances.[27] This
probably reflects a generally higher preference for text messaging among
girls, relative to boys (33 percent of boys versus 49 percent of girls opined
that their favorite method of communication in high school was text messaging.) Lots of other research has also noted that girls outpace boys in texting.[28] This marked preference for texting may help girls communicate
more (a good thing), but it may also make them more vulnerable to a digitally fueled escalation in their interpersonal conflicts. In any case, the potential for emotional escalation is one way that electronic interactions
clearly differ from in-person ones.

Inability of Targets to Get Away

Many children (and adults) today tend to see digital messaging or screens
as something that they never really get away from.[29] Middle-aged adults
(those born, for example, prior to 1970) may have a relatively harder time
understanding why electronic communication is so central to children today. However, the lives of today's children and teens are so impacted by
technology that they may assume there is realistically no alternative to
constant connectivity. For those who grew up with the landline telephone
as their primary means of communication, the fuss over cruelty on screens
may seem misplaced. I have noticed that some advice given to victims of
cyberbullying—"Just pull the plug!"—can be misguided because of this.
The growing population of "connected" adults knows that such a solution
is completely unrealistic, but they still often tell targets to simply block the
offending cyberbully (i.e., to disable the bully's ability to send a message or
posting directly to them). But by blocking one of the key players in the
drama (the bully), the victims no longer know what's being said to the
wider audience. So they may not want to block the cyberbully; or they may
comply with the adult's advice, only to unblock the person soon after.

These actions can be baffling, in much the same way that society used
to be baffled by battered women who stayed with their abusive husbands.

But behavior rarely occurs entirely without reason. By the 1970s, psychology had begun to realize that battered women were often motivated by fear of retaliation or financial dependence, rather than by masochism, although the standard diagnostic manual used in psychiatry didn't drop the masochism concept until 1994.[30] Just as in the case of battered women, cyber-victims have a rational reason to keep communications open with the peers who bully them; generally, they simply feel a strong need to be in the loop.[31] Being excluded from the communications is, for many teens, very anxiety provoking.[32] Indeed, teens are so strongly motivated to keep the flow of information going that they may not even tell adults about cyber-bullying, for fear their devices might be taken away.[33]

More Severe Impact Than Traditional Bullying

Another difference is that cyberbullying may have more of an impact than traditional bullying, at least for some subjects or in some circumstances. A 2009 study of about seventeen hundred Spanish adolescents compared the impact of in-person and online bullying, and found that subjects had a wide range of emotional reactions to traditional bullying, but tended to more extreme responses—either disregarding or being significantly impacted—with cyberbullying.[34] During the freshman study in 2012, subjects were twice as likely to categorize the most upsetting and serious threats they received during high school as digital (42 percent) rather than in person (21 percent).[35] One reason that cyberbullying may have greater impact is that the impossibility of controlling dissemination may particularly enhance the sense of helplessness so common to victimization.[36]

What Do Our Students Need to Learn About Cyber Communication?

1. Talking digitally isn't like talking in person. It is very easy to widely disseminate everything that is said.
2. Talking digitally can make you feel uninhibited and may lead to more thoughtless, casual cruelty.
3. Texting or posting back and forth about a feeling (like being annoyed) can cause that feeling to escalate and might make the situation worse.
4. It's hard to get away from an electronic problem. Understand that and help your friends if they need your support.
5. Sometimes cyberbullying has a bigger impact that bullying in person. Just because it's not face-to-face doesn't mean it doesn't hurt.

CONTROLLING TECHNOLOGY,
INSTEAD OF LETTING IT CONTROL US

Growing up during the Cold War, I vividly recall hearing laments about nuclear technology and our collective human failure to control our own technological advances. Whether or not our nuclear technology is better controlled today is questionable, but the same principle needs to be applied to digital technology. Electronic devices should be used to enhance our lives and to serve us—not enslave us. This is an important concept that children (as well as adults) need to consider, discuss, and study.

I mentioned briefly above the anxiety that subjects reported upon having to theoretically give up their devices for one hour. Both teens and adults have talked with me about their emotional response to being alerted to their device (e.g., by vibrating or ringing) but being unable to attend to it (e.g., being in a meeting or in class). One girl described the different possibilities that made her anxious; she talked about worrying that someone could be angry at her, or that others could be discussing her and she "wouldn't know about it." This was characterized as a potentially serious, even catastrophic, problem. Almost a third of subjects (32 percent) agreed with the statement, "not answering my phone right away makes me feel anxious." Almost a quarter (24 percent) said they would "worry that a text was about me," and 22 percent responded that "someone could get mad" if they couldn't respond immediately to a text or posting. These anxieties seem to lead some people to feel controlled by their device (i.e., they jump when it calls) and the constant link to a communications network, rather than in control of it. One researcher has coined a name for the fear of being without one's cell phone—*nomophobia*—and has noted the anxiety that accompanies even the *idea* of being without the device.[37]

The anxiety about not being connected isn't confined to children. For adults, this phenomenon may manifest in constant checks for work-related communications, even after work hours. Interestingly, an international company (Volkswagen) recently decided to take the bull by the horns and help workers balance home and work life by deliberately not forwarding e-mails to mobile devices after work hours.[38] A myriad of similar mobile applications ("apps") have been developed to help users artificially limit their access to e-mails or messages (e.g., BreakTime, Desktop Task Timer). From a psychological point of view, all of this is intriguing because it suggests that some people cannot or will not stop on their own, but require mechanical help to control their e-mail-checking behaviors.

But can education and awareness address this? Actually, awareness of this anxiety is the first step in controlling and mastering it, and in my fieldwork, I see very little awareness about anxiety around digital devices in general.[39] Kids see them as fun, entertaining, and connecting, but they seem less aware of any impact from being constantly connected. The novelty of this issue means that few adults are aware of it either, but awareness does seem to be increasing, and I'm optimistic that once we appreciate the differences between electronic communication and other forms of communication, and how they impact our lives, we will begin to better understand and deal with the incidence and types of cyberbullying.

What Complicates Our Ability to Teach Children About These Issues?

Cyberbullying isn't just different from bullying in terms of the media used. It's also a topic that fills many adults with a particular sense of unease and, sometimes, sheer inadequacy. We see the problem, but can't see ourselves as being helpful in the solution. One of the more persistent myths about children and cybertechnology is the belief that children know "everything" about technology, so there's no point in adults becoming involved in cyberbullying or cyber education, because the kids are so far ahead of us. If your teenager is your at-home tech support, then what can *you* possibly teach *her*?

Children themselves largely adhere to this belief. On a scale of 1 to 10, most subjects in the 2010 freshman study rated their knowledge about computers and using the Internet at 8, 9, or 10. However, when we actually *tested* their knowledge about using computers, the Internet, and social networking sites, they scored (on average) in the D or C range (60 percent to 77 percent correct). One computer science teacher pointed out that the largest subset of his students consisted of kids who knew very little about computers, and who didn't particularly want to know more.[40] The limitless sophistication of children's understanding of technology may therefore be something of a myth.

Children are, however, very *comfortable* with technology. While adults might worry about breaking an unfamiliar device, children generally aren't afraid to pick up new electronic devices and push buttons until they achieve the effect they want. This markedly comfortable use of digital devices is probably due to their superior grasp of the similar logic underlying many different digital devices. For example, most devices have some type of "back" key, and pressing that key causes the same action to occur. Once you know what the back key does on device 1, you can pick up totally novel device 2 and understand that purpose of the back key before you even use it. Many of the features and functions on digital devices are consistent in this way. People of all ages actually note these types of patterns in stimuli.[41] However, adults' greater life experience may make them consider both patterns and the possible exceptions to those patterns. Just because both buttons *say* "back," does it mean that they both *do* the same thing? Children, in contrast, tend to accept the consistency of patterns more readily, without considering the possibility of exceptions.[42] When they apply learned patterns to new digital devices, they're usually successful, and these successes increase their confidence in their own abilities.

So an adult may see children fearlessly using different devices and conclude that they're knowledgeable; but in fact, that adult may be confusing the skill of *using technology* with the skill of *using technology wisely*. Some of us will indeed be teaching children how to use technology, but for most adults, our role needs to focus on helping children understand the *impact* of what they do electronically. How can what we type or post be misinterpreted or misunderstood? How can electronic communications be disseminated? When is it appropriate to use more direct interpersonal communications, instead of technology? How does using technology intersect with mental health and relationships?

This can begin with teaching students about the ways in which digital communications differ from other forms of communication. Unfortunately, in my experience, this is still rarely, if ever, addressed either in school or at home. Most adults cannot teach children about these issues, simply because they don't understand them themselves. This doesn't represent a failure; it's just too new a field to have generated a broad degree of understanding.

But if our goal is to help children minimize abusive interactions, we've got to teach them to successfully communicate, and to interpret others' communications, in electronic realms. Despite our anxieties about knowing less than our students, the fact is that their mastery of technological mechanics doesn't always include the impact of using technology to communicate. We need to coach children on how their communications change in a digital environment, and how they can learn to master their anxiety so that their devices don't control them. We also need to discuss how what you intend to communicate can be very different from what the recipient subjectively hears, and that this is *especially* true in digital environments. If we're to help children control their use of technology, we need to understand what it is they need to know. So, before we can teach them to do that, we have to teach ourselves.

CHAPTER 5

New Times, New Troubles

Sexting, Self-Cyberbullying,
and Other Risky Online Behaviors

Survey Suggests "Sexting" Rampant in College[1]

Few Teens Sexting Racy Photos, New Research Says[2]

In 2010, there were an estimated 112 *million* episodes of drunk driving in the United States, according to a report from the Centers for Disease Control and Prevention.[3] But despite the risk and tragedy involved, the authors of that report never recommended that the use of automobiles be abandoned. That would have been an absurd suggestion, since cars are overwhelmingly a positive influence on modern life. Similarly, in this chapter I'm going to discuss some serious problems that occur with digital communications, but that shouldn't be taken as a recommendation that we abandon them. Most of our online experiences are positive, not negative, as a recent study from Pew found. Even teenagers, who are relatively more likely to report negative experiences, still experienced the Internet as generally positive.[4] It's important to remember that, even though my focus here is on problems.

Some of the issues that digital technology has brought up are truly novel—others are just reiterations of existing problems. It's also important to note that the topics covered in this chapter—sexting, self-bullying, and other risky behaviors—are not cyberbullying per se. There's little doubt, though, that some of these more peculiar online behaviors can be related to cyberbullying or to digital abuse in general. Understanding them can help us identify and perhaps reduce problems and bullying online, so it's worth taking some time to look at a few of the more prominent oddities. In this chapter, I provide some data and perspective on sexting, how and why kids cyberbully themselves, how the very young use technology, and how children view the very fluid issue of "privacy."[5]

I also share some research on what kids get away with in school; illicit cell phone use; and why children today might seek the anonymous opinions of total strangers online as a strategy for obtaining really candid, honest, and constructive feedback (and end up making themselves vulnerable to abuse). These issues seem to be risk factors rather than causes of cyberbullying—they may increase the likelihood of bullying online, but they don't seem to single-handedly and reliably cause cyberbullying to occur.

SEXTING

Sexting can be variably defined as "the electronic sending of pictures depicting nudity," the sending of pictures depicting "semi-nudity," or as "sending or posting sexually explicit pictures *or* writing." In the freshman study it was defined as "sending nude pictures of yourself." However you define it, if one judged this issue by the headlines, you might conclude it was epidemic. Stories in the press suggest that everyone seems to be doing it— sports stars, teenagers, retirees, even members of Congress.[6]

How Often Does Sexting Really Happen?

As with bullying and cyberbullying in general, surveys on the frequency of sexting tend to produce a wide variety of numbers. In my survey of college students, 30 percent reported they had sent nude pictures at some point during high school, and 45 percent said that they had received such pictures on their cell phones.[7] Similar numbers have been found in other surveys of college students.[8] On the other hand, a telephone survey by Mitchell et al. of a national sample of 1,560 children and teens revealed very different answers. In this poll—which was quite important, as it was the first to examine a nationally representative sample—only 2.5 percent of subjects reported making a nude image, and only 7.1 percent reported receiving one during the previous year.[9]

Those numbers sound very different, but closer scrutiny reveals key similarities. The *age of the subjects studied* is the primary difference between studies that found different frequencies of sexting. The Mitchell et al. survey included a wide range of ages (ten to seventeen), but at the older end of the spectrum (the sixteen- and seventeen-year-olds), rates of sexting were 31 percent and 41 percent, respectively. A second 2012 study of sexting among eleven- to eighteen-year-olds, conducted by Dake et al., found the same pattern; namely, that while "only" 17 percent of all students engaged in sexting, 32 percent of eighteen-year-olds did so.[10] Thus, all the different studies showed similar rates (about 30 to 40 percent) among older teens. Although the study reported by Mitchell et al. and Dake *appeared* to find lower rates of sexting, they actually found comparable rates when equivalent age groups were compared.

Putting all the pieces together, it appears that older subjects are substantially more likely than younger subjects to report that they sext, and that rates over extended time periods (more than one year, as with the freshman study) may be higher as well. Although all studies were done anonymously, it's also possible that subjects might be forthcoming about sexting if they are older, and are contacted by a familiar organization (versus by a stranger on the telephone).

The bottom line is that sexting is by no means as widespread as media reports might imply, but a significant minority of teenagers do engage in this online behavior. That said, I think that the scrutiny over the frequency of sexting is really a tempest in a teapot, and that a realistic focus on the social and emotional impact would be more productive. We shouldn't simply assume that sexting is associated with serious difficulties, or consequences, despite media cases that document the contrary. One important finding of the freshman study is that the majority of sexting doesn't appear to result in any significant trouble, although some types of sexting may be more problematic than others. What appears to be key is the reason *why* a teen chooses to sext.

What Motivates Sexting?

Indisputably, the most important motivation for sexting revealed in the freshman study (and others) was "pressure or coercion." A few years ago, I assumed that being pressured and/or coerced into sexting would be a very rare occurrence; but overall, about half of the freshman study sexters reported that they felt pressured, coerced, blackmailed, bullied, or threatened into sexting.[11] This proportion was consistent in my studies of eighteen-year-olds done in both 2011 and 2012.[12] I'm not the only researcher who picked up this trend: a qualitative report released earlier this year in the United Kingdom also identified coercive sexting as a major area of concern.[13]

In the freshman study, girls were more likely than boys to report that they had sexted, but this difference was entirely due to more girls reporting that they had been pressured, coerced, blackmailed, or threatened into sexting. The genders didn't differ on rates of voluntary or willing sexting.

When asked to rate, on a scale of 1 to 10, how upsetting it had been to send the nude picture, those who sexted voluntarily didn't experience it as very upsetting. Most of them (79 percent) selected the "least upset" ratings (a 1 or 2 out of 10). But those subjects who were pressured and/or coerced into sexting felt (not surprisingly) much more upset by the experience. In contrast to the willing sexters, only 17 percent of the pressured sexters selected the "least upset" rating.

Willing and pressured sexters didn't differ only on how upset they felt about sexting; they also differed on their motivations for sexting. Both types were most likely to report that a boyfriend or girlfriend wanted the picture, and least likely to say that someone at school or online had blackmailed them into providing the picture. But pressured sexters were three times as likely (55 versus 18 percent) to say that a *prospective* date (i.e., someone they weren't yet dating, but wanted to) wanted the picture, and they were also more likely to report that they were uncomfortable about providing the picture but ultimately decided that it "wasn't a big deal." As for any negative consequences following the sexting, almost a third of pressured sexters reported problems with peers or adults after they sent the picture (32 percent), but only 8 percent of willing sexters had those problems.

Taken together, this data suggests to me that it's really pressured or coerced sexting that represents the most significant problem. Pressure and/or coercion to sext may be twice as common among girls as it is among boys. For either gender, this type of sexting could be characterized as a form of sexual harassment. Pressured sexters were more upset by having sexted, and they were much more likely to have troubling consequences following sexting (primarily with peers). But it's also clear that not *all* social pressure to sext was experienced negatively. Teens who sexted willingly for an existing boyfriend or girlfriend experienced few negative outcomes and weren't apparently upset by the experience. But keep in mind that this study didn't track any long-term effects of sexting, and questions still remain about possible consequences years, or even decades, down the road. Given the highly publicized results for a few individuals, it's not such a stretch to envision the possibility of significant long-term costs and wonder, *What on earth were they thinking?*

What teens seem to be thinking about when they sext are their peer relationships. Although adults may worry that adolescent sexting can be solicited by predatory adults online, almost all the subjects in the freshman study who had received a nude picture (96 percent) reported that they recognized the person in the picture. Further, when I asked subjects, in the abstract, why sexting occurs, the most common reasons given were because a boyfriend or girlfriend wanted the picture, because the picture could attract someone you're interested in, or because it could demonstrate trust. Sexting was much less commonly attributed to reasons such as "it's the style now" or "it's just funny" or "it's a joke." All in all, subjects seemed to involve adults only rarely in sexting problems. Complications resulting from adults finding out about a nude picture were very rare, relative to problems resulting from peers seeing or hearing about the sexting. And if subjects had received a nude picture, the recipients' most common action was simply to delete it. Predictably, no subjects said that they had shown the picture to an adult, or even told an adult about getting it in the first place.

Characteristics of Nonsexters Versus Sexters

A few characteristics separated sexters from nonsexters more generally. Subjects who sexted were far more likely, compared to nonsexters, to report that they were sexually active during high school. Approximately 57 percent of nonsexters reported being sexually active, in comparison to 86 percent of those who engaged in sexting. Both pressured and nonpressured sexters were similarly elevated at 85 percent and 86 percent, respectively. Being sexually active was associated with sexting *in general*. Subjects who engaged in sexting were also more likely to report that they had also received nude photos. Most nonsexters (71 percent) reported that they hadn't received such images, while the opposite was true for both pressured and nonpressured sexters.

All sexters also reported more problems with anxiety, in comparison to subjects who had never sexted (55 versus 35 percent), and more problems with making friends (33 versus 22 percent). They described somewhat higher rates of violence in their family while growing up (20 percent versus 13.5 percent for nonsexters). Finally, sexters were also more likely than nonsexters to report that they had engaged in self-cyberbullying (described in detail next).[14] Only 8 percent of nonsexters had self-cyberbullied, but 18 percent of sexters admitted to this behavior.

But while sexters as a group tended to differ from nonsexters on some characteristics, on others, sexters weren't such a homogeneous group.

Unique Characteristics of Pressured Versus Willing Sexters

Some risk factors were elevated in all sexters, but were particularly elevated in either willing or pressured sexters. Willing sexters, when compared to pressured sexters and to nonsexters, showed higher rates of factors generally associated with psychological difficulties. (I was actually anticipating that pressured sexters would be higher in these factors, but the opposite turned out to be true.) Willing sexters were highest, pressured sexters were in the middle, and nonsexters were lowest, in reporting *depression* (67, 50, and 40 percent, respectively); *alcohol and substance abuse* (21, 11, and 8 percent); problems with controlling their *temper* (36, 29, and 20 percent); and problems making or keeping *friends* (39, 29, and 22 percent). Note that for most of these factors, pressured sexters still reported somewhat higher rates compared to their nonsexting peers.

Although willing sexters reported higher rates of these problems, the pressured sexters seemed more likely to report problems having to do with dating relationships. For example, prior dating violence was a specific risk that pressured sexters were the most likely group to report; almost half (48 percent) of pressured sexters, but only one-third of nonpressured sexters and one-fourth of nonsexters, reported prior dating violence. But this pattern didn't remain true for *all* types of previous violence; all sexters were similarly elevated in their history of family violence. The prior violence risk factor for pressured sexters seemed confined to violence in prior dating relationships. Recall also that pressured sexters were most likely to engage in sexting when a prospective date asked for a nude picture (a situation I compared to sexual harassment, above).

Overall, it seems that all sexters—even those who do so willingly—are higher in general psychological risk factors. Pressured sexters stand out, however, for problems in dating relationships. These difficulties may be at least part of the reason why some teens appear to be more vulnerable when they are asked to send a nude picture to someone with whom they're not in a trusting relationship.

RISKS ASSOCIATED WITH SEXTING

Apart from a teen's willingness to sext, the psychological issues associated with choosing to sext, or their feelings about having sexted, there are other consequences to consider. Although a teenager may envision sexting as a private affair between them and the photo's recipient, when others discover what's going on, unpleasantness may ensue. That appears to happen at times, regardless of whether the discovery is made by a peer, an adult, or the long arm of the law.

The Risk of Criminal Prosecution

In the United States, sending a nude photo of a minor is a crime, even if it's a self-portrait. When sexting first emerged as an issue, several high-profile cases of teens being prosecuted for child pornography were widely discussed. One result of these cases is that the possibility of criminal prosecution is sometimes emphasized to students above all else.

Does it matter what that risk really is? If there's even a 1 percent chance of prosecution, many would argue that it needs to be spelled out to students. That's reasonable, but I would still argue that probability does matter, simply because educators must have credibility to teach effectively. When adults headline risks that students feel sure are very unlikely (or even rare), they tend to sacrifice believability. Teens may suspect that adults don't like sexting because of its sexual nature, and are seizing on any potential risk (even a far-fetched one) to discourage its proliferation. Rather than lose the audience, it's probably better to assign prosecution a reasonable level of emphasis, even if it's hard to know what the true risk really is. Luckily, we do have some research that can help us estimate the probability of prosecution when a minor sends a nude picture of themselves or of a peer.

Although criminal prosecution for sexting does still occur, most jurisdictions appear to be backing off on prosecuting teens who sext as if they were adult purveyors of child pornography.[15] A national study found that by 2012, few teenage sexting cases were actually being prosecuted in a criminal court.[16] A 2011 survey of law enforcement found that the majority of cases that led to an arrest had serious aggravating circumstances (e.g., an adult was involved); only 18 percent of sexting cases that had no aggravating circumstances progressed to that point.[17] No one can, or should, say that sexting carries no legal risks; but implying that prosecution is common may be equally disingenuous.

Discovery by Peers or Adults

Some teens may regard trouble with parents or adults at school as a more probable result of sexting, but that consequence also doesn't appear to happen often. In the freshman study, slightly fewer than three-quarters (73 percent) of all sexters reported that to their knowledge, the picture(s) was never shown to anyone apart from the intended recipient. Willing sexters were less likely to say the picture was "passed around" (15 percent reported this), but even among pressured sexters, passing around wasn't overwhelmingly common. Still, slightly more than a third of pressured sexters said that the nude self-portrait was shown to others (34 percent). Clearly, pressured sexters (who were more likely to be sexting outside of an established relationship) were more likely to suffer through having a private photo shown to peers or adults.

Media stories tend to depict sexting episodes that involve a nude picture being seen, usually with lightning speed, by many, many others. That probably does happen—for example, a photo could easily be passed around to dozens or hundreds of other students—but the data doesn't suggest that this is typical. Overall, 19 percent of sexters reported that the picture was seen by one or two people after the original recipient, and only 8 percent said it was seen by three or more. Even when the picture was disseminated, it didn't always lead to trouble—although 27 percent of sexters said others saw their nude picture, only 18 percent said it caused trouble for them. Notably, when these images *are* seen by others, and then do cause problems, it doesn't seem to be the adults who generally see and respond to them. Sexters reported that their parents saw the image only 3 to 4 percent of the time, and both pressured and willing sexters reported getting into trouble with their parents because of the picture at very low rates (only 5.4 percent and 3 percent). Getting into trouble with the school adults was even lower—about 1 percent and 3 percent, respectively.

In contrast, trouble from peers was the most common type, for both pressured and willing sexters. About 14 percent of pressured sexters and 6 percent of willing sexters reported having trouble from peers because of the pictures that were shown around. I didn't ask subjects about specific types of problems with peers, but based on my fieldwork, it seems likely that problems would cluster around gossip and rumors, sexual harassment, and in more severe cases, social rejection and/or extreme humiliation and isolation. I think that the social impact of sexting, if taken to extremes by peers, can be potentially devastating. Luckily, such outcomes seem to be the exception, rather than the rule.

Raising a Red Flag on Coerced Sexting

Although my findings reveal that sexting is less likely to result in a backlash than the media might have led us to believe, the fact that kids may sext when coerced or pressured to do so is a problem that should not be minimized. As noted above, about half of the girls and a third of the boys who sexted said they did so at least once because someone else pressured or coerced them to send a nude picture. Pressure applied in the context of a relationship (i.e., with a current boyfriend or girlfriend) wasn't always experienced as a problem; what's of more concern are the subjects who did experience the pressure negatively, most commonly when the pressure came from someone the sexter wanted to date (most often a potential boyfriend). It's troubling to think that intimate pictures might be solicited from vulnerable, eager-to-please teenagers. Although I don't by any means think the higher rates of depression and substance abuse among all types of sexters should be ignored, the pressured sexters seem to be dealing with an additional set of troubles. They were the sexters most likely to have a history of dating violence and most likely to report that the picture(s) ultimately caused problems for them, usually with their peers and occasionally with adults. Thus, they may be the most vulnerable students—prior victims who are being revictimized.

SELF-CYBERBULLYING OR DIGITAL SELF-HARM

In 2010, following some perceptive conversations with teenagers, danah boyd [sic] published a blog in which she described incidents of "digital self-harm," which she described as teens "who are self-harassing by 'anonymously' writing mean questions to themselves and then publicly answering them."[18] This phenomenon was initially uncovered by the staff at a website, Formspring, who investigated some cyberbullying and found that the alleged victims had actually posted the cruel comments against themselves. I've referred to this phenomenon more casually as *digital Munchausen* because of its resemblance to the psychiatric disorder known as Munchausen syndrome.[19] The syndrome's central identifying symptom is the patient's infliction of self-harm in a quest for sympathy, attention, and admiration for their ability to cope with their "victimization." In 2012, I studied this type of online behavior in the freshman study, where 10 percent of the subjects told us that they had falsely posted a cruel remark against themselves, or cyberbullied themselves, during high school.[20] Interestingly, a higher proportion of boys (17 percent) admitted to this than did girls (8 percent). Half of these digital self-harmers had done this only once or very infrequently; the other half reported that they had cyberbullied themselves more regularly or had one ongoing episode that lasted at least several months.

Motivations for, and Success of, Digital Self-harm

Why might teens engage in this kind of bizarre form of self-harm? Boyd speculated on three possibilities: self-harmers might be uttering a "cry for help," they might want to appear "cool," or they may be trying to "trigger compliments." In my study, both male and female subjects were most likely to say they actually did this in an attempt to gain the attention of a peer, and were least likely to have done it "as a joke" on someone else. Girls were more likely than boys to say that their motivation was "proving I could take it," encouraging others "to worry about me," or to "get adult attention." Boys were more likely to say that they did this because they were mad, as a way to start a fight (presumably, they would falsely blame the person they were angry at).

Overall, I wouldn't characterize self-cyberbullying as a very successful strategy. More than half (57 percent) of the digital self-harmers related that the strategy didn't really work as intended. Many of those (62 percent) said that not only was the strategy unsuccessful, it actually made them feel worse afterwards. The remaining 38 percent said that despite the self-cyberbullying not working, they felt "OK" about it.

Slightly fewer than half (43 percent) of self-cyberbullies felt that this was a successful strategy because "I achieved what I wanted." The success of digital self-harm depended, at least in part, on the goal. For subjects who wanted to gain a peer's attention or "look tough," it was a much more successful strategy than for the subjects who were trying to start a fight or make a joke. But even among the subjects who felt the strategy worked overall, the picture isn't completely positive. More than two-thirds (72 percent) of the successful self-cyberbullies said that they didn't actually feel better afterwards. Out of all the subjects who said they self-cyberbullied, only 16 percent said that the strategy was successful for them *and* that they felt better afterwards.

If digital self-harmers are uttering a cry for help, we might expect them to be more likely to have other psychiatric issues. There is some evidence for that. There were no differences between self-harmers and non-self-harmers for depression and anxiety, but digital self-harmers were more likely to have had three or more psychiatric issues during high school and were also more likely to report being frequent users of drugs and alcohol.

Whether you call it digital self-harm or digital Munchausen, the fact that some students stage their own cyberbullying is an issue that educators should be aware of. I've noticed in the field that most adults accept printed transcripts as irrefutable proof of cyberbullying, but the existence of self-bullying suggests that we may be too innocent in this regard. Short of a confession or the utilization of digital forensics (beyond the desire or the capacity of almost all schools and parents), it may in fact be hard to know when a case of cyberbullying is "real." But this issue probably has a silver lining. Since a school's jurisdiction over an online bully is not unlimited, what this phenomenon really does is reinforce the need to focus on the targets of online abuse. When students claim to be victims of cyberbullying, they need our support and attention. That need should be front and center, regardless of whether the cyberbullying is real or manufactured. In fact, students who fabricate their own cyberbullying may need our attention most of all.

DIGITAL RISK-TAKING IN ELEMENTARY AND HIGH SCHOOL

Although adults have focused almost exclusively on cyber problems among children in middle and high school, such issues do in fact emerge during elementary school. My study of more than eleven thousand elementary school children helped shed light on how cyberbullying and cyber behaviors emerge prior to preadolescence.

Cyber Risk-Taking at the Elementary Level

When I decided to study school-age children in Massachusetts, I started with third graders for a couple of reasons.[21] First and foremost, I was conducting a study using a written survey, and children are generally comfortably literate by third grade. But also, third grade seemed like a reasonable place to begin when measuring the climb into digital technology. Although many elementary school teachers I interacted with were skeptical about the idea that their students spent any significant time interacting online, I already knew that that perception was not correct.[22] As it turns out, though, by starting with eight-year-olds, I would entirely miss the rising curve into online interactivity. Eight-year-olds are actually pretty "elderly" in the realm of beginning Internet users; that is to say, more than 90 percent of the third graders surveyed reported that they were *already interacting* with other children online.

Early online activity

According to data from parents, their elementary school–age children primarily played games online; the second-most-common activity was homework. When exactly most children begin to play online isn't clear from this data. As an educated guess, I would say that many, if not most, children in middle-class America play preliterate games online by kindergarten or first grade. Over the years, however, using the Internet for homework and for social networking has steadily increased, in addition to online game-playing.

The point is that eight-year-old students are already immersed in digital technology; this is not just an issue among middle- and high school students. The games young children play are significant because they frequently involve elements of social networking, such as chatting, information sharing, or interacting between children online, that could spill over into school the next day. In the field, I've noticed that during the earliest school years, both genders often play games together; by fourth grade, the boys begin to peel off into the action and adventure game genre.

Cell phone ownership in elementary school

The statistics on cell phone use were even more surprising. Among third graders, cell phone ownership was 20 percent in 2011 and 22 percent in 2012. Those percentages more than doubled to 52 percent ownership among fifth graders by 2012. Half of the third graders who owned devices indicated that they (probably) owned smartphones (i.e., they indicated that their cell phones could send text messages and access the Internet). As the children progressed through their school years, the same proportion (about 10 percent of subjects in each grade) reporting owning more-basic cell phones, but the proportion owning smartphones increased dramatically and accounted for all the growth in cell phone ownership. Between 2010 and 2012, smartphone ownership increased, but basic cell phone ownership actually slightly *decreased* among elementary school students.

Accessing the Internet through a more conventional computer (desktop or laptop) is still dominant, and most cyberbullying that happened between grades 3 through 5 happened on games that were probably played on larger screens (i.e., computers). But I also found that cell phone ownership was related to cyberbullying, for both bullies and victims. For example, while 12.6 percent of all third graders and 18.9 percent of all fifth graders reported being targets of cyberbullying, rates of victimization were higher for young cell phone owners. In 2011, "only" 10 percent of third graders who didn't own cell phones reported being cyberbullied, but 21 percent of cell phone owners reported victimization; and an astonishing 39 percent of the smartphone owners said they had been cyberbullied. That pattern was very similar in fourth and fifth grades. There was, interestingly, no difference in traditional (in-school) bullying between the different cell phone owners and non-owners, and by middle school the cyberbullying victimization differences began to drop away. Smartphone owners were also more likely to report being a cyberbully; 12 percent of non-cell-phone-owning fifth graders admitted to being a cyberbully, in comparison with 13 percent of cell phone owners and 18 percent of smartphone owners. Again, the pattern observed was the same for third and fourth graders as well.

In summary, parents often view cell phones and smartphones as safety devices, and in ways they may be; but it also appears that owning any kind of cell phone—especially a smartphone—increases the risk of being both a cyberbully and a victim of cyberbullying during elementary school.

Risky Digital Behaviors During High School

I think there is a perception that children are constantly misbehaving with their cell phones in school, but the research evidence for this type of activity is very mixed. How do electronics and education collide, and how are bullying and cyberbullying related to this type of digital misuse?

Illicit use of cell phones

In the freshman study, 83 percent of subjects reported that they had sent a text during class at some time in middle or high school, though only 29 percent of these kids reported ever being caught. Even though 83 percent is a high number, it must be said that a quick text message as a class is beginning or ending can be a relatively mild infraction. (Unfortunately, I didn't record the specifics of exactly when the text was sent—midclass, just prior to the start of a lesson, etc.) Although virtually every school bans texting during class, even midlesson cell phone use to contact friends is regarded by some as a violation only moderately more serious than chewing gum—banned, certainly, and generally, though not universally, enforced.

Of course, there are more serious infractions involving digital devices. Using phones to cheat has become a problem, although, on the positive side, only 17 percent of the respondents in the freshman study reported doing that (less encouraging is that only 1 percent of these also reported being caught). A more disturbing finding was that 20 percent of subjects had taken a surreptitious picture or video of their teacher, and 6 percent had posted the photo or video. Even when the intent is relatively harmless, it is an invasion of privacy; the seriousness escalates if the teacher is being *cyberbaited*—provoked to anger and then surreptitiously recorded and exposed.[23] In an international study of nineteen thousand subjects, about 20 percent of teachers reported that cyberbaiting had happened to them.[24]

But illicit use of cell phones doesn't stand alone as a problem; it's also associated with cyberbullying and bullying in school. Illicit cell phone users were much more likely, compared to their peers, to be cyberbullies (35 percent versus 15 percent), or bullies in school (30 percent versus 18 percent). Like gateway behaviors, taking sneaky photos or cheating with a cell phone might be viewed as a minor infraction; perhaps the same students who tend to rationalize the use of eye rolling or cruel laughter are more likely to similarly justify the inappropriate use of digital devices.

Cyberbullying of teachers and administrators

I found that it was fairly common for kids to discuss online why they don't like a particular teacher (39 percent), but it's very questionable whether that type of discussion can truly be termed misbehavior or "bullying." It's true that grousing about teachers online is essentially a public (and thus indiscreet) grievance, but in school hallways the grumbling is often at least partially public anyway. The relative seriousness of such comments relies more on their specific content than on their arena; defamatory postings that suggest an administrator is an alleged alcoholic or child abuser are very serious, while others that complain about more mundane issues, like the amount of homework a teacher assigns, really aren't. About 17 percent of subjects said they had made fun of a teacher online, and 16 percent said they discussed their teachers in a derogatory way (e.g., criticizing something specifically, such as their hairstyle or their voice). Interestingly, students who attended schools with stricter cell phone policies were less likely to post or text derogatory remarks about teachers or administrators. When the school's policy was "no cell phone use," 15 percent of students admitted sending or posting remarks; but when the policy allowed some use (e.g., during lunch or between classes), 25 percent had sent or posted such comments.

Although it's debatable whether such behaviors are truly "cyberbullying," I did find that the use of them was related to bullying behaviors in general. Students who made fun of teachers or administrators online were also more likely to admit to cyberbullying peers (39 percent, versus 17 percent for students who didn't make fun of adults online), and to bullying peers in person (38 percent versus 19 percent). As with early cell phone ownership and illicit cell phone use in school, commenting unfavorably about teachers online seems to be a somewhat risky digital behavior that is related to cyberbullying behaviors toward peers, and sometimes to bullying behaviors in school as well.

Higher numbers of "friends" online

Perhaps surprisingly, having a high number of Facebook "friends" online could also be tagged as a risky digital behavior, simply because the more digital "friends" someone has, the greater that person's general exposure online. More online friends means more eyes viewing personal information and more people who can potentially copy and disseminate that information. Among teenagers, it could be presumed that the number of online friends is a reflection of popularity, rather than of higher risk tolerance; but I didn't find that a high number of online friends correlated with popularity in general. There does, however, seem to be a relationship between the number of online friends and digital risk-taking.

Overall, 22 percent of subjects in the freshman survey had more than five hundred online friends on a social networking site (designated as a *high* number of friends in the study), and another 28 percent reported having between two hundred and five hundred friends (*medium*). Those who had a high number of online friends were characterized by more risky online activities. For example, 50 percent had used their cell phone illicitly in class, compared with 35 percent with a medium number of online friends, and only 23 percent of those with a low number of friends (fewer than two hundred). The subjects with a high number of friends were also slightly more likely to admit to cyberbullying (29 percent, versus 24 percent of the medium subjects and 17 percent of the low subjects) and slightly more likely to report being victims of cyberbullying (4.3 percent, 1.1 percent, 1.9 percent).

Why is digital risk-taking related to bullying and cyberbullying?

Overall, there seems to be a relationship between higher-risk digital activities and engaging in cyberbullying, and a somewhat weaker relationship with engaging in traditional bullying. It's possible that getting accustomed to exploiting technology in questionable ways (e.g., criticizing your teacher publicly online) can lead to more bullying or antisocial behaviors, especially in digital realms. This may be especially true during the elementary years. To my knowledge, there's no long-term or prospective data confirming that one leads to the other; but one high-profile case is suggestive—the case of Tyler Clementi, the Rutgers freshman who committed suicide days following his roommate Dharun Ravi's webcam spying. Ian Parker noted in his detailed article about the case that Ravi had a history of attempting to use webcams to record unwitting subjects.[25]

What's the takeaway? Simple and direct: first, delaying digital literacy and Internet safety education until middle school years makes no sense whatsoever. Trying to educate eleven-year-olds about digital literacy when they've been online for the past five years probably does little except underscore how out-of-touch many adults can be. Most importantly, by failing to discuss digital issues like risk online during childhood, we're missing an important window of opportunity. Because there is a correlation between risky online behaviors and cyberbullying, a broader discussion of risk online (including topics like illicit cell phone use and gossiping about people online) may be an important route to take with students, and the earlier we have these discussions, the better.

PRIVACY ONLINE

Privacy, as it applies to digital media, is really two different issues. First, it's about how well kids understand *how* to be private in the digital age; second, it's about their understanding of why this is even a desirable goal. Many subjects do seem to understand, at least to some extent, how to be private. Overall, about 54 percent of subjects in the freshman study said that their parents had talked with them about Internet privacy and why it matters, and those subjects were more likely to have set their Facebook profiles to *private* (86 percent versus 69 percent of other subjects). (Because any online friend can disseminate any private information publicly, it's questionable how much protection there is in setting a social networking profile to "private"; but doing so indicates that a subject is at least knowledgeable enough to take a basic first step.)

When I asked subjects some general questions about privacy online, most answered correctly about issues such as how easy it is to copy and redistribute photos, or that something on Facebook could be seen by an unintended party. The lack of knowledge about privacy seems to be concentrated in what I would characterize as a substantial minority, generally around 33 percent. For example, about a third of subjects seemed unclear on how easy it is to redistribute photos. A third also said it was very unlikely or only moderately possible that unintended viewers might see a photo posted on Facebook. A similar proportion (32 percent) also reported that they had given out their password/login to someone. Girls were more likely to share passwords (35 percent) in comparison to boys (23 percent).[26]

There was also a substantial minority that didn't seem to see the point of online privacy. About 30 percent of subjects felt that they "didn't have any private information worth worrying about" (that may be part of the "it can't happen to me" perception so common during adolescence). Only 29 percent said they were concerned about how their information might be tracked and compiled by marketers, and 37 percent thought that publishing their private information could compromise their future opportunities (it will be interesting to see what that risk truly is, as this generation progresses through adulthood). Finally, about 10 percent of the subjects in this study of college freshmen reported that, prior to this survey, *they had never considered these issues at all.*

Cyberbullying, Privacy Ignorance, and Boys

It's probably a stretch to say that privacy ignorance can lead to cyberbullying incidents. Overall, subjects whose parents spoke with them about online privacy were just as likely to become cyberbullies as those whose parents didn't have the "privacy talk" with them. Those who had set their profiles online to "private" were just as likely as others to be cyberbullies or targets of cyberbullies. There were some gender differences, however. Among boys, cyberbullies and cyberbullying victims were less likely to set their profiles to "private" and more likely to believe that a digital photo was "very unlikely" to get around (33 percent of male versus 9 percent of female cybervictims). The same could not be said for females in the study. So if cyberbullying and privacy ignorance are related, it appears to be more true for boys than for girls.

Confiding in YouTube or Formspring, Instead of in Your Friends

A final type of digital risk-taking occurs when individuals expose themselves needlessly to criticism or abuse. This seems to happen when an Internet audience is substituted in place of friends or family. Friendships and family relationships have a unique place in our lives; they provide us with the support, affection, and intimacy we need for optimal psychological functioning. One important purpose of these relationships is to provide you with a person who can tell you the truth when you need to hear it; someone you can trust to be truthful and not attempt to hurt your feelings or to simply provide amusement for themselves or others. It's trusting that person enough to expose your own vulnerabilities, and having them support you in response, that helps facilitate strong interpersonal connections.

But there are drawbacks to asking for candid feedback from the people who matter the most to you. Most of all, there's always the risk that once weaknesses are exposed, a trusted confidant might actually turn on the person who has trusted them. It's also true that we want people to think well of us, so pointing out our own flaws can feel scary. Perhaps predictably, therefore, a modest trend may be emerging in which preteens and teens pose sensitive questions online to strangers, instead of approaching family or friends. For example, a preteen girl might ask on YouTube, "Am I pretty?" In 2011 and 2012, several media outlets reported on a spate of young girls posting videos of themselves, plaintively asking viewers if they were indeed pretty or ugly.[27] At least one such video has been exposed as a hoax, and many of the viewer comments on the presumably legitimate postings have been supportive or at least fair, probably reflecting candid opinions. Nevertheless, asking such sensitive questions in public does elicit a fairly large number of abusive comments. Some sample responses to a typical video are listed next (translations in the brackets):

- Seriously . . . you obviously love yourself so idk [I don't know] why you need people to say your pretty or not. Stop being so . . . conceited and grow up. (: btw . . . youre pretty
- U R GuD LukiN BuT Did U mKe Diz For CompliMentz:) [you are good looking but did you make this for compliments]
- Ugly ass
- Attention seeking little rat, ugly fucking dog
- EXCUSE ME???? I think she's ugly you have your own opinion so back the fuck off
- you KNOW ure decent looking, ujust uploaded this to recive compliments . . .
- Dont listen to other people there just jealous btw why would u post this vid who cares wat others think
- This video should be titled "Count how many times I say 'That's Me!'"
- Ignore haters!
- Your very pretty, their just jealous of you

At first blush, it seems bizarre to expose one's vulnerabilities to strangers on the Internet, but such posters may be inclined to give more weight to the opinions that are (presumably) anonymous and thus less likely to be biased, rather than considering that the quality of the feedback is likely to be spotty at best. In the long run, choosing to air confidences online rather than with friends (or family) could theoretically weaken personal relationships by depriving them of trust-building interactions. I say *theoretically*, because there is to date no research that I'm aware of on this topic.

Another phenomenon that illustrates this trend is the use of Formspring, a social networking website that enables users to post questions or comments to another user, all anonymously. About a third of freshman study subjects (33 percent) reported that they had a Formspring account, and 66 percent of these users said that they like using Formspring because without it, "they might miss something." However, of those who had an account, two-thirds reported that they had had cruel remarks posted on it. Among the subjects who said they had received a cruel message, slightly more than half (54 percent) said that despite the anonymity of the site, they knew (or believed they knew) who had posted it. It's also interesting that 48 percent of users said they like Formspring because "it's anonymous and you can say whatever you want."

Why do teens open themselves up to such abuse by posting a personal question, either on YouTube or on Formspring? Apart from avoiding the perils of exposing their doubts about themselves to others, I think that this is an opportunity issue. I'm guessing that in *any* generation, young girls might have asked these questions publicly on the Internet, if they had had the opportunity, rather than making themselves vulnerable by discussing their insecurities with friends. Still, perhaps if we ask students to think about and discuss these issues, greater awareness will make them more conscious of the possible disadvantage of posing sensitive questions to total strangers, instead of close friends and family.

This is a chapter for which I could be accused of portraying all teens as cybermonsters. But although media stories abound about the terribly risky things that kids do online, I found that despite these challenges, most subjects I studied did *not* engage in high-risk digital behaviors of the type reviewed in this chapter. That said, there's little doubt that there is (at least some of the time) some risk when children and adolescents engage in sexting, self-cyberbullying, or illicit cellphone use and lack knowledge about online privacy. How common these behaviors are, and how commonly they harm people, is an open question for future research. In a book about bullying and cyberbullying, you might wonder why I've used precious real estate to discuss risk-taking, which in and of itself isn't a cause of bullying. But among those who did take risks, a pattern emerged. My research reveals that digital risk-taking does seem to be associated with cyberbullying, for both bullies and victims. To a lesser extent, digital risk-taking is associated with bullying in general. These behaviors are also important because they may, with more research, emerge as gateway behaviors. Perhaps, eventually, we may come to realize that risky cyber behaviors help clear the way for cyberbullying or cyberabuse to occur. For now, we can recognize that these are potentially harmful behaviors, and that the use of them may indicate, to adults, a student whose use of digital technology needs a little extra attention.

Which brings us, quite neatly, to our next question. How should we apply that attention, and how should we respond, likewise, to more obvious forms of bullying and cyberbullying? In the next chapter, we'll begin to explore the concrete side of bullying and cyberbullying prevention—what to *do*. Don't touch that dial.

CHAPTER 6

Responding Effectively to Bullying

The "9-Second Response" and
Other Informal and Formal Strategies

During the 1980s (and the first few years of the 1990s), violent and property crimes rose steadily in most major cities in the United States. (Indeed, it's because of that crime wave that I began my graduate career studying violence and abuse.) Yet during this crime wave, New York City, with its notorious reputation as an ineptly policed microcosm of simmering violence and psychopathy, adopted a strategy that turned out to be exceptionally successful. Based on the sociological theory known as "broken windows," the New York City Police Department stopped focusing limited resources on only the most serious crimes (an approach that would have been entirely understandable), and instead focused some of those resources on community well-being, including the *least* serious (but very visible) crimes—the gateway behaviors of crime, if you will.[1] Police intervened in graffiti writing and broken windows; they walked the streets, rediscovered community policing, and interacted with citizens in a way that, generally speaking, conveyed their expectation for the peacefulness of their neighborhood beats. Although crime dropped everywhere across the country in subsequent years, the reduction in New York City (and in other cities adopting the theory) was especially impressive. The case had been made: if you want to reduce antisocial behaviors, interact and connect with the people in the community, effectively convey expectations in a consistent manner, and address minor incidents before more serious ones erupt.

Although U.S. cities may have come to a reasonable comfort level with the presence of community policing and expectations as part of a reduction in crime, no such comfort level can be seen in schools today. But the broken windows theory may have application in the field of bullying, too. We seem to be pretty good about conveying our expectations about physical aggression to our students, but many schools I work with struggle to frame expectations regarding psychological bullying. While it's fine to emphasize that physical violence should *never* be tolerated, most bullying, as we've seen, isn't physical anymore. So our first line in responding is to address bullying that happens through the use of gateway behaviors and online behaviors.

RESPONDING TO GATEWAY BEHAVIORS

As I noted in chapter 1, gateway behaviors are socially inappropriate behaviors used to convey contempt and dominance—whispering about people in front of them, laughing at others openly, eye rolling, ignoring, name calling, encouraging peers to drop friends, and so on. Children nowadays typically bully using gateway behaviors—not physical aggression.[2] These behaviors represent an advantageous way to bully, since they usually don't break any formal school rules and can thus be used in front of adults. But they also muddy the waters: *gateway behaviors can be used to tease, to be mean just once,* or *to bully.* Even if you become an expert at recognizing these behaviors, you won't always know *why* they're being used. Two boys laughing pointedly at a third might be doing it for the first time or the hundredth time, and there's usually no obvious way to know which it is. So what should the response be, if you're not sure which you're seeing?

In the field, adults who observe such gateway behaviors may pause and attempt to do an on-the-spot motive analysis: "Maybe she only meant it as a joke, or it could very well be just a passing, minor bit of nastiness." If what they see is definitely bullying—an overt threat, for example—then they know that they must respond. But if they see an inappropriate behavior and don't know if it's being used to bully, they're as likely as not to decide it could be counterproductive to stir the waters. That type of decision isn't rare, apparently; subjects in my freshman study in 2011 reported that adults were only about half as likely to respond to bullying via gateway behaviors as they were to bullying that played out through more obvious actions (such as physical fighting).[3] But don't despair. There *are* ways you can respond, even if you're not sure exactly what you're seeing.

Your Goal

Your goal in responding to gateway behaviors, *regardless of whether they're being used to tease, bully, or be mean just once,* is simple: you want the children in your school to understand that *you expect them to behave in a reasonably civilized and considerate manner at all times.* This includes, by the way, times when they're mad, when their feelings have been hurt, and even when someone is being disgusting, irritating, or annoying. Feeling irritated or disgusted is not a license to behave however you like.

If you see gateway behaviors (rude social actions that convey contempt), remember that it's not necessary to establish the motive of the offending student(s) (e.g., teasing versus bullying). All you need to ascertain is the presence of an inappropriate social behavior. For the moment, forget your sensitive side and disregard the offending child's intention. If necessary, you can always go back to it later.

Respond, but Don't Necessarily Report

It's important to be aware that you won't always use formal discipline when responding to gateway behaviors. Formal discipline can be very effective with more obvious types of bullying, but its application for behaviors that don't break any rules, and that may or may not be being used for bullying, is obviously limited.[4] Furthermore, using formal discipline for teasing or every random mean comment is not only overkill, but probably impossible. What you need is a response that can be used *before* behaviors rise to a level that requires formal discipline. It has to be one that is also appropriate in the event that the child has merely gone too far with a tease, or has, in a rare spiteful mood, thrown out a single mean comment or gesture.

Although most behaviors used by bullies today may not be appropriate for a more formal response, if you repeatedly see a child doing something mean, particularly to the same target, you should of course continue to respond but you should also go up to the next level. Two reports should be made: (a) you suspect that bullying is going on—this is no longer a one-time event; and (b) you are asking this student to stop being offensive and he or she is ignoring you and persisting. Both counts should be subject to formal discipline.

THE 9-SECOND RESPONSE

If you think about gateway behaviors as the "litter" of the psychological climate in a school, then responding is the same as responding to any other type of littering. The only way to deal with litter is to make sure that everyone knows that it's not OK to toss your garbage on the floor, because a garbage-strewn landscape affects everyone in school. Gateway behaviors are like litter because, individually, each is a small problem; but when they're permitted to accumulate, they fundamentally alter the psychological landscape in a school. Like paper litter, the way to deal with gateway behaviors is to make sure that everyone knows it's not OK to toss around psychological garbage, because everyone has a stake in the school's landscape. If you saw a student ball up a piece of paper and toss it on the floor, you wouldn't stop to consider if he did it on purpose, or if he's doing it just this once; instead, you would simply stop and tell him to pick up the paper. You would be enforcing the social good for yourself and for all the other people who have to share and inhabit this space together.

Based on this approach, I've developed a response set for gateway behaviors that has several advantages. It's quick; it's easy to do; it makes sense to everyone; it takes the onus off the target, and puts it on the entire community; and it can't be debated or argued with. It avoids the entire can-you-prove-I-did-this conundrum (brought up, sometimes, by students and/or their parents), and it addresses bullying behaviors while not branding the casual litterers with a scarlet B that will follow them for life. Most importantly, this response will clearly convey to all the students who see it what your expectations are.

Step One: Consistently Notice Gateway Behaviors

This is the difficult part of the response, because the idea of having to respond to every snicker and rolled eye may indeed be seen as, at best, overwhelming, and at worst, simply impossible. But remember that the goal of setting expectations is not to find yourself obliged to constantly point out violations, but rather to change the students' behavior so that those violations *no longer occur*. Once children understand a clearly stated expectation for their behavior, most will comply with it (the exception being those who have too many other challenges). In other words, notice and respond consistently, and you won't have to do it for long. One high school teacher I've worked with closely pointed out to me that he figures, each fall, he'll have to be tirelessly on top of things for September—but after that, the kids know the score and they mostly cease the behaviors (at least while he's present—an issue I'll discuss later).

Talking once with a group of teens, they pointed out to me that the kids always know which adults notice and respond and which don't; and they adjust their behaviors accordingly. Hearteningly, one girl who was a frequent target told me that she loved the classes where teachers never failed to respond to gateway behaviors; she described how safe she felt in such environments, not needing to keep 25 percent of her attention on the other students, waiting for the blow.

Step Two: Respond by Owning the Impact

Now the easy part: once you've noticed, responding is simple and quick. When you see a child who behaves contemptuously or rudely toward another child, simply tell the offending child that *you*—not the target—are offended and bothered by the behavior and they must stop. That's it. Clocked, this takes about five seconds, although I call it the *9-second response* because it takes another four seconds to pull your mind together when you're not accustomed to responding. Teachers who are used to doing it tell me they can respond in three to four seconds.

The critical element here is to *not* emphasize the damage being done to the target ("How do you think that made Kristin feel?")—they probably know exactly how it made Kristin feel. Putting the onus on the target can also make her very uncomfortable and may increase the likelihood of retaliation at a later time or date. Instead, emphasize the damage to yourself and to the entire school community. In fact, if the target of the cruel remark or gesture is present, you can ask that child to simply move along—implying to any watchers that the target is really not the problem. If needed, you can always talk with the target later, but for now, you're driving home the message that the use of socially cruel behaviors impacts the entire school by poisoning the school climate—and that it is not the target's job to bear the responsibilities for the hurt.

Some educators prefer to emphasize the community's norms (e.g., "We don't do that here!"), but I think a broad, conceptual argument like that is less effective than telling a child that *you*, personally, are being harmed by their behavior. The fact that you are directly impacted (offended, bothered) emphasizes the message that gateway behaviors don't simply harm people in the abstract; people who use them are being truly hurtful to the school community, and there are very good reasons for the social rules that forbid such behaviors. Most children who engage in these behaviors are focused only on wounding the target, and haven't particularly considered that they could be having a much broader negative impact.

Consider a situation where you see a few girls whispering and giggling about another student who is standing a few feet away and trying hard to appear indifferent. Your response could be:

> *Excuse me, girls? I don't know what you're talking about, but it's not OK to whisper about another person in front of them. That's very inconsiderate, and it really bothers me. Please stop it immediately.*

As you speak, you can sternly shoot them The Look (as an educator, you know which one I mean). If you have a moment, it's best to pause and meaningfully watch them as they scatter or their chattering trails off.

Potential Problems with the 9-Second Response

Now, I don't really imagine that that's the end of it. If you've ever day-dreamed about coming up with an effective response to a challenging situation, you know as well as I do that reality is always more complex. The 9-second response is simpler in the abstract than in actual, more intricate human interactions, but it's designed to be a flexible response. Here are some of the questions and problems that will arise, and how to deal with them.

What if the student(s) simply responds: "No, we weren't doing that."
It's quite likely that you'll get this answer. Your pleasant response is easy—just remember your goal: to make sure they know your expectations for so-cial behaviors.

> *I'm so glad to hear that, because it's really offensive to talk or laugh about somebody right in front of them. We won't have this conversation again, then!*

Now this is key: under no circumstances should you engage in a "Yes you did"/"No we didn't" type of debate. If they say they didn't do it, be-lieve them (at least appear to believe them), but underline the message any-way. Whether they protest or not, you've now taught them—and every other child within earshot—that you consider laughing and talking about someone else in front of them a rude and unacceptable behavior. Keep it up, and generally speaking, they will stop doing this in front of you.

What if they say, "I wasn't talking about you, *so why are you bothered?"*
This statement represents a truly excellent opportunity, because you then get to explain that when people are inconsiderate, rude, or even mean (you can feign shock here), it impacts everybody—not just the target. You can point out that you know they weren't whispering about you, but that doesn't mat-ter—it still bothers everyone who sees it. That's why we call whispering in front of others "rude" and why there's a social rule that forbids it.

What if they really weren't *giggling or laughing pointedly at someone else?*
Although the whispering and giggling behavior is generally unmistak-able, in the unlikely event that you're wrong and they weren't being inap-

propriate, you've done no harm. You simply express your pleasure that they weren't doing what you thought they were doing. It's fine to even (briefly) apologize for your suspicions, if you like. The students aren't being forced to take any punishment they don't deserve, and no one is being demeaned, disbelieved, or dismissed. You're not damaging a child by bringing up the mere possibility of poor behavior; *nobody* gets through childhood without being asked to stop, at least once, something that they weren't actually doing.

Although the 9-second response does require you to say "Stop doing that," and you might give them a stern look in the bargain, it should *never* turn into a lengthy argument or harangue. If they say they didn't do it, you just say that's OK—do not argue the point; it is not a dispute. I'd maintain, incidentally, that even if you *are* wrong, you're still achieving your anti-littering goal, because you're still using the situation as an opportunity to teach social expectations.

I see these behaviors all the time; I'm not sure I can be "offended," over and over, every day. What then?

It's easy to become accustomed to these behaviors, and it's natural that after a while, they begin to lose impact; but that's just more evidence that rude behaviors affect everyone—the entire school—and not just the target of the abuse. Research has maintained the hypothesis, incidentally, that bystanders are impacted just as much (or more) than bullies and victims by bullying behaviors.[5] The goal of the 9-second response is to remove all these bits of debris from the psychological environment, and then everyone will benefit. I don't deny that it takes effort, and occasionally some play-acting. But remember that the idea isn't to make more work for you; rather, it's to invest some effort up front in order to reduce problems down the road.

Also, consider this: in our legal system, if you commit a crime, the case is not between the aggressor and the victim (e.g., *Bully vs. Target)*; it's between the aggressor and the entire state or commonwealth (e.g., *Bully vs. the United States of America)*. If I assault person A, I'm not only hurting them; I'm offending against the entire community, and the entire community will be the victim of the crime.

What if they don't stop doing these behaviors even after I've used the 9-second response?

First, examine your performance. Are you being convincing? When you tell a student you're offended, are you doing it with a smile on your face? Since you're not sure the behavior is deliberate bullying, do you sound tentative? You need to believe what you're saying. This may be easier to do if you remember that you're calling them on the outward manifestation, not the intent, of their behavior. Even if a student's gateway behavior is for a neutral reason, such behavior is problematic for your school community.

Also, consider how long you've been using the 9-second response. Students need to see a noticeable sea change in you before they conclude that there's a new sheriff in town. And you will become more comfortable with the response as you repeat it.

What if they continue using gateway behaviors, but just not around me?

It's quite normal for children and teens to engage in forbidden behaviors when adults aren't around; this includes not just issues such as bullying, but eating junk food, drinking, and using foul language. Internalization about social rules takes years to achieve, and meanwhile, many rules are bent when parents aren't present. Having said that, I would argue that when children engage in behavior known to be expressly against the adults' rules, it feels very different from engaging in a behavior that they believe the adults don't care about. Consider drinking beer at a friend's party. The teen whose parents have clearly forbidden drinking feels very different (probably a little guilty) from the teen whose parents have never brought up the issue. Bottom line: there's no way to control behaviors that don't happen in front of you—but you can help mold students' values, so that if they do something wrong, at least they *know* it's wrong. That's the first step in internalizing rules and developing ethics.

How will they learn anything if I just tell them to stop, without an explanation?

Remember, the goal of the 9-second response is simply to convey your expectations. That doesn't mean that *why* we should treat each other decently doesn't matter, but changing behavior does not require constantly reiterating that *why*. Generally, students understand why we should be socially civil to each other, but they may forget or they may see school as a place where the rules are suspended. The 9-second response is really a prompting tool—a reminder that the rule is still in place. Childrearing is filled with such behavior prompts (imagine how different raising children would be if you only had to tell them each rule one time!).

When you use the 9-second response, the point is not to have a sociological discussion about why societies have rules; it's to remind them that their behavior bothers or offends you as a member of the community, even though you weren't the direct target. If you can, it's a great idea to have a more extended conversation at a later time or date about why these behaviors cause problems in the entire community, and how they make everybody feel that school is an unpleasant and possibly unsafe place.

Positive, Proactive Ways to Address Gateway Behaviors

Having a class discussion is a great way to examine the issue of gateway behaviors and their consequences. Begin by asking your students to identify behaviors that they consider rude or inconsiderate. Make a list on the board. If the kids don't think of common gateway behaviors, like name calling or eye rolling, you can include them on the list. Once you have a reasonable catalog, ask your students, "Why do we have rules about these behaviors? What's the purpose?" Encourage a discussion about how manners aren't just meaningless, arbitrary rules—they are guidelines based on consideration for the feelings of others, and by keeping everyone feeling OK, manners allow people to function at their highest level. The point of this class discussion is to remind children that social rules aren't pointless, and they aren't even just about kindness. Finally, you can encourage a discussion about why and how these rules are sometimes broken—sometimes by accident (such as with teasing that goes too far) and sometimes on purpose.

The Dangers of Responding Neutrally to Gateway Behaviors

I think the most useful way to consider these situations is from the student's perspective. Let's use the example of two teachers who walk past a group of three girls who are whispering and giggling and casting amused glances at a fourth girl—they may not be pointing fingers in a physical sense, but their whispering is decidedly directional. The teachers, seeing such a situation for the fourth time that day, may well feel that it's certainly not nice to whisper about someone right in front of them; but the three girls are not creating a disturbance or breaking any school rules, which effectively ties the teachers' hands. To discipline a student, their behavior needs to be disruptive or against the rules. The teachers, perhaps, view their own action (walking by) as essentially neutral; they're not stopping the situation, but they're not promoting it, either.

The difficulty is that *students* may not interpret this behavior as neutral at all, however impartial the adults intend to be. The whisperers (and any bystanders or witnesses) may see the adults' walking by not as passive distaste, but rather as *implicit permission*—if there is no objection, than the logical conclusion is that nothing offensive has occurred. From the target's perspective, it's clear that cruelty is happening; but the adults who walk by apparently either don't care, or perhaps even agree with the whisperers. In the freshman study, I told subjects to imagine that they were in this scenario and asked them why they thought the teachers walked by. The most common answer (34 percent) was, "The teacher doesn't see it as a problem." The next most common answers (tied at 25 percent each) were, "The teachers agree with the bullies" and "The teachers don't like me." Only 16 percent of subjects felt that the teacher probably didn't know what to do. Thus, behavior that adults believe is neutral appears to be viewed by students as indicating explicit permission and even *approval*.[6] These are definitely not the kinds of expectations we want to project.

But before we judge the teachers' actions too harshly, let's consider the situation realistically. It's unlikely that the teachers walking by truly don't care what happens to the kids in their school—most teachers enter the profession because they want to work with kids and to improve their lives. It's far more likely that they don't react because they conclude that the incident is probably a one-time case of teasing or meanness. Teasing, being mean, and bullying can all involve gateway behaviors, and to definitely untangle the three, you'd need to know the intentions of the possible aggressors. Bullying may be obvious to the children who are directly involved in the incident, but it's not always so obvious to onlookers. However, teachers should not have to worry about whether to take action. Inconsiderate and contemptuous behaviors—gateway behaviors— are really never OK, even if they began as a tease; so letting children know that they're not OK is *always* appropriate. It really doesn't matter whether it's bullying or not.

Why Don't All Educators Already Respond to Gateway Behaviors This Way?

In many schools today, educators are trained to discipline or respond only to behaviors that are clear violations of the student code of conduct. Vigorous protests that sometimes emerge from parents and students in the face of *any* disciplinary action place educators in the position of having to constantly defend themselves, and that in turn may inadvertently undercut the authority of schools to respond effectively to gateway behaviors that are bullying. It's ironic that parents, who very much want schools to control bullying, may actually make schools less able to do so by openly challenging procedure, thus weakening their authority.

One result is that schools tend to react by enforcing the idea that re-sponding to children's misbehaviors is appropriate only when those misbe-haviors violate formal, written rules, in which case formal responses (such as discipline) are most appropriate. This perspective renders educators un-able to respond to the gateway behaviors used to bully others. There's no rule about rolling your eyes, or laughing at others, or whispering about people, or staring, or laughing. These rules would be unenforceable—how could we codify what constitutes the "wrong" kind of laughter? But despite there being no formal rule about laughing, if we want to protect children, then we must respond to laughter that is used cruelly to abuse others.

This is not to say that formal discipline is irrelevant. Formal disci-pline does play an important role in a response set—but in the same way that a police department shouldn't devote all of its resources to the most egregious and serious crimes, a school shouldn't devote all of its responses to the most obvious cases of bullying. The difficulty is that all behaviors that are troublesome don't rise to the level of sending someone down the proverbial river. Thus we're in a double bind: we've both removed from teachers the will (and possibly the authority) to respond to minor misbe-havior and limited them to addressing more serious misbehaviors by del-egating the discipline to the administrators. While it's probably not an issue to delegate serious problems to administrators, it's most certainly an issue—and a critical one—to discourage responding to small, yet cumula-tive, behaviors.

Likely Arguments Against the 9-Second Response

I think that a great deal of my work has benefitted enormously from all of the interactions I have with educators, almost on a daily basis. Part of these conversations has been a pretty thorough hashing-out of the 9-second re-sponse—what works, what doesn't, and what kinds of questions emerge. Here are the issues that come up for debate most often. Every one of them represents, in my view, a valid concern.

We need to do more about bullying than just tell them to cut it out.

That's true, but remember, we're not talking about cases where we suspect there's chronic bullying or even cases where we know bullying is happen-ing; we're talking about the run-of-the-mill socially cruel behaviors that may *or may not* indicate a bullying situation. Obviously, repeated behaviors by the same offenders are another matter. Remember the point raised in chapter 1: if you find yourself wondering if that use of gateway behaviors reflects a bullying situation, then it's time to have a chat with the possible target and see what's going on.

It's also worth pointing out that a response is just that—a response. It's only one part of a truly effective prevention effort, which also has to include faculty, student, and parental education, awareness, and proactive behaviors, as well as support and input from the community.

Isn't it unnecessarily harsh to tell children who may be just teasing to cut it out?

I would argue, actually, that it's much more damaging to permit children to be rude to each other entirely unfettered by society's rules. The fact is that, as educators, we are charged with some responsibility for helping children prepare for life. Allowing them to believe that they are free to behave however they like (cruelly, thoughtlessly, or not) does not prepare them to behave in an acceptable way as adults. It's not "kinder" to let kids be mean. It may, in fact, just be kicking the can down the road.

What about using mediation instead of the 9-second response?

Mediation is a critically important skill that can help students throughout their lives. There has been a definitive trend toward training students and teachers to use mediation as the best method to resolve conflict in schools.[7] Most educators express a very high level of satisfaction with programs using mediation to resolve student-on-student conflicts.[8] Mediation is a very attractive option, as it involves student empowerment and restorative justice.

The very real success of this trend, however, doesn't rule out the possibility that mediation (both formal and informal, adult and peer) may not be appropriate for use with some types of conflicts—and bullying is one of them. Mediation and negotiation generally assume that two children in conflict possess relatively equal power, but as we know, bullying episodes are defined by their imbalance of power. Theberge and Karan argue that the presence of a power imbalance essentially rules out the use of mediation.[9] Other researchers have also noted that mediating between a powerful bully and his or her less-powerful victim is generally not recommended.[10] Even papers that actually recommend mediation for bullying cases typically specify that the cases can't involve noticeable power differences.[11] (And according to my definition, I would argue that if a case does *not* involve a tangible power difference, then it is probably not a bullying situation in the first place.)

In addition to the power imbalance issue, there are other problems with using mediation with students who bully. Some research has noted that at least some bullies are adept at being charming or lying during a mediation. Rather than being candid and up front, bullies may work hard outside of the mediation to attain their goal of dominance over the target.[12] Mediation, which deemphasizes fault and emphasizes both parties' responsibilities, may suggest to victims that they are equally responsible for the bullying.[13] In addition, the victims' fear of retribution may make it impossible for them to participate fully. In fact, in the freshman study, retaliation following mediation was tagged by subjects as the most common problem resulting from adult efforts to address bullying. When I asked subjects to specify *how* adults make it worse when they deal with bullying, the most common answer (with 64 percent) was, "They make you sit down with the bully and talk it over, and you know you'll get it worse later on." The trepidation that misused mediation evokes in students in the research should give us all significant pause. Worst of all, it may also make mediation—a valuable and important approach to conflict resolution—a much less attractive option even in the many cases where it is actually appropriate.

It should be noted, however, that mediation might theoretically have some uses in bullying cases. It could be very useful for bystanders and targets to take part in mediation, particularly bystanders who befriend bullies and help egg on their actions (casually referred to as *eggers* in MARC). Eggers may be more responsive to both discipline and mediation, at least during elementary school years. They typically underestimate the destructiveness of their own enabling behaviors, even when they themselves have been bullied.[14] Mediation could also, at least theoretically, be useful in cases where bullying has shifted into a more equal-power fight, which we know occurs in about half of all bullying cases that gravitate online.[15] However, I can't actually recommend the use of mediation in either of these cases, since I have not been able to locate any research on either situation.

One final point. I'm very aware that the prospect of a bully genuinely apologizing to a target and understanding the target's perspective could be extremely powerful and potentially very healing. The difficulty is that in the absence of both parties being genuinely motivated to change, it is too difficult to truly know whether a mediation would be helpful or hurtful for a victim. In an equal-power fight, both parties are typically unhappy, which offers a true incentive for change. In a bullying situation, the bully is effectively "winning" the social game, and therefore has little incentive for change. Wanting things to change is a key element in successful mediation.[16] Adults may choose to disregard this danger and instead rely on their own personal appraisal that the mediation was successful, and that the bully felt genuine contrition and offered genuine apologies. We may *think* we can reliably judge when an apology is genuine; but if we're wrong, the consequences can be quite serious for the victim. Apart from mental health and safety issues, we are also gambling that the victim hasn't ultimately learned that telling adults about bullying was a big mistake. That risk, in combination with all of the research suggesting that mediation cannot be effective with bullying, suggests to me that using mediation *in these cases* is at best imprudent and at worst very damaging. Again, I emphasize that this is in no way a criticism of the mediation process. While I strongly believe that peer mediation programs should exist in every school system, I remain very concerned about their use with emotionally fragile targets who may feel pressured into a repeat victimization by well-meaning counselors and administrators.

The good news, however, is that (a) mediation is always a technique that can be revisited if the power imbalance changes in a situation, as it often does; and (b) there are other methods for helping targets feel safer and more comfortable in school.

STEPS SCHOOL PERSONNEL CAN TAKE TO HELP A TARGET FEEL SAFER

While the following steps are meant primarily for use by administrators, school counselors, and school resource officers (SROs), it can be helpful for teachers to know these as well. Teachers are often on committees that form safety plans (which can use this type of data), and if they know what is reasonable to expect from counselors and administrators, they can help confirm that certain steps are taken in appropriate situations.

Establishing a Safety and Comfort Plan

Victims may need, or benefit from, a safety and comfort plan. This can include a safe person in school—someone the child likes and can go to, anytime. The student should choose this safe person, and the possibilities can include administrators, counselors, nurses, SROs, teachers, and other fulltime staff who are not always occupied with other students. The child's teachers should be told that this student should be permitted to see the safe person at any time. A signal can be set up (e.g., the student takes a tissue, or closes a book) so the teachers know that the child wants to see the safe person, without the student needing to announce that fact. Initially, do not be concerned if a victim appears to exploit their safe person as a way to avoid schoolwork. Focus instead on the child's sense of safety and comfort. Eventually, when the situation appears to be resolving, you can address a child who exploits the situation (if necessary).

Increasing Structured Interactions

Unstructured areas can pose particular concerns. Have a plan in advance for less structured areas, such as buses and the lunchroom (and the playground for elementary-age students). Victims should never be left to hope that they can find a safe place to eat lunch or a safe seat on the bus ride home. A seat should be reserved in advance near friends (or near friendly students).

Engaging Student Help

There's little doubt that students can be the most powerful elements in any bullying prevention or reduction plan.[17] Through MARC we've trained hundreds of students to be anti-bullying leaders in their own schools through a unique process where the students retain much of the control and responsibility for the programs they implement. I've even seen some bullies—those with real leadership qualities—become pretty committed anti-bullying activists in their own schools, and have been told anecdotally that this experience has "turned them around," although I have no data to back up these war stories.

Although students can achieve wonderful goals when addressing bullying in the abstract, my fieldwork experiences suggest that they might be more tentative about helping targets of bullying directly, possibly because they fear being singled out as well (by association). The good news is that students can help their peers without having to commit to either a new friendship, eating lunch, or playing with a target. In the freshman study subjects were given a scenario where a target has been told something mean; a second individual walks past and says, "Don't pay any attention to him." When the theoretical comment was made by an adult, 38 percent of subjects felt it would be very effective; but when it was made by a peer, 68 percent felt it would be very effective. Even just a simple comment as a student walks past appears to be potentially very helpful. Student interventions can probably be far more effective than adult ones (see chapter 7 for a discussion about engaging bystanders and other students).

Encouraging Strengths and Resources

While this section focuses on changing the behaviors and responses of the student who's the target of bullying, it's important to emphasize up front that I'm not suggesting that the only or even primary response to bullying should be to "fix" the victim. In fact, implying that students have power to change the dynamic of the relationship may suggest that *they* are the problem, which can further harm a victim of peer abuse.[18] Yet, while it's clearly important to target the bully for intervention and possibly consequences, two difficult truths are also evident.

First, despite discipline, unless all contact between the bully and the target is eliminated—unless they are not even within eyeshot of each other (very difficult, even impossible, in many school settings)—there is no way to be 100 percent certain that the bully won't retaliate against the target, even if the retaliation is only a future promise (such as looking pointedly at the target). Second, even if total isolation from each other is possible, other students may engage in retaliatory actions. In many school settings, therefore, it's difficult to be sure that intervention with a bully means that the bully's target is now 100 percent safe.

Because of that difficulty, and because of the injury that may have already been done to the target's self-esteem, it's usually worthwhile to ask how we can help targets feel better about themselves and feel more resilient in the face of any comments or actions by other students. The essential rule of thumb here is to work off existing strengths. What friends does this student have, either in school or in other settings? Are there outside groups he or she is involved with, such as a church group or other activities? Does the student shine in musical, artistic, mechanical, or other abilities? Is the family close? Are family events and visits largely positive occasions? Sometimes an increased emphasis on areas of the victim's life that are really affirmative can help make the student feel better about herself and thus better able to withstand cruelty from peers. Generally speaking, adults are better than children are at shifting their focus to more positive things following an unpleasant encounter, but this is definitely a skill that children can (and will) learn. And parents who are casting around for ways to help their child who's a target may feel more productive if they have a focus for their efforts.

RESPONDING TO BULLYING ONLINE

Much of what I've discussed in this chapter applies mainly to traditional in-person bullying. But just as cyberbullying introduces an entirely new dimension to bullying behaviors, so does it introduce a new set of responses, and generally speaking, these are less developed then the interventions commonly used for in-person bullying.

A Nonlawyer's Take on the Legal Issue

Unlike traditional bullying, much cyberbullying takes place off campus, most typically in the child's home. This means that the behavior falls into a different legal category. While behavior that takes place at school is clearly under the jurisdiction of educators, behavior at home is usually viewed as being under the jurisdiction of parents.[19]

One important exception to this rule is off-campus behavior or speech that makes a "real threat" or "substantial disruption" in the school climate.[20] Exactly what a "substantial disruption" means is not clear. Different courts have used different definitions for this term. For each cyberbullying case, school administrators must decide if the cyber behavior is making, or will make, a substantial disruption before they decide to discipline a cyberbully.

However, even if a school decides that cyberbullying is not making a substantial disruption to the school environment, *there are still important steps that all schools can take to help cope with and resolve cyberbullying incidents.*

What Schools Can Do

The fact that bullying takes place online doesn't really permit schools to wash their hands of it. There are responsible actions that can be taken *regardless* of the disruption to the school environment (or lack of it).

When to Involve the Police

Let's make this simple. If the behavior in question involves criminal activity, threats, significant violence, or electronic or physical stalking, I believe (as a nonlawyer) that consultations with police should occur. When in doubt, it's a good rule of thumb to run the situation past the local police, with whom I hope you have a good working relationship. If you don't, take a morning to stop by your local police department and introduce yourself. Find out which officer specializes in juvenile affairs or school issues, and make sure he or she knows who you are. Then, when you have doubts, you have a phone number you can call for a quick consultation.

Other Actions You Can Always Take

It's often worthwhile to have an educational discussion with the cyberbully and with cyber bystanders. It may be important to point out that this discussion is *not* discipline; it is educational, about the dangers of cyberbullying and the fact that everyone is now aware of the situation. If relevant, discuss future legal problems the child may incur if these behaviors continue. You can involve an SRO or police officer in the discussion, and the child's parents, if possible.

If you're informed about an online situation, be sure to inform potential cyberbullies and cyber bystanders about the consequences for bullying or cyberbullying while in school. If the cyberbully or cyber bystanders engage in any bullying or cyberbullying in school, follow through on consequences immediately. Inform all relevant adults—teachers, coaches, counselors, and bus drivers—about the situation between the two children. Ensure that they are aware of the potential for bullying and that they keep a very sharp eye on these children. If it were me, I would document everyone I had informed of the situation.

Follow up with parents, especially parents of victims. Do not wait for them to call you; let them know that the above actions are being taken. Many parents want to know what disciplinary actions are being taken against a cyberbully, and you may need to educate them about confidentiality laws. Be sure that they know you are not merely refusing to furnish information because you personally wish to protect a bully.

RESPONDING AT THE LEVEL OF FORMAL DISCIPLINE

It's a funny sort of paradox. On the one hand, I've encouraged you to disregard the "Is it bullying?" question entirely if you witness an incident of mean behavior, and to respond instead to the inappropriate conduct directly. This is true in the moment, when you are faced with a student who's actively engaging in a gateway behavior. But in more formal situations, such as when you're deciding whether bullying is actually happening, or when you're evaluating a student's overall pattern of behavior, drawing the distinction between what's bullying and what's not is *very* important.

I defined bullying as an abusive behavior that involves intent, repetition, and power imbalance. Most researchers and experts also use those three elements to define bullying. The point here is that while drawing the bullying/not bullying distinction isn't important when dealing with minor behaviors *informally*, it is important when dealing with behaviors using formal responses or formal discipline. Without a clear definition of bullying, situations where adults should focus their energies on a child's misbehavior can degenerate into an argument over whether or not a situation merits the "bullying" label. I'm constantly asked questions like this one, submitted to an e-mail list recently by a social worker at a middle school:

> *My son was named a bully by the principal . . . he had taken another boy & held him up against the wall & threatened him . . . now my son had never got in trouble before & was never in a fight before . . . I agree that this was hurtful behavior, but I do not believe that he was a bully as the principal said . . . What are your thoughts on this?*

Notice that the question is not, "What's the best response that will help my child learn not to repeat his aggressive behavior?" but, "We think it's not bullying; they think it is bullying—who's right?" Thus the attention has focused on how the adults will classify the behavior, instead of focusing on the children involved, how to help the target cope with the situation, and how to teach the bully that what he did was wrong. Parents who push to have a behavior labeled as "bullying" often do so because they worry that otherwise, the problem won't be taken seriously. It's up to school personnel to make sure that parents know that they take these behaviors very seriously—regardless of the label.

Keep the Focus on the Child's Behavior

Although I always encourage parents to focus on the behavior itself, rather than on the label, educators in many states are obliged to make an official determination about whether or not a child's behavior constitutes "bullying." When discussing the rationale behind this decision, a few cautionary points are in order.

1. Never use the word *bullying* itself unless you must. It's emotionally loaded, and likely to generate an emotional response. Refer to a child as a bully only when you are absolutely required to.
2. If you must label a situation as bullying, make clear the criteria used for that label and how you see the case fitting these criteria. For example:

> *In this school and in this state, there are three criteria for a situation to be called bullying. The behavior has to happen more than once—we can see that this is true here. The behavior can't be an accident—I think it's obvious that Bill's throwing rocks toward a bull's-eye he had painted on Henry's car wasn't an accident. And there must be a power imbalance. This last criterion is the trickiest, but I think in this case we can agree*

that Bill is one of the most popular boys in school, and he had a group of friends laughing and congratulating him as he did this. Henry's a great boy too—he is more shy, though, and doesn't seem to get support from other students over this matter.

3. The parents of the bully will often disagree, and it's a good idea to let them save some face. That may permit them to focus on their child's behavior without being distracted by a debate about the word *bullying*.

   I think the critical issue isn't whether or not this is bullying, but how we as adults respond to Bill's behavior. Many kids try out these kinds of behaviors, since they're so strongly associated with popularity. Let's just focus on how we can get Bill to understand how seriously we take his behavior. I see so much great potential in him; I don't want him to get sidetracked.

4. On the other side, the parents of the target may disagree if you *don't* think the situation is bullying, in which case it's often a good idea to redirect them to the behavior in question and how safe their child feels:

   I think that whether or not this is bullying really isn't the most important thing; what's most important is making sure that Henry feels we addressed the situation and that he feels safe coming back to school. Let's focus on how we can support Henry.

Never cite confidentiality without explaining it—this point cannot be overemphasized. Many parents don't understand that federal law (and possibly state law, depending on the state) forbids administrators from discussing another parent's child in any way. To an upset parent, you may appear to be stonewalling or even protecting the other student. It's critical to point out that you don't have a choice—you understand how they feel, but you must obey the law.

WHEN SHOULD YOU *NOT* RESPOND?

I've argued that some small amount of meanness is probably, in the long run, advantageous (if unpleasant) for children—sort of like going to the dentist. If the meanness isn't significantly traumatic or damaging, then it's a training ground for dealing with all the difficult situations that life inevitably produces. Having said that, when do those situations occur, and when should adults *not* respond?

Let me begin by saying that I truly believe that there's no way to get this issue exactly right, all the time. No matter how hard we try, it's likely that at times, children who would benefit from our intervention won't get it, and at other times, children who would benefit from working things out on their own don't get to do that, either. There's no way to be 100 percent accurate because there's always the possibility that only the child has all the relevant information about the situation. In addition, educators are only human, and are thus subject to influences that have nothing to do with the situation at hand. An example would be telling kids to "just work it out" not because that seems appropriate, but simply because the situation seems too much to deal with at the end of a long day.

Still, there are some general guidelines that may help minimize the mistakes.

- *Evaluate the balance of power*: Ask yourself if one of the kids has much less power than or is afraid of the other. If the answer is yes, then taking a closer look is a better approach than dismissing the incident.
- *Weigh the content of the dispute*: Ask yourself if the dispute appears to be relatively inconsequential. A quarrel over whether someone's mother is an alcoholic is not inconsequential, but an argument over who gets to go first on the slide can be. Is the content of the quarrel something that can be really hurtful? Is it important? If the answer is no, then encouraging the kids to work it out for themselves is probably merited.
- *Consider whether the dispute is a repeat occurrence*: Regardless of content, is this a situation or problem that is appearing repeatedly? Even if the content seems very trivial, students who are engaging in problem behaviors together over and over again are essentially struggling with a larger issue. That's a signal that a talk is merited.
- *Look for an obvious ulterior motive*: Be careful here, and be sure to read the section on "tattling" in chapter 2. An obvious ulterior motive is always a signal to take a situation more (not less) seriously, although the situation may be different from the one being reported. For example, a young child persistently telling you that so-and-so is butting into line, and they want the person punished, is a signal for a talk with the "telling" child. You may ultimately decide that so-and-so is indeed guilty or you may find yourself uncovering something entirely different, such as a situation where the teller is actually the guilty party.

- *Determine whether the situation has escalated*: Any situation between children that appears to be escalating should be attended to by adults. Children often don't understand how their behaviors can contribute to an escalation, including their digital behaviors. Some education is often in order.
- *Always respond to fear*: If a child is afraid, that situation always merits your close attention. Always.
- *Always offer a safety hatch*: Even if you tell kids to work something out for themselves, or tell them not to "tattle" (an approach I do not recommend), finish your comment by letting the children involved know that you will listen if this is important. You may not be able to listen right now, but you will soon.
- *Even if you ask them to work it out, cue them with the process*: Rather than just saying, "You two work this out," prompt the children with the process that's needed. Ask them, "How could you two work this out for yourselves, without having to ask for help from a grown-up? Can one of you propose a solution?" If the students respond with a reason why they came to you (e.g., "But he never does what he says he'll do"), then help them negotiate a compromise, but also stay put, to help enforce the results. Hopefully, the extra minutes you spend there will mean that in the future, these children will be able to work out small problems for themselves.

• • •

In this chapter I've talked about responding to bullies and their targets. But what about responding to bullying by working with bystanders? If you've picked up a newspaper in the last five years, you've probably read about how bystanders are key. So let's dive in: on to chapter 7.

CHAPTER 7

Engaging Bystanders and Other Peers

A Developmental Approach to Cultivating Prosocial Behavior

Bystanders—the silver bullet. If only we could get bystanders to do what we want them to do: actively intervene when bullying happens; discourage bullying wherever they see it; and immediately report anything they witness to an adult. Then, perhaps, the bullying issue would abate.

So what's the holdup?

WHO DO WE MEAN BY "BYSTANDERS"?

The term *bystander* is vague; there are several peripheral peer groups that are potentially important in bullying situations. Some students actually witness episodes; others may not be physically present, but may become aware of incidents. I call these groups *witnesses* (who can be either *allies* or *non-allies*) and *aware peers*. Still other peers may encourage bullying by befriending and supporting bullies, even if they may not know about specific bullying instances; these I refer to as *bully-friends*. Rather than assuming that the same prevention approach should be taken with each of these groups, I think it's more interesting to study them first and see if key differences emerge. However, the fact is, most research doesn't differentiate; so in the rest of the chapter, I usually refer more generically to "bystanders." I *was* able to draw some comparisons between witnesses, aware peers, and bully-friends in my studies of students in grades 3–12 and college freshmen, and I cite those findings were applicable.

ARE BYSTANDERS ALWAYS PRESENT
OR AWARE OF BULLYING?

A variety of studies have suggested that most bullying incidents are done in the presence of bystanders. One endlessly cited report is a Canadian study that found that peers were bystanders in 85 percent of bullying instances.[1] What's not always noted is that this study examined only twenty-seven children in one elementary school, and did so almost fifteen years ago. However, the researchers (Atlas and Pepler) used a clever tactic: they observed bullying episodes directly in a school and were thus able to watch, and literally to count, the number of instances in which peers were present or observing. Using a similar approach, O'Connell, Pepler, and Craig recorded playground bullying episodes in two Toronto schools and found that more than half the incidents (53 percent) involved bystanders or witnesses.[2] (The authors speculate, reasonably, that the lower percentage in the second study may be due to the difficulty, on a video, of observing more subtle bullying, such as the use of comments or psychological tactics.)

While these studies counted the percentage of incidents that included bystanders or observers, other studies have simply asked children if they've *been* a bystander. Generally, pretty high proportions of students report that they've observed bullying. One study found that 88 percent of students had witnessed bullying; another, 68 percent.[3] Another, the Youth Voice Project (YVP), found that 54 percent of students were exposed to verbal bullying.[4] (The YVP is a unique piece of research conducted by Stan Davis and Charisse Nixon, who asked thirteen thousand children how different adult and peer strategies affected the outcomes of bullying situations.) In my freshman study, 70 percent reported that they had seen bullying or cyberbullying.[5] Finally, another recent study found that a similar proportion of students (88 percent) reported that they had witnessed peer cruelty online (although, importantly, only 12 percent said they saw it "frequently").[6]

A fundamental difficulty here is that although the two types of statistics are often cited together, the percentage of students who *see* bullying isn't the same as the percentage of bullying incidents that include observers. For example, it could easily be the case that a single bullying incident is observed by multiple bystanders, which would inflate the percentage who saw bullying but wouldn't change the proportion of incidents with witnesses. In short, these numbers tell us that lots of kids see bullying and cyberbullying, but only the direct observation studies have actually suggested that a high proportion of incidents have witnesses.

And once again, digital communication complicates the issue. The direct-observation methodology may be, in many ways, the best method for measuring the proportion of in-school incidents with bystanders, but cyberbullying can rarely (if ever) be directly observed by researchers. If researchers hang around a school, there's a good chance that they'll witness some bullying; but the Internet is a much bigger area to cover. To ensure that they witnessed cyberbullying, researchers would have to cultivate hundreds of online contacts ("friends") and hang around social networking sites for potentially a long time. They still would probably not see cyberbullying from other sources, such as through text messaging. This reality necessitated the use of a different method for measuring the presence of bystanders online and in school, and I decided to simply ask victims directly if other kids knew that they were being targeted (*aware peers*), and if other kids actually saw the bullying or cyberbullying happen (*witnesses*). Predictably, there were more incidents where kids were aware of bullying and cyberbullying then there were incidents with direct witnesses. For in-school bullying victims, 37 percent of the victims said there were witnesses, but 42 percent said there were aware peers. Online, 23 percent said they had witnesses, but 30 percent said that other kids knew about the cyberbullying.

Measuring bully-friends also reminds us that bullies are not socially isolated in schools; 25 percent of elementary students reported that they were friends with kids who were bullies; and an additional 18 percent said that they have, at some point, been friends with bullies. A high proportion of victims themselves were friends with their bullies at one point or another prior to the bullying (40 percent in elementary school and 46 percent in middle or high school). Although I wouldn't expect a victim to actively support their bully (even if the person is a friend), one could argue that by befriending a bully they had inadvertently supported an environment that promotes or tolerates bullying.

Going by the numbers, this might suggest that friends of bullies, those who know about bullying at the school, and direct witnesses are all fairly common. That suggests, in turn, that (consistent with the jist of Atlas and Pepler's study) many bullying incidents are either seen or talked about between peers, in person or online (but especially in person). Sixty-one percent of bystanders in the freshman study talked with peers about bullying they saw (in school or online), yet only 15 percent said that they reported it to an adult at school. It's students, not adults, who may have the best idea of what's happening at school; and while some targets undoubtedly feel humiliated that others know what's happening, perhaps we can use this peer awareness to help address these situations.

WHY BYSTANDERS MATTER

Bullying is widely described as a "whole school" process.[7] Bystanders are fundamentally involved, both as facilitators and as preventers. If bullies are seeking power and status, then having others who witness or know about bullying activities is desirable.[8] This motivation to have witnesses is a key difference between peer abuse and other types of interpersonal abuse, and it has important implications for prevention. Adult-perpetrated child and spouse abuse are typically hidden behaviors where secrecy is key (legal reasons and social norms may call for such secrecy). Peer abuse (bullying and cyberbullying) *are* often kept secret from the adults, but in the child-only world, peers are encouraged to observe. One result is that we have a tool in combating bullying that we don't have against more concealed types of abuse. Peers who know about bullying and cyberbullying represent a unique opportunity to prevent these problems, but we don't pursue their help only because they may help the target of bullying. Whether or not they realize it, bystanders are direct stakeholders in the school climate, and they in turn impact that environment, as well.

Bystanders Can Cause or Exacerbate Bullying

As stated above, the presence of witnesses is often seen as a key reason that bullying occurs. Konstantina and Pilios-Dimitris felt that the presence of bystanders is one of the primary reasons for bullying, because witnesses confer social prestige upon the bully.[9] O'Connell's study found that (averaged across all episodes) more than half of bystanders actively supported bullying by watching it and thus (perhaps unintentionally) reinforcing the bullies' behavior.[10] O'Connell, Pepler, and Craig's study of recorded playground bullying episodes went further; they found it wasn't simply that a witness could be the reason for bullying, but that more witnesses actually exacerbated an episode. While (on average) four children witnessed each bullying episode they recorded, the more witnesses there were, the longer the episode lasted.[11] In spite of the data, my field experiences suggest that many students believe that "just watching" is neutral and has no impact in bullying incidences, but these studies suggest otherwise. Like adults who observe (see chapter 5), perhaps bystanders can't really take a neutral stance—if they watch and do nothing, they may actually be reinforcing the bully.[12] So lesson number one to bystanders could be, "No, you're not being neutral when you watch bullying," along with a discussion of the many possible ways witnesses can respond, including simply removing yourself from the scene. That may often feel uncomfortably like abandoning the victim, but if the removal is combined with other tactics (e.g., getting friends or adults to help), it might be a very good solution. Indeed, one international study found that leaving the scene, combined with a secondary goal like getting the teacher, was actually a preferred strategy.[13]

Bystanders Are Impacted by the Bullying They See

Several studies have found that bystanders are psychologically affected by observing bullying.[14] Carney, Jacob, and Hazler studied the impact of bullying on bystanders during 2011.[15] They found that bullying was a psychological trauma that resulted in both psychological and physiological changes in both victims and bystanders. The level of anxiety, trust in relationships, and physiological indicators of stress (cortisol levels) were all related to exposure to bullying (as either a victim or a witness).

Rivers completed an important study examining the impact of bullying on bystanders in 2009.[16] In that study of over two thousand children in the United Kingdom, significant mental effects were found among those who observed bullying, including (among other symptoms) anxiety, hostility, phobias, depression, somatic complaints, and obsessive-compulsive behaviors. Importantly, these effects were observed even in observers or bystanders *who were not themselves victims of bullying or other forms of violence.* How does seeing bullying affect those who were prior victims versus those who weren't? Rivers theorized that among bystanders who were prior victims, psychological revictimization may be an important cause of trauma. However, even those bystanders who weren't prior victims might feel significant tension between their belief that they *ought* to confront a bully and their failure to do so; such tension (termed *dissonance* by psychologists) could account for bystander hostility toward targets. It's presumably more comfortable for bystanders to decide that a victim deserves the bullying, rather than to conclude that they are personally failing as bystanders because they're not actively confronting the bully. This raises the somewhat disturbing possibility that programs and adults who emphasize to witnesses that they "should" intervene in bullying could be inadvertently contributing to the hostility that witnesses sometimes exhibit toward the victim.

Bystanders Can Be Powerful Allies for Targets

Bystanders have power—no doubt about it—but they don't often see what another student's bullying situation has to do with them. Slogans often used to encourage students to intervene in bullying episodes don't always, unfortunately, convey the key role they might play. For example, the slogan "Tell an adult" may mistakenly give children the impression that other students are not really part of the equation when it comes to peer abuse. It highlights the role of adults and thus fails to emphasize the responsibility that *all* people (including children) have to be solicitous of one another.

Bystanders may also not understand their responsibility with regard to bullying if they don't realize how much bullying impacts the entire school. *All* community members suffer when bullying happens in their midst, so all community members have a stake in the problem and thus a motivation to stop or reduce bullying. Children in any school need to understand and think about how bullying of any child affects them personally. Although many kids I encounter in the field don't always recognize how bullying affects the school in general, they do perceive that witnessing or knowing about bullying impacts them personally. I've yet to hear a child say that bullying in their school doesn't affect them at all and they couldn't care less if it happens, as long as they're not personally targeted.

WHAT SHOULD BYSTANDERS DO?

In this discussion of what bystanders should do, I don't address long-term strategies—such as changing the school climate or getting parents more involved. Rather, I suggest immediate strategies that we can encourage students to engage in when they see bullying or cyberbullying, or soon afterward—actions such as telling an adult, telling a bully to stop, helping a target escape a bad situation, or fostering peer support.

The emphasis on telling adults is very visible, so I'll start there; but a lot of the following discussion focuses on the kinds of responses that students *actually* use, based on my data (and others').

Action 1: Reporting to Adults

In the field, I often run across two different beliefs that surprise me. First is the assertion that children must be encouraged to report to adults, without any acknowledgment that an enormous amount of data indicates that they are far more comfortable (usually) in reporting to peers. The second belief that surprises me is the implicit assumption that reporting to adults is, in fact, an effective way of stopping a bullying situation. Because my goal is retain credibility with students and adults, I think it's important to consider these assumptions.

They may report—just not to you

Children do report, or they don't, depending on how you define *reporting*. A number of studies have found that despite encouragement, many students don't report bullying to adults.[17] Clearly, if they see or experience bullying and don't tell anyone, then they're not reporting. But most subjects report that they frequently *do* discuss the bullying with a friend or sibling. Under the "tell an adult" strategy, this isn't considered reporting. But I would argue that talking to friends about a distressing situation is most definitely reporting—and reporting in a potentially productive way. My freshman subjects knew how to help friends who came to them to talk about a bullying situation. Almost two-thirds said they would talk about the situation with their friend and try to make them feel better; 41 percent said they would discuss, or help their friend act upon, the possibility of telling an adult; 27 percent said they would help their friend report cyberbullying to the relevant website. Friends can help friends frame or reframe situations; they can point out inconsistencies or ask questions that help the reporter better understand the incident. Friends can also offer emotional support and can help plan and carry out strategies, if any, that should be taken. Last but definitely not least, as children grow, they seek out peers more and more for reporting purposes; this is not pathological but is developmentally very normal and even adaptive.

The tendency to increasingly shift reporting from adults to peers throughout the school years was documented very clearly in my study of twenty-one thousand schoolchildren in 2011. Elementary students preferentially reported to parents and teachers; but by middle and high school, the students had placed teachers near the bottom of the list, and peers had assumed their developmentally appropriate place at the top. Older students continued to report the more serious incidents to parents, but after elementary school, single-incident or minor social cruelties were reported much less often to parents. Reporting to teachers simply declined, and reporting to peers increased, as children grew.[18]

In the freshman study, the largest group of students who reported were those who reported *only* to peers (41 percent). The remaining 60 percent were about equally split between 20 percent who only reported to adults, 20 percent who said they didn't report to anyone, and 20 percent who said they reported to *everyone*—adults *and* peers. Combining these groups, we can see that overall, 37 percent of students reported to adults (school adults and/or parents) but 60 percent reported to peers, revealing a preference that really shouldn't surprise anyone reading this book. Some gender differences shouldn't be too surprising either; the shift from telling adults to telling peers is a more marked preference among the female subjects. Altogether, 66 percent of girls told peers, versus just 45 percent of boys. Similar proportions told adults, but boys were more likely to prefer reporting to no one.

We could look at this data and regard the reduction in reporting to adults over the span of childhood as representing a failure; but I would argue that it is not a failure for children to shift some emotional needs to their peers during adolescence. Rather, I contend that it represents a normal trajectory and that we as educators have been less than successful in encouraging children to report to us precisely because we've been rowing upstream, instead of working *with* the inevitable juggernaut of cognitive and social growth. It's important to note that teens are not choosing to report to insignificant acquaintances; in the freshman study, both boys and girls who reported to peers overwhelmingly chose to confide in their "closest friends" rather than "other kids" (85 percent versus 15 percent). If we look at the data from the perspective of normal adolescent development, it may be easier to see why we should expect that so many teenage students will report to peers rather than to adults.

Of course, there's nothing wrong with encouraging your students to report bullying to adults. The problem is that, realistically, they have a range of choices (educator, parents, friends, siblings), but the message "tell an adult" implies there is only one choice (educator). How many programs discuss with children the emotional benefits of talking about their situation with anyone they're close to—friends, siblings, *or* adults? It's somewhat ironic that we don't encourage children to discuss their difficulties with their friends, even though this is precisely the tactic that most individuals ultimately learn to use in life. The fact that we may be omitting this obvious resource could also make adults look clueless, and therefore even less attractive as confidants. If we truly want students to talk with adults, we've got to be a credible alternative. But there are two sides to this coin. If we want to be realistic about encouraging victims to go to their friends for help, then we should also consider asking students to think in advance about *how* they would help friends who approach them for assistance with a bullying situation.

But even apart from of the fact that kids may prefer to report to peers, there is another problem with our emphasis on adult reporting. The "tell an adult" plea is predicated on a very important assumption: that reporting to the powers that be will make the situation *better* for the victim. But does it?

Does reporting work?

Data from the freshman study suggests that reporting works, in the sense that students who reported felt that adults responded very positively. Adults most often told reporters that they would deal with the situation; they made the reporter "feel better" and told him or her "not to worry." Negative reactions, like telling the student to "mind your own business," were rare. But in many other respects, reporting cannot always be viewed as a satisfactory solution to bullying. When my youngest was in kindergarten, he described a playground scene in which another little boy was (slightly) mean to a girl. "She should go tell the teacher," was my (reflexive) advice. "Mom," he said soberly, "that's not good advice. If you're always telling the teacher about every little thing, no one will play with you." He had made a serious point. We often fall back on "tell an adult," and while we say this with the best intentions, its usefulness as advice is probably more limited than we'd like to admit.

The literature on reporting effectiveness is decidedly mixed. For example, a 2004 study on more than twenty-seven hundred children in the Netherlands reported that most adult intervention was not effective.[19] A different study found that the effectiveness of adult advice depended upon the age of the children; namely, that younger teens found adults' advice to be more effective than older teens did.[20] A survey of students themselves found that most teens didn't believe that teachers' interventions were effective, although some did.[21] In a large study of Toronto schools, students reported that teachers' actions following reporting were largely ineffective, although teachers themselves felt that they were responding well.[22] Finally, I did find in the freshman study one suggestion that reporting to school adults is relatively effective. Although we could debate whether disciplining a bully is a measure of "success," 80 percent of the students who reported bullying to a school adult also said that the bully was ultimately disciplined, in contrast with only 20 to 30 percent of nonreporters, and 30 percent of peer-reporters.

One possible explanation for some of the variability lies in the expectations that we place on reporting. What is reporting supposed to accomplish? Should it resolve the bullying situation (perhaps immediately), or is reporting more useful as a way of helping targets cope emotionally? The YVP found that adult responses that emphasized alliance and emotional support were experienced by victims as the most helpful. These included "listened to me," "checked in with me afterwards to see if the behavior stopped," and "gave me advice." Strategies that were more focused on resolving the situation (punishing the bully, mediating, increasing adult supervision, and promising to talk with the other kid[s]) were sometimes helpful, but were also sometimes harmful. Subjects in my freshman study similarly ranked talking and being supportive as the most helpful action adults can take (64 percent endorsed this). About half felt that having adults check in with them frequently was helpful, and a similar proportion said that speaking with other teachers (so more people are watching out) helped. These studies suggest that you can't just ask if reporting was effective, because different people might define that concept differently; to measure efficacy in reporting outcomes, we need to explain what we mean by *effective*.

But using imprecise terms like the word *effective* isn't the only possible reason for mixed outcomes about reporting. Another possibility is that some studies ask about abstract situations, while others ask about situations that subjects have actually experienced. These two approaches can yield different results. For example, in the freshman study, I asked about both the effectiveness of reporting in the abstract (e.g., "If this were to happen, should kids report it to an adult?") and whether subjects found it effective to report bullying they had actually seen or experienced. For abstract situations, most subjects endorsed some kind of reporting. Subjects who were willing to report in real life were the most positive about reporting, either because it would make the reporter feel better to talk about the situation, or because it would help resolve the situation. Kids who reported to no one, on the other hand, were the most negative: 22 percent believed that kids should learn to cope with bullying by themselves, and 7 percent felt that reporting would make the situation worse. Except for the nonreporters, these beliefs were very rarely endorsed. In the abstract, therefore, most saw reporting to adults as a good idea.

But when I asked subjects about real situations that involved their own personal reporting, a somewhat less positive picture emerged. This part of the study asked subjects if their reporting had "worked" for them and offered four possible answers:

- It definitely worked.
- It worked somewhat.
- I didn't see an impact, but I believe the adult was working behind the scenes.
- It didn't have any effect.

Most kids said that there was an impact from reporting, but only about 26 percent responded that it "definitely" worked. The highest proportion (38 percent) felt that reporting made "a little bit" of a difference. This suggests a generally positive, but somewhat tepid, endorsement. (We'd rather hear, of course, that reporting is unquestionably successful most of the time.) The kids who told *only* adults (not peers) were the most positive about the outcomes. Girls were more likely than boys to give the adults credit, even if obvious evidence of impact wasn't present; in fact, that was the top answer for girls. Perhaps adults are more likely to follow up with girls, and to reassure them that even if they see no obvious signs, action is being taken (this is a step I *always* recommend, since not following up often leads reporters to conclude that you've forgotten their report or are ignoring it). Boys were the more lukewarm group overall, but girls weren't vastly more enthusiastic. Only the girls who reported just to adults were likely to feel that reporting made a difference.

This study, combined with the YVP, suggests that when you ask subjects in the abstract, they are more enthusiastic about telling adults; but when you ask them about their personal experiences with reporting, they are less positive and more mixed in their responses. This difference could be due to subjects feeling pressured to supply the "correct" answer—namely, that students should report to adults. That kind of pressure would be experienced more in abstract situations, but less when subjects are discussing what really happened to them. It's also possible that in real life, the effectiveness of reporting to adults is truly mixed, or (as noted above) that subjects differ on how they define "successful" reporting. My takeaway from these studies is that we really don't understand why reporting to adults seems so checkered as a strategy, and this is an area where we need more research. The situation isn't dire—neither my studies nor the YVP were extremely negative about reporting—they just weren't extremely positive, either.

Does reporting result in peer retaliation?

One final issue with reporting is a fear many students express— that even if reporting to adults does help, retaliation or attacks from peers could negate any positive effect. To explore this, I asked subjects first if they were concerned before they reported about how their peers might respond, and then whether, after reporting, they experienced any problems with their peers. In general, about 22 percent of students told me they were initially very worried about peer reaction, and another 33 percent were "somewhat" worried. The good news is that most subjects apparently worried excessively. While overall 55 percent were worried about peer reaction to their reporting, only 27 percent reported any negative reactions from peers, and 70 percent of these were characterized as mild, rather than significant.

The one exception to this trend was the segment of students who reported only to adults, and not to peers. They were the least worried about peer responses (only 39 percent were worried) but had the highest rate of actual trouble from peers following the reporting (39 percent reported having trouble, mostly mild). Therefore, it would appear that reporting is most likely to lead to retaliation if the student reports only to adults and does not discuss the situation with his or her peers as well. It seems likely to me that students who report only to adults have other social problems with their peers, which probably magnifies any negative peer responses.

Bottom line: we can probably make reporting a more successful experience for students by framing it as an action that can either make you feel better, help resolve or stop the situation, or both. As adults, I think we should emphasize strategies that have been identified as helpful in my research and in the YVP (strategies that build alliance and support). The fact that students are more likely to endorse reporting in the abstract reminds us that we should probably give less credence in general to situations in which students may feel pressure to give a "right" answer.

Action 2: Saying "Stop"

The runner-up for favorite adult-endorsed tactic is a simple one: encourage students to be more active as bystanders—to confront bullies when they see an incident, and tell them to stop. The "just say no" approach is attractively straightforward and assertive (in a way that many of us wish we were), and in many ways intuitively commonsense. It's true that adults who are appropriately assertive often do better on a myriad of life skills and situations. Still, general research on the utility of being assertive in the face of bullying suggests that it's a complex issue, where a standardized, "one size fits all" approach is unlikely to work. Most of the research on the success of confronting abusive behaviors has been done in the context of psychotherapy, where it's been repeatedly found that direct confrontation, even by highly skilled adult therapists, is ineffective in changing abusive behaviors.[23] Yet in my fieldwork, I've encountered a number of adults who feel deeply committed to encouraging young children to use this tactic.

Despite its broad appeal, I see two major problems with this approach. First, it recommends an exceptionally difficult course of action. We know from many studies that victims of bullying lack assertiveness.[24] Only 20 percent of subjects in the freshman survey said that they actually confronted their bully assertively. Victims also rated themselves as shyer than any other subjects, and victims with weaker social skills who attempt to assert themselves have been observed to be unsuccessful and to continue to be victimized.[25] Yet, it's these very students—those who are among the least likely to be assertive—who are being asked to be exceptionally brave. It's frankly difficult to see how simply encouraging children to be more assertive in the face of peer abuse would be very effective.

Second, confrontation may either be ineffective or may backfire and actually *increase* bullying against the bystander, the victim, or both. A Canadian study did find that about half the time, the immediate incident ceases when an assertive peer steps in to confront the bully.[26] That's encouraging, but other research has pointed out that the approach appears to fail as often as it works. A more recent study by Stiller et al. found that saying "stop" was effective only about 15 percent of the time, although it was rated as sometimes helpful another 50 percent of the time.[27] Studies of children's opinions are somewhat less positive. A survey of 285 middle schoolers in the United States found that pledges, rules, and telling bullies "No bullying!" (a version of "stop") were rated as among the least effective methods.[28] The YVP found that a peer's confronting a bully and telling her to stop was at best a checkered approach. Almost three-quarters of the time (73 percent) it had no real impact, or even made things worse for the victim in the long run.[29]

Despite these studies, I think failing to be effective 100 percent of the time really isn't a strong argument against using this method; if being assertive toward a bully stops even a small percentage of incidents, isn't it worth trying? But the real gamble isn't just that confrontation is difficult to achieve and only questionably effective; it's the risk that confrontation may actually *increase* bullying. While being assertive may stop a bullying incident in the moment, in the long term, it may worsen the situation (for either the confronter or the victim). Witnesses often perceive confrontation as a risky strategy, because it can result in their becoming a victim. This does appear to be a real risk. Witnesses who confront can be socially (and sometimes physically) targeted themselves; this has been noted particularly for girls.[30] But it's not only witnesses who can suffer as a result of direct confrontation; victims can find their situation worsened, too. In one longitudinal study, teens who tried to avoid victimization by being assertive actually ended up being more victimized than their peers.[31] Even when the victim isn't the one doing the confronting, bullies may become more aggressive against the victim in the long run, even if it causes the immediate incident to stop.[32] The YVP, which has compared the differential impact of several specific short-term and long-term strategies, found that a peer's telling a bully to "stop" helped the victim's situation 27 percent of the time, but also made it *worse* 30 percent of the time.[33] Taken together with the proportion of incidents where confrontation had no impact, we can see that 73 percent of the time, telling a bully to "stop" may be either ineffective or detrimental for the victim.

This doesn't mean that we should throw out the baby with the bathwater. It's entirely possible, especially in light of the variably effective use of assertion in general, that some children or some situations can use the "stop" approach successfully. Unfortunately, we don't yet understand *which children* or *which situations*. For example, perhaps schools with trained faculty, or children with strong social skills, can use the tactic successfully. Perhaps saying "stop" works when it's used in conjunction with other strategies (e.g., saying "stop" and then helping the target leave). Unfortunately, at this point it's all just conjecture.

In light of all this, does the evidence justify investing time, money, and effort in programs that center on training students to engage in active confrontation of bullies? Second, even if we decide the answer is no, should we encourage children who feel able to assertively confront bullies (i.e., students who don't require an investment in training) to do so? Standing up for a peer can make a child feel powerful and kind, and it can both reinforce positive social norms in the children who witness it and make targets feel much better.

There are research-based, effective programs that include the "stop" method, but these programs also combine it with a variety of other actions, such as teacher training, positive reinforcement of prosocial behaviors, and active student involvement.[34] This makes it difficult to tease apart the effectiveness of these different specific approaches. All we truly know is that there *is* evidence of effectiveness for whole-school programs that include, but are not limited to, a "stop" strategy, with these caveats:

- Assertiveness is not a panacea, as it doesn't always work.
- The "stop" strategy harms victims as often as it helps them, although we don't know why/where/how.
- The YVP's comparison of different strategies makes the "stop" strategy appear decidedly weaker than other strategies.

In light of these three facts, adopting programs whose core is the "stop" strategy appears unwarranted and possibly even unwise. Of course, future programs using new approaches might be able to utilize this technique; it does hold potential for effectiveness, but I don't think we know enough yet to harness that potential.

Apart from the issue of adopting programs designed to train children in being more assertive, there's the issue of the few students who feel easily able to confront bullies without additional training. Should we encourage *anybody* to pursue the "stop" strategy, given that we know that it might make the situation worse for the target of bullying about a third of the time? I wish I had an easy answer for this dilemma, but I don't. I certainly don't like the thought of discouraging children who feel inspired and brave enough to try to stop bullying in its tracks. On the other hand, I like even less the idea that they may be gaining their empowerment on the backs of the victims, who could then be subject to retaliation. Perhaps the best answer is redirection, rather than discouragement. If a particularly assertive child wants to move aggressively to stop bullying, the best option might be to use their natural assertiveness to focus on the victim directly (e.g., by taking the victim away from the scene), rather than focus on the bully. That tactic has the added advantage of modeling kindness and prosocial behaviors.

None of this should be taken as a contention that children should meekly accept powerlessness and helplessness in the face of peer abuse. Because students often feel at a loss when faced with difficult social situations, we ultimately want them to learn that they actually have a variety of possible responses at their disposal. Perhaps, though, instead of focusing only on tactics that are more risky and less reliable, it would be more productive to consider more positive strategies that have evidence of broad effectiveness. These are discussed in the next sections.

Action 3: Refusing to Be the Bully's Audience or Admirer

In MARC's fieldwork, discussions with children often tend to coalesce around the concept that simply *not watching* (e.g., walking away, not providing the bully with an audience) can be a low-risk strategy that's easy to engage in. The difficulty is that walking away or ignoring doesn't feel very empowering; in fact, it often feels like an abandonment of the situation. But we've found that feeling may begin to change following a discussion and some recognition that the presence of more witnesses likely means that the bully will persist for a longer time.[35] Indeed, I typically encounter much more resistance to this idea from adults than I do from children themselves. The kids may be right to think that by refusing to watch, they could ultimately benefit the target.

However, it's important to note that *used by itself*, ignoring the situation was definitely not an effective strategy (at least during middle school), according to both the YVP and the freshman survey, where only 35 percent of subjects felt that ignoring the situation was a good tactic. With that in mind, in MARC we train children to pair "not being the audience" with other strategies (e.g., conferring with an adult, getting other peers to help, helping a target feel better, etc.).

Action 4: Peer Friendliness and Peer Alliance

Apart from simply *not* watching an incident unfold, or telling an adult, there are other options that research has demonstrated to be reasonably effective—that is, these strategies may not always stop bullying in its tracks, but they are significantly more likely to make the situation better than to make it worse. One such possibility is friendly actions by peers.

Victims of bullying suffer particularly from a lack social support from peers.[36] Friendly actions by peers can, therefore, be particularly powerful. In the freshman study, 85 percent of subjects said that a friendly remark by a peer would be extremely helpful in a bullying situation, but only 29 of subjects felt that a friendly remark by an adult would be similarly helpful. In the YVP, the most helpful action by peers ("spent time with me") was effective 54 percent of the time; the most effective action by adults ("listened to me") was slightly less likely to be effective at 43 percent of the time.

An interesting study examining two Italian middle schools found not only that friendly actions by peers were among the most effective interventions, but also that their major impact was to make helpers and victims *feel* better.[37] Anecdotally, many kids have told us that when they are feeling bad about themselves socially, after being bullied, there's nothing that makes them feel as good as a peer who reaches out to them. The YVP found that from the victim's perspective, the most helpful strategies by peers were those that were *emotionally* supportive. These included, in order of helpfulness:

- Spent time with me
- Talked to me
- Helped me get away [from the situation]
- Gave me advice
- Called me
- Helped me tell an adult
- Made a distraction
- Told an adult

These are arranged in order of impact; the top of the list catalogs the most effective (and least potentially harmful) tactics. This list is interesting both for what's on it and for what's *not* on it. As Davis and Nixon wrote: "It is notable that the peer actions reported as most helpful are also the safest for peers as well, *and represent acts of alliance rather than of confrontation* [original emphasis]. Even the relatively silent and thus totally safe action of calling a student at home to give support was reported to be helpful much more often than it was unhelpful. Consistent with our data about teachers, these data suggest that students feel that giving advice is most helpful when the peer is giving encouragement."[38] Although the YVP focused on in-school bullying, it's likely that its findings pertain to cyberbullying as well. There's no plausible reason to suppose that socially supportive actions wouldn't similarly help children who are suffering through their peers' digital cruelties.

The broad conclusion that I take from all of the data is that we may be misplacing our efforts by focusing intently on "fixing" bullying and cyberbullying situations. What targets experience as the most consistently helpful actions aren't efforts to assertively stop bullying, but rather, actions by adults and peers that help a victim cope emotionally, usually through simply talking, connecting, and providing social support. This feels counterintuitive; wouldn't stopping the situation always be best? Perhaps, if it can be done successfully, but clearly adults cannot always stop bullying. Taking the emotionally supportive route can feel frustratingly slow or even inert in a society that reveres action, but I don't think the consistency of these findings can be ignored. Besides, there's no rule that dictates all-or-nothing. In rallying peers to do their part, we can emphasize both creating emotional connections and actively helping victims.

Early in this chapter, I pointed out that fellow students are a key part of the idea of the "whole school" approach to bullying prevention. Of course, there's another group that forms a critical part of that community, but it's one we haven't yet examined. So in the next chapter, let's turn to the role that parents can play in the bullying dynamic. Perhaps I've saved the best for last.

CHAPTER 8

Working with Parents

Shared Goals, Different Perspectives

What about the parents in your school community? While I do think that most parents and educators work in tandem on issues such as bullying and cyberbullying—they are both invested in putting a stop to them—you don't need to be Sigmund Freud to pick up an occasional undercurrent of tension. Schools are held responsible for the actions of children, even though there's no doubt that outside influences can substantially determine those actions. Despite the impossibility of constant monitoring, and the reality of the child-only world, schools are pressured to guarantee that bullying behaviors stop. Parents, on the other hand, may suffer from a lack of information due to confidentiality laws; in the face of what feels like inaction or indifference they may be frantic enough to take inappropriate actions or even threaten lawsuits in defense of their children. Parents of accused bullies can deny the severity of their children's behaviors, deny the actions altogether, or insist that appropriate (but lengthy) investigations be undertaken. The need to stop bullying can run headlong into realities that sometimes prevent that very goal. It's that tension that we need to think about.

Let's begin by examining a study I conducted of 1,940 parents of children of all ages across the state of Massachusetts, using the data to examine some key questions. How do parents feel about their child's school's response to reported bullying incidents? How much do their children tell them, and how much do they, in turn, tell schools? But most important, how can we help parents understand their role in these issues; how can we understand, and help parents get through, at least some of the denial; and how can we actively promote a more cooperative environment?

HOW MUCH DO PARENTS KNOW?

Approximately one-third of the Massachusetts schools that surveyed students and/or faculty also wanted to survey parents, and were given a secure

143

link to an online questionnaire, which they then forwarded to parents on their mailing lists. Ultimately, only 3 percent of respondents were screened out because they didn't have children in the local schools. No other identifying or demographic information was gathered on the respondents, since that action might cause parents to feel concerned that their answers were not completely anonymous; also, of course, I wanted to encourage parents to complete the survey by keeping it succinct.

Overall, the sample was fairly equitably distributed across the grades: 916 of the respondents had a child in elementary school, 789 had a child in grades 6 through 8 (middle school), and 823 had a child in high school. A number of parents had children at more than one level (which is why the numbers add up to more than 1,940). Contrary to my expectations, the sample wasn't solely—or even mostly—composed of parents whose children were victims of bullying (see more details on that later in the chapter).

When considering what parents hear from their children, and what they in turn expect from schools, it can be tempting to just throw in the towel and decide to accept the fact that parents are always likely to overestimate the ability of schools to fix bullying. However, some of the tensions between schools and parents arise from real differences in what parents and children (and thus schools, which is where most of these episodes take place) know about bullying incidents. So understanding what parents know about the bullying experienced by their children is where we have to start. Comparing the data from parents to that obtained directly from students can give us clues about constructive ways to approach this difficulty. What really struck me in looking at all the surveys was that it appears likely that parents and educators are actually seeing *different pools of information*, and it's that difference that may lead to some problems.

Parents Do Not Hear About All Bullying Incidents from Their Older Children

As I noted in chapter 7, the data from students and parents suggests that K–8 children usually report many kinds of incidents to their parents, but older children are much choosier about what they report. Consider this survey data: for the younger grades, a similar proportion of children said that they were victims and had reported incidents to their parents. For example, among K–5 students, about 45 percent of parents had received a child's report, and a similar number of children (38 percent) stated that they were victims on the grades 3–12 student survey. I observed a comparable situation for the students in grades 6 to 8; about 52 percent of those surveyed said they were victims, and 44 percent of parents were aware of those victimizations. These numbers aren't identical, but they're in the same general ballpark.

For the older children, though, some real differences emerged. On the student survey, 50 percent or more of the children said that at some point during high school they were targets either in school, online, or both; but in contrast, only 30 percent of high school parents were aware that their children were bullied. This suggests that high school victims are only selectively reporting to their parents. As I've pointed out in past chapters, I don't think this represents a failure of parenting, but a natural outgrowth of teens' social development. Indeed, a second nugget of information is reassuring in that regard. In addition, it begins to shed light on the differences between what parents and educators see and hear.

Kids Report the More Serious Incidents to Their Parents, Particularly as They Grow Older

At every grade level, more of the incidents reported to parents were just one-time events; but parents appear to disproportionately hear about the more serious problems as their children grow older. For example, the elementary parents knew about almost three times as many one-time problems as ongoing, repeated bullying situations. But as the kids grew up, I observed that they were less and less likely to report one-time problems; still, they remained likely to reveal repeated bullying. Perhaps, as they get older, they're simply less inclined to report the more commonplace, insignificant, or transient cruelties. Other pieces of data lead me to the same conclusion. Just as older kids are more likely to continue to report *repeated* bullying, they're also more likely to report *physical* bullying, which is often perceived as more serious than psychological bullying. (This is not to imply that psychological bullying is unimportant, but being physically threatened can certainly increase the urgency of a problem.[1])

In all age groups, parents do appear to hear reports that are skewed toward physical bullying. More than half (52 percent) of elementary parents characterized the bullying of their children as at least partly physical; and about a third of the middle school and high school parents (30 percent and 33 percent, respectively) said their child had reported being physically bullied. When high school students report bullying, in contrast, only about 10 percent of all their reports concern physical bullying. If we assume that the lion's share of the physical attacks are reported to parents, then an extrapolation of these numbers would suggest that about three-quarters of the psychological bullying that happens to high schoolers is not reported to parents. This is one factor that starts to skew parents' perception of the kind of bullying that goes on, and their perception of the responses of schools, which are dealing with many more incidents on many different levels (I go into more detail about this later).

Parents Often Don't Report to Schools

One more piece of data that dovetails with the findings above is that parents frequently do not report to schools, at least when children are adolescents. Parents who believed that their child was a victim of bullying were much more likely to report to school authorities if their child was in elementary or middle school. Rates of parental reporting dip precipitously as the child enters high school. Meanwhile, the rate at which the parent instructs the child do the reporting rises as the student ages, but only slightly.

To sum up, during elementary school, students appear to tell their parents about many the incidents that happen to them—both small and significant—and their parents, in turn, frequently report these issues to the school. But as children get older, students tend to focus more and more on telling parents primarily about the more serious incidents of cruelty. Furthermore, high school parents themselves appear to be less willing to report bullying to the schools, which probably means that when they *do* report, the incident is quite serious (or they *believe* it's serious, which is admittedly something quite different). When a high school parent reports a problem, therefore, that issue has already made it through two filters—first, the student would have considered it serious enough to report it to his or her parents; and second, the parents would have considered it serious enough to report to the school. Parents go to the ensuing meeting at the high school already certain that the problem is very serious; educators, on the other hand, may walk into that meeting with the idea of exploring the problem to determine how serious it is. Those two agendas can certainly clash.

HOW DO PARENTS VIEW THEIR CHILDREN'S SCHOOL ON THE ISSUE OF BULLYING AND CYBERBULLYING?

Parents—and communities—tend to form impressions about their school's interest in reducing bullying and cyberbullying. I won't say that these impressions are always wrong, as I frequently find myself taking the temperature, so to speak, in a school where I'm working. But impressions aren't always correct, either. Right or wrong, though, parents' sense of a school's commitment matters because it can determine whether they approach a bullying problem with an olive branch or a baseball bat.

Do Parents Know if Their School Works on Bullying Prevention?

Here's the first problem: overall, too many parents remain unaware of the anti-bullying efforts at their child's school. Parents at the middle school level were the most likely to be aware of the bullying- and cyberbullying-prevention efforts at their child's school, probably because bullying and cyberbullying provoke more anxiety at that age. Parents at every level, however, should know that their child's school is actively working on prevention (particularly in a state like Massachusetts, where every school is mandated to be doing exactly that). It's striking that between one-third (33 percent) and one-half (47 percent) of parents said they didn't know about any such efforts at their child's school. Making parents aware of these efforts is the first step in communicating to them that yes, their local school does care about this issue.

Parents' Views of the Schools' Response to Their Reporting

When surveying parents about their child's possible bullying victimization, I was well aware that parents sometimes overuse the term *bullying* to describe a wide assortment of social problems. As a way of taking this into account, parents were given the option of reporting their child's victimization as either a one-time incident of cruelty or as a repeated targeting. These two choices were used to tease apart the single-incident cases from those that more closely resembled true bullying (intentionality, repeated occurrence, power imbalance). Parents who reported that their child had been exposed to *repeated* bullying were subsequently asked a series of questions about the school's response to the situation:

- How satisfied do you feel with the school's response to this report?
- Did the school do a good job at communicating and "checking in" with you?
- Did the school make your child feel better and safer about attending school?

I realize that the tenor of these questions implies that the onus is entirely on the *school* to resolve the bullying situation—but keep in mind that the goal of asking these questions was in fact to see how successful parents viewed the school's actions in these situations. The good news is that parents of elementary school children were more positive overall than parents of older children: they were more satisfied with the school's response to their child's bullying situation, they were more likely to feel that the school did a good job of "checking in" with them, and they were more likely to feel that the school made their child feel safer about attending. The bad news is that even the elementary school parents were not very positive, and the parents of older children (particularly middle school parents) were mostly negative about their school's reaction to bullying. There's clearly plenty of work to be done.

PROBLEMS BETWEEN SCHOOLS AND PARENTS

All of this can be very important in helping us understand the perspective that parents take and the problems that arise between parents and schools. We've all heard plenty of stories about parents overreacting to bullying; but I've also heard many stories from parents who feel that their distress and their child's situation simply aren't being taken seriously by the school. Looking at the data from students and parents, I'm left with the strong impression that parents and educators approach these conversations from two fundamentally different perspectives. Educators see the whole gamut of misbehaviors, and they see all of them on a regular basis; what happens, therefore, rarely feels like a crisis to them. Their perspective is shaped by the entire group of students they see daily. Parents, on the other hand, have only the one child (or perhaps a few), and they see only the problems that get through their child's "seriousness" filter. They hear about problems so rarely, and the nature of the problems they're told about tends to be so significant, that they may well regard any problem their child brings to them as potentially very serious. If they then decide to approach the school, they've undoubtedly decided that it's very serious indeed.

So when you and a parent sit down, you're not at the same starting point; that parent is already halfway around the track. This doesn't mean that you necessarily need to change the content of what you have to say (e.g., "I don't think this is a critical issue for Jennifer"), but appreciating where they're coming from can help you adjust your approach:

> *I realize how serious this is—that's why you're here today. I absolutely see how a situation like this can be serious; but I'm seeing some behaviors that are leading me to sense that Jennifer's actually coping really well with it on her own. Let me tell you some details about what I see,*

and then I would really like to hear what you think about that, and learn what you're seeing at home that's leading you to feel concerned.

The idea, ultimately, is to let parents know that you understand that from their perspective, the issue is indeed serious, that you want to hear specifically why they think this is so, and that you want to share why you either agree or don't agree. The clue is to listen to what parents say: their data has likely gone through two "seriousness" filters, so the situation *could* in fact be more grave than you perceived it at first. Remember that if students are truly being traumatized, they are more likely to report it first to their parents rather than to any educator.[2]

Parents May Insist That a Situation Is Bullying, Even When It Doesn't Meet Legal or Policy Criteria

Bullying is a word that almost universally evokes anxiety; conversely, it may also reveal anxiety. Parents who are anxious to have their child's situation resolved may insist that a situation is bullying in an attempt to get educators' attention, sympathy, and (they hope) ruthless action. It's also possible that they simply lack knowledge about what constitutes bullying (or, like many, are working from their own personal definition). Regardless, I very rarely find that it's fruitful to debate whether or not a situation is truly bullying. The rule of thumb is to respond to the anxiety, rather than to the content, in the parent's appraisal of the situation. Reassure parents that you're taking the situation *very* seriously indeed and focus the conversation back on the problem at hand—the actual situation—rather than on what label should be used:

> *I want you to know that I am very committed to resolving this situation and to making Kevin feel safe here at school. What I'd like to do now is focus not so much on the label for the problem; instead, let's focus on what we need to do today to make sure that he feels OK about coming to school tomorrow. Do you think he would find it helpful if I had a talk with him, one-on-one, first thing in the morning, to let him know that he can always come and see me anytime he feels threatened? Do you think that would be a helpful first step?*

Tip: Parents who insist that something is bullying likely feel anxious enough about the situation that they are not apt to accept any suggestion that the incident is not bullying. They may worry that "not bullying" means that no follow-up or action is needed. If they call a situation "bullying," then it needs your attention—regardless of whether it's actually bullying or not.

Parents May Not Believe Their Child Is Involved in Bullying

Although there are certainly the rare pathological types who would deny their child's misbehavior regardless of the circumstances, for most parents, a small amount of denial is commonplace. I divide parental denial into three types: type I, where parents simply don't see the bullying; type II, where parents see the behavior but believe the teacher or the class is the real problem; and type III, where parents think the behavior is normal.

Type I denial

Type I denial is when parents simply do not see the behavior you're referring to and don't believe it's happening. The more general and vague the information you give them, the more likely they are to pursue this course. The solution, therefore, is to be as specific as possible when reporting a misbehavior. Ideally, a list of exactly when, where, and what took place is best; it's hard to maintain that a child has done nothing in the face of such specifics. So the conversation shouldn't be about how "Meredith is bullying someone in her class," but about how "on Tuesday morning, the teacher in Meredith's homeroom reported to me that Meredith had, with other students, pointed at a disabled student and laughed aloud, mocking her inability to pronounce certain letters."

Tip: Avoid, if possible, the dreaded "B" word. Its use often simply throws gasoline on the fire. Use it only if you must (e.g., if the problem behavior, because it is classified as bullying, has triggered a response required by your school's bullying procedures).

Type II denial

Type II denial is when the parents essentially accept that there's a problem, but decide that the genesis of the problem is the teacher or the class—not their child. These parents usually focus on how the teacher has "picked on" or singled out their child for criticism; or how their child is bored by the class and so is acting out; or how the teacher has neglected their son or daughter. Sometimes parents deflect blame onto another student, rather than onto a teacher; they may suggest that the other student is the "ringleader" or that their children were only tangentially involved.

Responding to type II denial is really all about gathering your data before this discussion ever takes place. If children are engaging in abusive behavior, they likely are doing it in more than one place—so you need to have a conversation with the other teachers who teach and supervise that child. What are they seeing? If they are observing similar issues, then the response to a type II denial is to point out (gently) that this isn't happening only in your class; rather, you're simply the one who's bringing it to the parents' attention. If other teachers truly see no indication of what you're describing, then more work is needed before you approach the parents. Why is this child acting out only in your class? Perhaps he or she is taking advantage of a unique situation; for example, maybe your class is the only place in school that provides access to a preferred target (although that is unlikely). Or perhaps there is a challenging psychological dynamic between you and this student. (Unpleasant to consider but, realistically, this is a possibility that should never be simply dismissed out of hand—teachers are, after all, human beings.)

> **Tip:** Type II denials often come from parents who are very anxious and unhappy about the idea that their child may be a bully, and they may need to save face while they digest the evidence they're presented with. It is smart strategy—not capitulation—to adopt the tactful attitude that many children engage in these behaviors from time to time ("Yes, we do need to respond firmly; but between us adults, this isn't the end of the world"). The more judgmental and disapproving you appear, the more they will dig in their heels. If you can get past this type of denial at the first offense, then if the child repeats the problem behavior, the parent is much more likely to accept that this is now a serious problem that requires professional help.

Type III denial

Type III denial is actually very common, and it emerges from the fact that parents have one (or a few) kids at home, and you have a thousand (or several hundred) at school. Parents in this kind of denial do see and acknowledge the behavior you're referring to, but mistake it for normality—they just don't have the comparison group that you have. Sure, they see their son acting out, but isn't that what all boys do? You know, because you have a comparison group of hundreds of boys, that, no, that's not what all boys do. Lacking that context, it's hard for a parent to know what's normal and what's not.

> **Tip:** Parents in type III denial need to know that you find it really useful to hear that they see the same things you see. You also want to assure them that there are ways to deal with these behaviors, and that (again) many children will try them out, and the important thing is to respond appropriately. Sometimes they need to hear that it's harder to recognize a challenge when you don't have hundreds of other kids to compare, and that working in a school full of children provides a useful perspective. Although I think it's fine to draw general comparisons (e.g., "You're right, Tom is a very active boy, but I have twenty-four other students who can sit through a lesson without throwing spitballs at another student; that's why I'm concerned"), you should never draw specific comparisons to another student.

A final word of advice: when you talk to parents about these difficult topics, always be sure to "sandwich" what you say between positive comments, as we'll discuss next.

Parents May Demand More Information Than You Can Legally Disclose

When parents of both supposed targets and bullies hear about or report incidents, they often want to know the identity of the other children involved. This raises the very sensitive issue of confidentiality. When educators respond to information requests by saying "That's confidential," they may be misinterpreted as stonewalling, avoiding a conversation, or even protecting the bully. The problem, I think, is a communication issue.

Educators know what *confidentiality* means, so they refer to it as anyone might speak of any familiar rule—without explanation. Unfortunately, parents often don't know the meaning as understood in schools, and so they may think that your lack of a detailed explanation suggests a different agenda. To avoid this problem, make sure that whenever you cite confidentiality, you do it with a brief explanation:

> *I completely understand why you want to know this; I would want to know also, in your shoes. But federal [and state, if applicable] law forbids me from talking to anyone about another parent's child. No matter how much I sympathize, I would be breaking the law if I gave you that information, and I just can't do that.*

Repeat as often as needed, even to the same parent—and make sure you continue to do it gently. Check out the free brochure online, which you can download, print, and pass out to parents.[3]

Parents May Demand That the Other Child Be Disciplined

Just as information about the other child cannot be disclosed, actions taken in regard to a child who bullies (or is perceived to bully) can't be discussed specifically with the parents of the target. However, you can review with the parents the specific steps that your school takes in all bullying cases.

Right here is a problem area: many schools *don't* have a series of specific steps they take in bullying cases. In that event, you'll need to consider developing those, since it's useful to be able to discuss what happens in the abstract, especially when confidentiality law forbids you from discussing what happens on a personal level to other children. Then, if a parent demands that another child be expelled, your answer could focus on two points: first, that although you can't discuss that child's situation specifically, you can describe the steps that are taken in all bullying situations, and that will also be taken in this situation; and second, that you want to focus on the target, and what steps you and the parents can take to make sure he or she feels safe at school.

> **Tip:** Visuals help a lot. They provide a physical focus at what can be a difficult moment and can even help calm parents down. Have a printed handout that reviews the steps taken in all bullying cases, and include even the steps that you may consider obvious (e.g., "interview the target"). Go through it with the parents, and ask for their help with any step as appropriate (e.g., in gathering information from their child). Anecdotally, several schools founded by religious orders have told me that a brief prayer with the parents of a victim can help reduce the emotional level of a meeting, but that option is obviously not available to public schools.

Parents May Not Understand the Limits of What Schools Can Do

One thing that cyberbullying has done is to make everyone much more conscious of the limits of school jurisdiction, but some of the psychological "leftovers" of earlier decades may lead parents to believe that schools can intervene in problem behavior no matter where it happens. The tricky part here is that while it's a good idea for parents to let the school know what's going on in off-campus or online bullying cases, parents can't always expect the school to take disciplinary action against the offender.

The jurisdiction that schools have in disciplining off-campus offenders is actually a heated, divisive legal issue, and therefore one I'm not going to touch here, since I'm not a lawyer. However, schools can, and should, take other steps, even when bullying takes place off campus. Notably, children who are targets of off-campus bullying or cyberbullying may well need the support of school personnel, and regardless of your legal obligation to respond to the offender, your humane obligation toward the target means that that support should be forthcoming.

Tip: Never simply wash your hands of a situation, or tell an upset parent, "There's nothing I can do." Always emphasize what you *can* do, and you can always say that you're ready to support a child who's a victim.

Tip: Cyberbullying sometimes targets teachers, counselors, or administrators. Try not to overreact if a child says something mean about you on the Internet. Just as they are in the hallways, children are very interested in discussing their feelings toward their teachers when communicating online; it's usually not anything truly personal, even when they mention you by name. Casual comments (even mean ones) about your appearance, your teaching style, your intelligence, and so forth should probably be utilized as a teachable moment (or ignored), rather than responded to vehemently. (For the curious reader, yes, my students have said very unflattering things about me online.) Obviously you have to protect yourself from serious libel or slander. But I do believe that part of the new digital reality is that we all need to grow a thick skin about casual online comments, because so many of us will be the subject of kids' posts. If you feel up to it, there's nothing wrong with using such comments as a learning opportunity about the public nature of social networking sites (assuming, of course, that you viewed them legitimately), and how easy it is for unintended audiences to see the posts one intends only for the eyes of peers.

Parents May Not Make the Effort to Understand the Facts About Bullying or Cyberbullying

Parents often list bullying as one of their primary concerns today, and you, as an educator, may hear from parents incessantly about this problem. So it may be a surprise to see how few really want to attend those informational evenings. I've personally spoken at hundreds of events aimed at parents. Some of these have drawn only a few people; many have drawn about a hundred or two hundred; some have drawn several hundred or more. Over the years, I've come to observe several factors that can help educate parents in a school district.

1. *Use multiple methods to communicate*: Don't just offer parent education evenings; use a variety of methods to get the information out there. Put up a dedicated page about bullying on your school's website, and make it easy to find. Send out a paper flyer telling parents about that page, and post the flyer around your town or neighborhood. Start a committee and invite parents to serve alongside educators and local police. Partner with your local cable access channel to produce a show or two about bullying and cyberbullying, and what parents can do about these issues. Invite students and parents to be on the show. Write articles for the local newspaper. E-mail a survey for parents (you can get a free one from MARC).[4] Approach your local police department and ask for their help and ideas. (If this sounds like a lot of work, consider how many phone calls all of this readily available information might eliminate.)

2. *Make live presentations noteworthy*: If you do put on an evening program, make it count—it is usually more effective to put on one noteworthy evening rather than several less enticing evenings. When I say *noteworthy*, I mean that you should try to have a speaker who is not from the school system but who is recognized and will draw parents in. Look for local authors of relevant works, and offer to help sell their books at the event. Partner with the other schools in your system; a districtwide event is often seen as more important than one for just one school. Engage parents; ask for their feedback and ideas prior to the evening. Promote the evening as you traditionally might, but also make sure there is information online that is easy to find. I think every event involving parents should be featured on the school's home page as well. (I have received many disappointed e-mails from parents who told me they looked for information about an event on the school's website, but weren't able to find it.) Offer students extra credit if they attend the evening with their parents. Ask your local cable access channel to film and/ or broadcast the event (with the speaker's permission, of course). Then, regardless of the in-person attendance, you can run and rerun the event on local cable, and you will be certain to reach more parents.

3. *Offer information and resources*: You can list these on the webpage that you devote to bullying and cyberbullying. Think about these resources in advance, and have some printed lists of helpful websites that you can give to parents. This does take some effort but it really helps demonstrate your interest in being effective.

PARENTAL ATTITUDES THAT CAN HINDER EFFECTIVE RESPONSES TO BULLYING SITUATIONS

As a parent myself—of teens and a younger child who, I hasten to point out, are most definitely *not* always perfectly behaved—I'm loathe to begin pointing fingers at mothers and fathers who are doing their utmost to keep up with their children digitally. As I pointed out in chapter 4, parents today often struggle with a persistent sense of anxiety when it comes to technology and the accompanying belief that, being less knowledgeable, they really aren't in a position to supervise or teach their kids about cyber issues. If they do too little to monitor their offspring's digital behaviors, they're criticized as neglectful. If they do too much, they're criticized as "helicopter parents" or "spies." It's no wonder so many parents have the sense that they can't win.

Still, I think parents can adopt attitudes that, while understandable, may contribute to their children's misbehaviors. Listening for, and being prepared to address, these attitudes can help parents see the connection between their child's cyber behaviors and their behaviors in school (and in life).

Nice Kids Wouldn't Do That

Parents can be misled by their own preconceptions of who could, or who would, bully someone else. Adults often retain a ready-made profile of who might be a bully: a seriously maladjusted misfit, someone without friends and with lots of academic and emotional problems. With that profile in mind, they may reject any implication that their own child might have done something bad to someone else. Since adults tend to expect online behaviors to align closely with offline behaviors, they regard the volunteer work and good grades their children achieve as evidence that their kids can't possibly have done anything cruel on the Internet. But we know that there are children who misbehave online who *do not bully in person*. Can it be that otherwise "nice" kids might cyberbully?

As noted in chapter 4, the factors that affect electronic communications can result in cyberbullying or cyberfighting that otherwise might not occur. The lack of tone in electronic writing (especially short tweets or text messages) can result in misunderstandings that sprout, in turn, intro full-blown conflicts and bullying. The lack of nonverbal feedback cues (e.g., facial expressions) can result in digital writers blithely pursuing what they believe is only mild criticism, without realizing that it's actually having a hurtful impact—a phenomenon I've termed *negligent cyberbullying*. Digital environments can feel deceptively private and confidential. Factors like these mean that it's far from impossible that an essentially well-behaved child could express feelings, with unexpectedly severe consequences, from a place of perceived safety. Relying on the offline personality, therefore, to predict any propensity to get into online trouble, is probably a shaky proposition. The truth is that misbehaving online is an understandable mistake that *any* child can make.

If I'm a Good Parent, My Children Will Never Lie to Me

In the field, I often have parents approach me with essentially the same problem: the school has contacted them about a bullying incident their child has allegedly engaged in, but the child denies everything, and as a result they simply can't believe it. This sometimes happens even in the face of pretty strong evidence (e.g., they may have found evidence of their child's cyberbullying on their own home computer). If you peruse the Internet, you can find many blogs written by parents who are "shocked" and "stunned" when they discover their child in a lie. Parents seem unaware that surveys of teens pretty consistently demonstrate that lying to parents is normal, not abnormal. Self-report data from one study of 120 teenagers (average age about sixteen) found that almost all of them (98 percent) reported that they had lied to their parents.[5] Another study of forty-three thousand teens found that 83 percent reported lying to their parents.[6] My freshman study found that 77 percent of the students who were facing discipline in a school situation lied to their parents about their role. Adults tend to believe that they can reliably tell when a child or teen is lying, which probably contributes to their perception that they haven't been lied to.[7] (This conviction is, by the way, a normal holdover from parenting toddlers; during toddlerhood, a lying child is usually ridiculously transparent. "I didn't eat any ice cream," a three-year-old may insist, with ice cream all over her face. Because they were once so obvious, it's easy to forget that they may not be that way anymore.)

The difficulty, of course, is that refusing to accept any child's normal propensity to lie (especially to save their skin) can make parents part of the problem instead of part of the solution.

PARENTAL ATTITUDES THAT CAN HINDER RESPONSES TO CYBERBULLYING PREVENTION

A major part of dealing with cyberbullying situations is prevention and education about how to use digital technology. In my opinion, this doesn't mean that teachers and parents have to become computer experts; but it does mean that they have to talk with youth about what's going on with them online. Sometimes, however, I've noticed that the adoption of certain perspectives can prevent positive conversations of this sort. Let's go through them briefly.

Teens Have an Unhealthy Addiction to Cell Phones

Many teens seem unable to function without cell phones in hand. Their reluctance to put them down, even for a moment, causes specters of addiction to haunt parents (and teachers). In the freshman study, subjects readily acknowledged that cell phones do interfere with daily life; they estimated that cell phones intrude on social situations 57 percent of the time, and on school or work 59 percent of the time. Despite this level of awareness—which I think bodes well for efforts to teach children how to control their devices—it's still true that many of the subjects expressed anxiety when asked how they would feel if they could not check or handle their cell phone for *one hour*. About 28 percent of boys and 35 percent of girls reported that they would feel anxious and worried if that were the case; 29 percent said it would be boring for the hour. The good news is that despite those high levels of anxiety, 42 percent said they could handle an hour of not being connected without having any significant feelings, one way or the other.

Because such knowledge is just emerging, it's not surprising that parents are still struggling to understand why their children are so single-mindedly committed to being connected at all times. In trying to explain this discomfort with being disconnected to parents, I often use driving without a seat belt as a good analogy. If you're accustomed to driving your car with your seat belt buckled, then you may find that it feels peculiar not to use one, so much so that even if you're only moving your car from one parking space to another, a mere thirty feet away, you still want to buckle up. Perhaps by the same token, a generation of children who have grown up with constant connectivity find it uncomfortable to be untethered from each other, even if only for a single hour.

Children Can Be Supervised Online

Pew's survey of teens and their parents in 2010 found that parents are reporting increased supervision of their children online—77 percent of parents reported that they had reviewed where their children go online and what they see, and 41 percent had "friended" their child on a social networking site.[8] I think that parents' efforts to watch what children do online, however, is to a great extent being thwarted by the rapid proliferation of Internet-enabled mobile devices. While a parent might be able to see what happens on the family desktop, what about the Internet-connected cell phone? The tablet or iPod that goes online? The laptop that the child borrows when doing homework? And of course, there are all the devices that they use in different locations: the computer at the library, the friend's cell phone, etc. etc. Following each and every device is potentially such a daunting task that it's not surprising that many kids report being able to surf the web without parents looking over their shoulder, either literally or virtually. In the freshman study, subjects were asked to rate, on a scale of 1 to 10, how much they felt their parents *intended* to supervise them online, versus how much they were actually supervised. They reported that their parents intended to supervise them, on average, a 3.45 out of 10; not terribly high, but higher than their estimate of *actual* supervision, which rated, on average, 2.75. Almost 40 percent of subjects said that their parents exercised literally zero supervision. This wasn't necessarily due to parental ineptness with digital devices, either; on the same scale, students rated their most knowledgeable parent a 6.05 out of 10 on technological know-how. The low rating seems more likely to be due to the impossibility of supervising every possible Internet-connected device, as well as Pew's finding that 85 percent of kids use the Internet outside their homes.[9]

As the number of connected devices increases, and the availability of Internet connection everywhere grows, the ability of adults to literally follow children around the Internet may well decrease or disappear altogether; but at least we will always have the ability to help them use the best safety device of all—the one between their ears.

TIPS FOR PREVENTING PROBLEMS

Ultimately, of course, what we want is to help parents overcome any problem perspectives or denial, and to appreciate what they hear and what they know about their own children. So working with parents is not just about reactions; it's about taking steps to help prevent parents from feeling that you are criticizing them, ignoring them, picking on their children, taking the other child's "side," or other tribulations. Here are two basic tips to help parents see that you're on their side.

I've come across two really good techniques that can go far in convincing parents that you're not attacking them when you discuss their children's shortcomings with them. The first is the positive phone call. If, at the beginning of each school year, you spend a few moments leaving each household a message just to let them know that things are going well so far and that you are really enjoying teaching their child, and would welcome any questions or concerns they have, you will buy yourself a lot of capital for those less-pleasant phone calls when something does go wrong. (A letter or e-mail is a good second choice.)

A second technique is to always "sandwich" your concerns between two comments about the student's potential, abilities, or just general wonderfulness. There's a big difference between hearing, "I'm calling because we're having a problem with Joey," and "I wanted to touch base with you about Joey. He has so much potential and is such a terrific boy; I am concerned that we're seeing some behaviors that could get in the way of his success. I really don't want to see that happen to such a smart student." Generally speaking, even cynical parents who are sure that "every" teacher says agreeable things about "every" student feel much more positive about that teacher, and often that school.

CONCLUSION

Moving the Field Forward

Sometimes I think that the biggest obstacle facing the field of bullying and cyberbullying is the sheer volume of variable-quality information. Sifting through all of this data in an attempt to get to the bottom line is a real challenge. I know very well that many educators are overwhelmed by, and may even avoid, the subject of bullying. In the interest of making the topic re-emerge as both refreshingly interesting and accessible, I haven't presented a truly exhaustive analysis here; instead I've tried to highlight the main issues and make better sense of what happens with children in the real, day-to-day world.

Understanding bullying and cyberbullying involves both learning new topics and reminding ourselves about the underlying issues and techniques that have always been germane, but are sometimes forgotten in the cascade of anxiety and information overload that accompanies a constantly publicized social problem. Many of the messages and prevention efforts we already know about bullying remain the cornerstones of our efforts to reduce it. The *goal* in bullying prevention is still equable, civilized, self-controlled behavior among children, even when angry or irritated (actually, especially when angry or irritated). The *tools* are still knowledge and awareness about the impact of cruel behaviors on others, ways to intervene and help, healthy and successful relationships, and, today, a good grasp of how digital communications are different from more traditional forms of social interaction. The *mechanisms* remain clear and effective education, an eye trained on the different developmental needs of children, the emotional connections we make with our students, and our common sense.

Without a doubt, bullying *has* changed. The major changes are the shift from physical to predominantly psychological bullying, and the ways that cyberbullying and cyber behaviors interact with the social lives of children today. These changes, in turn, mean that adults have to change

161

their prevention efforts. For example, the shift to psychological bullying means that similar types of behaviors are utilized by bullies and by those who aren't attacking seriously (e.g., teasing). This may mean we need to focus less on bullying per se and more on preventing all types of cruel, mean, or just thoughtless behaviors. As always, the consistency of the adult response is key in guiding the development of social behaviors in children, but the response itself may need to take a new tack at times. We have to take care not to dismiss behaviors that don't meet the technical definition of bullying, and to emphasize that a behavior doesn't have to be bullying for it to matter. It's always been true that there's never a justification for being mean or cruel. It hurts if someone else was mean first, and other people can make you feel annoyed, disgusted, or even mad, but none of these are a license to do whatever you like. That doesn't mean we should teach children to disregard how they feel about someone. But it does mean that there is an important distinction between constructive and appropriate responses to interpersonal difficulties, and responses that are both destructive and likely to worsen a tense situation.

Cyberbullying *is* new, and bullying and cyberbullying are different, but they often coexist and closely interact (especially in older children). It can be difficult to accept new realities, especially those that gallop at lightning speed across our landscape (as the digital revolution has). The very rapidity of these transformations challenges us emotionally and intellectually, but it's the old techniques—being connected to, and communicating with, our students—that can mitigate our anxieties and even our ignorance. Sometimes adults take pleasure in demeaning electronic communications, rather than listening to their students and learning alongside them about how to coexist with digital life in a healthy way. Children (and adults, for that matter) need to learn to control their devices, and not permit their devices to control them. Technological advances have brought us great benefits, but of course there are costs as well; and there are always circumstances where communicating face-to-face is best. Although it may be hard to believe, I've never talked with a group of kids who completely failed to perceive this.

Adapting commonsense education to new types of risk has certainly been done before. What can be challenging is teasing apart the different types of risk associated with new issues, like cyberbullying. One way of conceptualizing different types of risk is to separate what I call horizontal and vertical risks. I define *horizontal risk* as simply the likelihood that a bad thing will happen. *Vertical risk*, on the other hand, is the seriousness of the hazardous outcome if it does occur. When people are feeling anxious about a situation, they tend to consider both horizontal and vertical risks. And in the case of bullying, the anxiety is often truly terrible. Parents can worry that bullying will cause their child to commit suicide (horizontal), which would be the worst outcome they might ever deal with (vertical). But when "experts" address risk, they may ignore vertical risk. So a blog or an editorial in the newspaper might discuss only the fact that bullying seems to lead to suicide very rarely. It's good to hear that horizontal risk is low, but it doesn't address the anxiety around vertical risk (i.e., "It may be rare, but if it does happen to me, it will be completely devastating"). In educational efforts, it's important to acknowledge high vertical risk to avoid appearing indifferent; but for a very rare event, it's still wise to emphasize the low horizontal risk.

In spite of all of our efforts to be sensible about risk and trauma, when it comes to children, it's easy for common sense to curtsy to anxiety. Too often, we allow our nervousness about our effectiveness as caregivers to sideline our collective understanding that some negative social experimentation is simply part of childhood development. Instead of accepting that *any* child or teen (even a typically kind one) might make the mistake of "trying on" cruelty as a social lever, we perpetuate and legitimize the adults' anxiety through finger-pointing at parents or schools. We need to stop looking for someone to blame, and acknowledge our common burden, successes, and failures, as adults who raise children. The fact is that children are *supposed* to try out different roles and different behaviors. Sure, some of these roles and behaviors will land them in trouble. That's just part of life.

Our anxieties also tend to attach themselves to impossible expectations. Every person reading this book hid some things from their parents. Knowing that, it never fails to astonish me when adults today insist that a child hides *absolutely nothing* from them. Children, remember, live partly in a world of their own. You, as an adult (even an adult who is very important to them), don't get access to that world. Rather than sensibly accepting that all children will at times be avoidant or deceitful, we attach far too much drama to their misconduct.

Not all parents are educated about developmental differences in children, but I think it benefits all educators to be. A focus on developmental issues has always been an important part of bullying prevention, and it remains so today. How do bullying and cyberbullying change as children grow and develop? Who is most impacted by, and vulnerable to, bullying and who is more resilient? Keeping a focus on vulnerability and resiliency can help empower targets to live successfully with the meanness that is an inevitable part of life, and help children vulnerable to aggression develop better coping mechanisms. A developmental focus can also help us assess what children need at different ages to develop the social skills necessary to avoid and cope with antisocial peers. For example, both the Association for Childhood Education International and the American Academy of Pediatrics have come out with official positions expressing concern over the reduction of play in the lives of many young children and the (possibly associated) reduction in social, cognitive, and academic skills.[1] Although there is some controversy in the field of early childhood education over the value of "academic" versus "play-based" preschool and kindergarten, the consensus among researchers and practitioners seems to be that enriched, educational play is the best method for young children to learn.[2] Because we know that the play is associated with social skills, particularly with the kind of social skills that children use to cope with challenging social situations, it has been hypothesized that the reduction in children's play may be a contributing factor to the increase in bullying and cyberbullying. While some play situations are outside of education's purview, others are not, notably playtime in preschool and kindergarten.

WRAP-UP: THE FINAL CHALLENGE

Could I have condensed this entire book into one bullet list (a *short* bullet list)? Here you go: ten bullets that say it all.

- What we call bullying has changed; it's now more often played out as psychological, rather than physical, attacks.
- What we call cyberbullying is often simply cruel or thoughtless digital behavior, but it may be experienced as bullying by the recipient.
- What happens online and what occurs offline are inextricably linked, especially among teens.
- Kids start online interactions very young—early in elementary school. The older they get, the more bullying migrates online.
- It's critical to recognize the beginning level of abusive behaviors—gateway behaviors—and stop them when you see them.
- Teach your students how digital interactions lack a lot of social information, and how that can lead to problems with others if they're not careful.
- Encourage friendships and friendly actions between peers. That's the best defense.
- Throw parents a bone. Most are trying their best. It's not easy.

- Don't minimize the concerns of kids who seek you out. Connect with them. Connect with them. Connect with them. *Working with children is never just about the academic content.*
- The Massachusetts Aggression Reduction Center website has quite a few free downloads. Use them! (www.MARCcenter.org or www .elizabethenglander.com)

Fundamentally, I think that bullying prevention is like exercise: anything you do is better than doing nothing, and collective efforts can particularly pay off. You won't do everything perfectly, but who ever has? You won't know everything, either, but children can learn very well from adults who are willing to learn alongside them. Maybe bullying prevention is really about learning to be more accepting of others, and more skeptical of ourselves. Take a deep breath, and take the first step.

Research Discussed
in This Book

For those interested in methodology, here are a few details about the sources of the data that I discuss in the book. With a few exceptions, all findings that are presented are differences that reached statistical significance at or very near the $p < .05$ standard (through chi square, regression, ANOVA, or MANOVA). For fluency's sake, and because this is not intended as a book for fellow researchers, I did not specify statistical details (e.g., "$X^2 = 456.77$, $p < .000$"). When differences did not reach statistical significance, but were interesting nonetheless, I used the word *slightly* (as in, "Boys were slightly more likely to like the color blue"). Many other researchers' findings are cited too, of course.

ANNUAL STUDY OF COLLEGE FRESHMEN AT
BRIDGEWATER STATE UNIVERSITY

Each year my students and I anonymously survey hundreds of college freshmen at Bridgewater State University, most of whom are enrolled in the introductory course in psychology. In this book I primarily share findings from the 2010–2011 and 2011–2012 surveys of 1,234 students (617 in each year). These students aren't representative of all eighteen-year-olds across the country, but they do come from a variety of backgrounds. However, most subjects come from white, working-class to middle-class families in Massachusetts and surrounding states (New Hampshire, Maine, Vermont, Rhode Island, and Connecticut). This is both an advantage, in that social class and ethnicity are (for the most part) naturally controlled covariates in this study, and a disadvantage, in that the sample is not representative of teens across the country. However, this survey has as a significant asset very detailed information, with more than three hundred variables studied, and I ask questions not only about bullying and cyberbullying, but also about family life; relationships with teachers, peers, friends, and others; social behaviors; substance abuse; indicators of mental health; sibling relationships; cyber behaviors; and many other variables. It is a retrospective study (meaning that participants have to remember past conditions), although high school is a pretty recent memory for eighteen-year-olds. Most of the data collected is about high school, but some questions ask students about earlier events in their childhood.

WAVE ONE OF 21,000 CHILDREN IN GRADES 3–12

Beginning in 2010, we started anonymously surveying children in grades 3 through 12 across Massachusetts and New Hampshire. Unlike the freshman study, this data is collected primarily from within Massachusetts and New Hampshire, from a variety of social classes and from urban, suburban, and rural areas. Most of the data considered here was measured between January 2011 and June 2011. During those months, we surveyed more than 21,000 children—approximately 7,000 at each level (elementary, middle, and high school). This survey was broader than the freshman study but also shallower: it examined fewer variables but gave me a great way to assess how bullying and cyberbullying develop and change between elementary school and high school.

SURVEYS OF ADULTS

Between September 2010 and June 2011, 3,715 teachers and administrators and 1,941 parents were anonymously surveyed. Unlike parents, who took the survey only if they were personally motivated to do so (and thus were an almost certainly biased sample), faculty were generally asked to complete the survey because their schools were participating in the survey of students. Neither sample was nationally representative, but the faculty data is probably a closer match to the population in general. As I discussed in chapter 8, the sample of parents was (somewhat surprisingly) not overwhelmingly composed of mothers and fathers whose child was a target of bullying. Still, simply because this sample of parents was self-selected, it is not likely to be representative of all parents.

ANECDOTAL DATA FROM CHILDREN AT THE
SCHOOLS IN WHICH MARC WORKED

In the Massachusetts Aggression Reduction Center, I train college-aged students to deliver programming to schoolchildren. Having these older teens and young adults work with their slightly younger peers is a deliberate strategy, intended to facilitate a strong rapport and to provide positive role models to younger children. Because of that rapport, younger children often regale my students with interesting and informative anecdotes and personal stories. This type of data cannot definitively answer questions, but it can provide illustrative examples and raise new issues that in turn can help inform the direction of the research we conduct.

APPENDIX B

The Massachusetts Aggression Reduction Center

The Massachusetts Aggression Reduction Center is a university-based center, designed to increase access to high-quality, research-based bullying and cyberbullying prevention services, to train future educators in bullying and cyberbullying prevention, and to facilitate professional relationships around the Commonwealth. We achieve those aims by partnering with K–12 educators, guidance counselors, administrators, law enforcement, and public servants in the legal sector (e.g., district attorney's office). The ultimate purposes of such a partnership are to:

- Provide free or low-cost research-based and high-quality prevention programs throughout K–12 communities (including faculty, guidance counselors, administrators, parents, and students) about the causes of aggression, bullying, cyberbullying, and cyber behaviors in children
- Train future educators, by having Bridgewater State University faculty and students deliver many services through their participation in the center
- Conduct research and disseminate current research findings in that area in a speedy and comprehensive manner
- Provide K–12 faculty and personnel, law enforcement, physicians, attorneys, and other stakeholders with the knowledge and understanding to cope with aggression, bullying, and safety issues in schools, including effective responses and intervention techniques

Undergraduate and graduate students at Bridgewater State University in the fields of psychology, sociology, education, social work, and related areas of study can apply to become student associates in MARC. Students can become involved in research, training students at local area schools, giving assemblies, and many other center activities. Students do not provide training and programs for faculty, parents, or administrators (faculty in the center provide this training for schools and communities), but beyond that each student freely chooses the areas he or she would like to become involved in.

University students are powerful role models to younger students in a way that many other adults (such as parents and teachers) cannot be. Adolescents, who may turn a deaf ear to parents and teachers, tend to respond to college students, who are regarded as high-status peers.

GOALS OF THE STUDENT TRAINING

A MARC student undergoes training at the center, and thereafter provides training to younger peers. These undergraduate students, who receive course credits for their work in MARC, help high school and middle school students:

- Learn how to *recognize* and *label* the problems they see, and how to use small-group discussion to more precisely identify what they consider to be the most pressing problems in their own school
- Learn to brainstorm and problem-solve about how about they, as a group, can lead an engagement in their specific school culture to work against violence and bullying

The power of this method lies in the fact that it is the teenagers themselves who both *identify their schools' challenges* and *come up with their own ideas about how to address them*. Neither the problems nor the solutions are defined or imposed by adults. We utilize a unique training method that shows students how to transform free-floating ideas into concrete plans.

This student training is designed to help the school successfully launch a student-initiated program, or programs, aimed at reducing violence and bullying or accompanying problems (for example, such a program might work to reduce gossiping or cyberbullying). MARC starts the ball rolling, but it is up to the school to provide some format and structure for their student group to continue its activities.

Student Training Format

The length of a student training session is generally two to three hours. Training often also includes thirty to sixty minutes of educational pedagogy.

MARC facilitators are training teenagers to become leaders and "peer helpers." Peer helping is a model wherein teens are trained to become educators and counselors for their peers. Benard pointed out that while peers can destroy a child's sense of safety, they are also among the most powerful providers of support.[1] Benard's study found that peer helping was a valid intervention strategy resulting in reduced at-risk behaviors. The MARC program aims to teach teenagers how to identify what they consider to be issues and challenges in their own school, and to coach them in coming up with their own ideas for improving their school climate. The Innovation Center released a review of peer helping programs that identified important characteristics and tenets that made such programs successful.[2] These were, among others:

- Being "youth-run and led"
- Raising awareness in young people without taking too much power from them
- "Meeting young people where they are"
- "When young people have full ownership, they step up to the tasks"
- "Teen trainers are more effective than adult trainers"

Because MARC seeks to supplement and not replace other types of bullying prevention programs, the program opted to develop student programming for teenagers based on the peer helping model. This approach is particularly attractive for an academic center, which has a ready pool of college students to serve as high-status peer models for high-school and middle-school children.

Student Training Procedure

1. The MARC supervisor begins by introducing the university team and orienting everyone to what will happen. S/he discusses the content of the training and explains that they are there to learn about what the students see happening in their school and to help them think of ways to work on it.
2. A short PowerPoint presentation is given to get the students thinking and focused. Remote polling may be used during the presentation to engage the students and to assist the facilitators by revealing facts or issues of interest in the school.
3. If we have school-specific survey data from the student group, we share it with them.

4. The high school or middle school students are divided into small discussion groups of three to seven students each. Each small group sits down with one or two university students (facilitators). One student is asked to take notes.

5. All students go through a process where they transition between small groups and the larger group. During this process the students learn how to produce original insights and ideas and to transform them into concrete, usable plans.

6. Students usually have many ideas, and facilitators are careful not to dismiss any of them, but to guide them toward practical or realistic goals. The critical point here is that the students must feel that they themselves have thought up these programs and that they will be the ones to implement them.

Notes

Introduction

1. E. Englander, *Freshman Study 2011: Bullying and Cyberbullying*, Research Reports from the Massachusetts Aggression Reduction Center (Bridgewater State University, June 2011), http://webhost.bridgew.edu/marc/research.html.
2. U.S. Department of Education, "Bullying: Peer Abuse in Schools," *LD Online*, 1998, http://www.ldonline.org/article/6171/.
3. A sobering report in the United Kingdom ("Teachers Tell Bullied Kids: Don't Be So Gay," *Echo*, November 5, 2011, http://www.echo-news.co.uk/news/local_news) found that bullied teens were told, far too often, that if they only "stopped acting gay" then the abuse would end. Statements such as these, which imply agreement with bullies ("it was justified"), place the blame and responsibility squarely on the victim, instead of supporting teens who may be seeking to establish their own identities. (It is important to note that well-intentioned adults who are unaware of the repercussions of their statements may at times say such things. It is a testament to the necessity of training adults who work with children.)
4. J. Medina, "Kids Lie Every 90 Minutes—And That's a Good Thing," *Huffington Post*, January 15, 2011, http://www.huffingtonpost.com/john-medina-phd/kids-lie-every-90-minutes_b_807775.html.
5. L. Bond et al., "Does Bullying Cause Emotional Problems? A Prospective Study of Young Teenagers," *BMJ* 323, no. 7311 (September 1, 2001): 480–484, doi:10.1136/bmj.323.7311.480; A. Brunstein Klomek et al., "Bullying, Depression, and Suicidality in Adolescents," *Journal of the American Academy of Child & Adolescent Psychiatry* 46, no. 1 (January 2007): 40–49, doi:10.1097/01.chi.0000242237.84925.18.
6. C. Winsper et al., "Involvement in Bullying and Suicide-Related Behavior at 11 Years: A Prospective Birth Cohort Study," *Journal of the American Academy of Child & Adolescent Psychiatry* 51, no. 3 (March 2012): 271–282.e3. I am being deliberate with my language use here. The media, and many experts, have linked bullying victimization to the suicides of several children. I use the term *possible* because others have pointed out that it's difficult to assess the level and severity of many actual bullying cases (more on that later in the book) and it's typically the case that among suicide victims, multiple stressors are present (suggesting that bullying may not be the only cause of suicide). This is in no way intended to dismiss the very real trauma that abuse such as bullying can wreak upon its victims.
7. E. Englander, "Spinning Our Wheels: Improving Our Ability to Respond to Bullying and Cyberbullying," *Child and Adolescent Psychiatric Clinics of North America*

21, no. 1 (January 2012): 43–55, doi:10.1016/j.chc.2011.08.013; D. Olweus, *Aggression in the Schools: Bullies and Whipping Boys* (Oxford, England: Hemisphere, 1978), http://psycnet.apa.org/psycinfo/1979-32242-000.

8. U.S. Department of Education. "Bullying: Peer Abuse in Schools." LD Online, 1998. http://www.ldonline.org/article/6171/.

9. Englander, "Spinning Our Wheels"; E. Englander, "Is Bullying a Junior Hate Crime? Implications for Interventions," *American Behavioral Scientist* 51, no. 2 (October 1, 2007): 205–212, doi:10.1177/0002764207306052; P. Gradinger, D. Strohmeier, and C. Spiel, "Traditional Bullying and Cyberbullying: Identification of Risk Groups for Adjustment Problems," *Zeitschrift Für Psychologie/Journal of Psychology* 217, no. 4 (2009): 205–213, doi:10.1027/0044-3409.217.4.205; M. McKenna, E. Hawk, J. Mullen, and M. Hertz, "Bullying Among Middle School and High School Students—Massachusetts, 2009," *Morbidity and Mortality Weekly Report (MMWR)* 60, no. 15 (April 22, 2011): 465–471.

10. D. Olweus, *Bullying at School : What We Know and What We Can Do* (Oxford, England: Blackwell, 1993).

11. E. Englander, *Study of 21,000 Children in Grades 3–12 in Massachusetts*, Research Reports from the Massachusetts Aggression Reduction Center (Bridgewater State University, June 2011), http://webhost.bridgew.edu/marc/research.html.

12. H. Cowie and R. Olafsson, "The Role of Peer Support in Helping the Victims of Bullying in a School with High Levels of Aggression," *School Psychology International* 21, no. 1 (February 1, 2000): 79–95, doi:10.1177/0143034300211006.

13. University of Wisconsin-Madison, *At the Table: Making the Case for Youth in Decision-Making* (Innovation Center for Community and Youth Development and National 4-H Council, 2003).

14. S. Davis and C. Nixon, *The Youth Voice Project* (Penn State Erie, stopbullyingnow .com, March 2010), http://www.youthvoiceproject.com/.

15. For the sake of readability, and because this isn't a book for fellow researchers, the research findings I cite in the chapters don't include statistical or methodological details. Those can all be found in appendix A. All differences I cite in this book are statistically significant, with a few exceptions. Findings that approach significance but don't achieve the p <. 05 standard are worded as "slightly different" or something similar.

Chapter 1

1. "Special Edition: School Bullying," *Education.com*, n.d., http://www.education .com/special-edition/bullying/schoolbullying/.

2. D. Olweus, *Aggression in the Schools: Bullies and Whipping Boys* (Oxford, England: Hemisphere, 1978), http://psycnet.apa.org/psycinfo/1979-32242-000.

3. T. Parker-Pope, "Web of Popularity, Achieved by Bullying," *Well* (blog), *NYTimes .com*, February 14, 2011, http://well.blogs.nytimes.com/2011/02/14/web-of-popularity-weaved-by-bullying/.

4. Olweus, *Aggression in the Schools*.

5. S. Davis and C. Nixon, *The Youth Voice Project* (Penn State Erie, stopbullyingnow .com, March 2010), http://www.youthvoiceproject.com/.

6. U.S. Department of Education, "Bullying: Peer Abuse in Schools," *LD Online*, 1998, http://www.ldonline.org/article/6171/.

7. E. Englander, "Preliminary Report: Bullying and Cyberbullying in Massachusetts 2011–12" (presented at the Workshop: PCP Interventions, Freehold, NJ, 2011).

8. E. Englander, "Cyberbullying—New Research and Findings" (presented at the 2012 National Cyber Crime Conference, Norwood, Massachusetts, 2012).

9. R. Faris and D. Felmlee, "Social Networks and Aggression at the Wheatley School" (Department of Sociology, University of California, Davis, 2011).

10. D. Finkelhor et al., "Trends in Childhood Violence and Abuse Exposure: Evidence from 2 National Surveys," *Archives of Pediatrics & Adolescent Medicine* 164, no. 3 (March 2010): 238–242, doi:10.1001/archpediatrics.2009.283.

11. Davis and Nixon, *The Youth Voice Project.*

12. W. Craig, D. Pepler, and R. Atlas, "Observations of Bullying in the Playground and in the Classroom," *School Psychology International* 21, no. 1 (February 1, 2000): 22–36, doi:10.1177/0143034300211002.

13. Englander, "Cyberbullying—New Research and Findings."

14. G. Hinsliff, "Why Have We All Become So Casually Cruel?," *Comment Is Free* (blog), *The Observer/The Guardian*, July 3, 2010, http://www.guardian.co.uk/commentisfree/2010/jul/04/steven-gerrard-twitter-facebook; S. Oden and S. R. Asher, "Coaching Children in Social Skills for Friendship Making," *Child Development* 48, no. 2 (1977): 495–506.

15. Parker-Pope, "Web of Popularity, Achieved by Bullying,".

16. Englander, "Preliminary Report: Bullying and Cyberbullying in Massachusetts 2011–12."

17. J. Vohs, "Vulnerable Targets: Students with Disabilities and Bullying," Federation for Children with Special Needs, http://fcsn.org/newsline/v30n3/bullying.php.

18. "2009 National School Climate Survey: Nearly 9 Out of 10 LGBT Students Experience Harassment in School," GLSEN: Gay, Lesbian and Straight Education Network, http://www.glsen.org/cgi bin/iowa/all/library/record/2624.html.

19. Englander, "Cyberbullying—New Research and Findings."

20. U.S. Department of Education, "Bullying: Peer Abuse in Schools."

21. Depending upon your location, the issue of repetition may be legally moot. In some states, no repetition is required in the legal definition of bullying. However, most researchers and psychologists do recognize that repetitively cruel behavior is psychologically distinct from one-time events, and thus likely to be experienced very differently by the target.

22. U.S. Department of Education, "Bullying: Peer Abuse in Schools."

23. Davis and Nixon, *The Youth Voice Project.*

24. X. Wu et al., "Peer and Teacher Sociometrics for Preschool Children: Cross-Informant Concordance, Temporal Stability, and Reliability," *Merill-Palmer Quarterly*, July 1, 2011, 1–5.

25. E. Englander, *Study of 21,000 Children in Grades 3–12 in Massachusetts*, Research Reports from the Massachusetts Aggression Reduction Center (Bridgewater State University, June 2011), http://webhost.bridgew.edu/marc/research.html.

26. E. Englander, *Freshman Study 2011: Bullying and Cyberbullying*, Research Reports from the Massachusetts Aggression Reduction Center (Bridgewater State University, June 2011), http://webhost.bridgew.edu/marc/research.html.

27. J. Wolak, K. Mitchell, and D. Finkelhor, "Does Online Harassment Constitute Bullying? An Exploration of Online Harassment by Known Peers and Online-Only Contacts," *Journal of Adolescent Health* 41, no. 6 (December 2007): S51–S58, doi:10.1016/j.jadohealth.2007.08.019.
28. S. Hughes, "Alone Together," *Pennsylvania Gazette*, May/June 2010, 1–4.
29. R. Clements, "An Investigation of the Status of Outdoor Play," *Contemporary Issues in Early Childhood* 5 (2004): 68–80.
30. Centers for Disease Control and Prevention, "KidsWalk-to-School: Resource Materials," Department of Health and Human Services, February 25, 2008, http://www.cdc.gov/nccdphp/dnpa/kidswalk/then_and_now.htm.
31. Englander, *Freshman Study 2011*; W. Bösche, "Violent Content Enhances Video Game Performance," *Journal of Media Psychology: Theories, Methods, and Applications* 21, no. 4 (2009): 145–150, doi:10.1027/1864-1105.21.4.145.

Chapter 2

1. http://www.safeandcaringschools.com.
2. http://www.ashleypsychology.com.
3. http://www.theneweditor.com.
4. S. Woloshin and L. Schwartz, "Giving Legs to Restless Legs: A Case Study of How the Media Helps Make People Sick," *PLoS Medicine* 3, no. 4 (2006): e170, doi:10.1371/journal.pmed.0030170, http://www.plosmedicine.org/article/info:doi/10.1371/journal.pmed.0030170.
5. E. Thiegs, "Stageoflife.com Reports 91% of Teenagers Have Been Bullied," *MarketWire.com*, August 25, 2011.
6. E. Englander, "Spinning Our Wheels: Improving Our Ability to Respond to Bullying and Cyberbullying," *Child and Adolescent Psychiatric Clinics of North America* 21, no. 1 (January 2012): 43–55, doi:10.1016/j.chc.2011.08.013.
7. Harris Interactive, *Teens and Cyberbullying Research Study* (Washington, DC: National Crime Prevention Council, 2007), https://docs.google.com/viewer?a=v&q=cache:MZW2k0_UqtIJ:www.ncpc.org/resources/files/pdf/bullying/Teens percent2520and percent2520Cyberbullying percent2520Research percent2520Study.pdf+&hl=en&gl=us&pid=bl&srcid=ADGEESgaYyB_ccy50DELeT9LK098sm20_Pkc2NyVC2qR08yGuB1qVUoCH2fvlgDlPiIrDSXd Do7F2w3hIyJJLUi62ZnvyqWlYCaSFEshwu6ruuAq2zDIUB3MeUr3qOElJHKq A0nwnA4Y&sig=AHIEtbT9NOXWtZ8y5yTEa1hJJyRf3Bm5Rg.
8. R. Dinkes, J. Kemp, and K. Baum, *Indicators of School Crime and Safety: 2008* (Washington, DC: U.S. Department of Justice, April 2009).
9. *Student Reports of Bullying and Cyber-Bullying: Results from the 2009 School Crime Supplement to the National Crime Victimization Survey* (Washington, DC: U.S. Department of Justice, 2009).
10. M. McKenna, E. Hawk, J. Mullen, and M. Hertz, "Bullying Among Middle School and High School Students—Massachusetts, 2009," *Morbidity and Mortality Weekly Report (MMWR)* 60, no. 15 (April 22, 2011): 465–471.
11. D. Finkelhor, H. Turner, R. Ormrod, and S. Hamby, "Trends in Childhood Violence and Abuse Exposure: Evidence from 2 National Surveys," *Archives of Pediatrics & Adolescent Medicine* 164, no. 3 (March 2010): 238–242, doi:10.1001/archpediatrics.2009.283.

12. K. Mitchell, J. Wolak, and D. Finkelhor, "Trends in Youth Reports of Sexual So-licitations, Harassment and Unwanted Exposure to Pornography on the Inter-net," *Journal of Adolescent Health* 40, no. 2 (February 2007): 116–126, doi:10.1016/j.jadohealth.2006.05.021.

13. S. Hinduja and J. Patchin, "Cyberbullying Research in Review," Cyberbullying Research Center, 2010, http://www.cyberbullying.us/Cyberbullying_Research_In_Review.pdf.

14. K. DeLong, "Survey Shows 17 Percent of Students Are Victims of Cyber-bullying," *FoxNews.com*, n.d., http://fox6now.com/2012/02/16/survey-shows-17-percent-of-students-are-victims-of-cyber-bullying/.

15. E. Englander, "Cyberbullying—New Research and Findings" (presented at the 2012 National Cyber Crime Conference, Norwood, Massachusetts, 2012).

16. E. Englander, *Study of 21,000 Children in Grades 3–12 in Massachusetts*, Research Reports from the Massachusetts Aggression Reduction Center (Bridgewater State University, June 2011), http://webhost.bridgew.edu/marc/research.html.

17. Harris Interactive, *Teens and Cyberbullying Research Study*.

18. Englander, *Study of 21,000 Children in Grades 3–12 in Massachusetts*.

19. M. Borg, "The Emotional Reactions of School Bullies and Their Victims," *Educational Psychology* 18, no. 4 (December 1998): 433–444, doi:10.1080/0144341980180405.

20. E. Englander, "Preliminary Report: Bullying and Cyberbullying in Massachu-setts 2011–12" (presented at the Workshop: PCP Interventions, Freehold, NJ, 2011).

21. Ibid.

22. E. Englander, *Understanding Violence*, 3d edition (Mahwah, NJ: Lawrence Erl-baum Publishers, 2007).

23. K. Sofronoff, E. Dark, and V. Stone, "Social Vulnerability and Bullying in Chil-dren with Asperger Syndrome," *Autism: The International Journal of Research and Practice* 15, no. 3 (May 2011): 355–372; *From Teasing to Torment: School Climate in America—A National Report on School Bullying* (GLSEN: Gay, Lesbian and Straight Education Network, October 11, 2005), http://glsen.org/cgi-bin/iowa/all/library/record/1859.html.

24. M. Langevin, "Helping Children Deal with Teasing and Bullying," Minnesota State University, Mankato, October 22, 2001, http://www.mnsu.edu/comdis/isad4/papers/langevin.html.

25. L. Bowes et al., "Families Promote Emotional and Behavioural Resilience to Bullying: Evidence of an Environmental Effect," *Journal of Child Psychology and Psychiatry* 51, no. 7 (February 3, 2010): 809–817, doi:10.1111/j.1469-7610.2010.02216.x.

26. A. Wolbert Burgess, C. Garbarino, and M. Carlson, "Pathological Teasing and Bullying Turned Deadly: Shooters and Suicide," *Victims & Offenders* 1, no. 1 (April 2006): 1–14; Clayton R. Cook et al., "Predictors of Bullying and Victim-ization in Childhood and Adolescence: A Meta-analytic Investigation," *School Psychology Quarterly* 25, no. 2 (2010): 65–83; A. Brunstein Klomek et al., "Bully-ing, Depression, and Suicidality in Adolescents," *Journal of the American Acad-emy of Child & Adolescent Psychiatry* 46, no. 1 (January 2007): 40–49; W. Craig, "The Relationship Among Bullying, Victimization, Depression, Anxiety, and

Aggression in Elementary School Children," *Personality and Individual Differences* 24, no. 1 (January 1998): 123–130, doi:10.1016/S0191-8869(97)00145-1.

27. Englander, "Preliminary Report: Bullying and Cyberbullying in Massachusetts 2011–12."

28. Harris Interactive, *Teens and Cyberbullying Research Study*.

29. S. Jaffee and R. Gallop, "Social, Emotional, and Academic Competence Among Children Who Have Had Contact with Child Protective Services: Prevalence and Stability Estimates," *Journal of the American Academy of Child & Adolescent Psychiatry* 46, no. 6 (June 2007): 757–765, doi:10.1097/chi.0b013e318040b247.

30. R. Faris and D. Felmlee, "Social Networks and Aggression at the Wheatley School" (Department of Sociology, University of California, Davis, 2011).

31. J. Wang, R. Iannotti, and T. Nansel, "School Bullying Among Adolescents in the United States: Physical, Verbal, Relational, and Cyber," *Journal of Adolescent Health* 45, no. 4 (October 2009): 368–375, doi:10.1016/j.jadohealth.2009.03.021.

32. K. Sinclair et al., "Cyber and Bias-based Harassment: Associations with Academic, Substance Use, and Mental Health Problems," *Journal of Adolescent Health* Short Communication, February 2012, doi:10.1016/j.jadohealth.2011.09.009.

33. In-school bullying: $r = .749$, $p < .000$; online bullying: $r = .76$, $p < .000$.

34. E. V. Hodges et al., "The Power of Friendship: Protection Against an Escalating Cycle of Peer Victimization," *Developmental Psychology* 35, no. 1 (January 1999): 94–101; M. J. Boulton et al., "Concurrent and Longitudinal Links Between Friendship and Peer Victimization: Implications for Befriending Interventions," *Journal of Adolescence* 22, no. 4 (August 1999): 461–466, doi:10.1006/jado.1999.0240.

35. L. Bond et al., "Does Bullying Cause Emotional Problems? A Prospective Study of Young Teenagers," *BMJ* 323, no. 7311 (September 1, 2001): 480–484; M. Busko, "Anxiety Linked with Increased Cell-Phone Dependence, Abuse" (presented at the Anxiety Disorders Association of America 28th Annual Meeting, Savannah, GA, 2007); Craig, "The Relationship Among Bullying, Victimization, Depression, Anxiety, and Aggression in Elementary School Children."

36. K. Sugden et al., "Serotonin Transporter Gene Moderates the Development of Emotional Problems Among Children Following Bullying Victimization," *Journal of the American Academy of Child & Adolescent Psychiatry* 49, no. 8 (August 2010): 830–840, doi:10.1016/j.jaac.2010.01.024.

37. R. Kaltiala-Heino et al., "Bullying, Depression, and Suicidal Ideation in Finnish Adolescents: School Survey," *BMJ* (Clinical Research Ed.) 319, no. 7206 (August 7, 1999): 348–351.

38. C. Arata, "Child Sexual Abuse and Sexual Revictimization," *Clinical Psychology: Science and Practice* 9, no. 2 (May 11, 2006): 135–164, doi:10.1093/clipsy.9.2.135.

39. T. Messman, "Child Sexual Abuse and Its Relationship to Revictimization in Adult Women: A Review," *Clinical Psychology Review* 16, no. 5 (1996): 397–420, doi:10.1016/0272-7358(96)00019-0.

40. ($X^2 = 29.7$, $p < .003$).

41. S. Davis and C. Nixon, *The Youth Voice Project* (Penn State Erie, stopbullyingnow .com, March 2010), http://www.youthvoiceproject.com/.

42. Ibid.

43. E. Englander, "New Findings in Bullying and Cyberbullying Research" (keynote presented at the Wellness Conference for Brevard County, Satellite Beach, FL, September 10, 2012).

44. S. Oden and S. R. Asher, "Coaching Children in Social Skills for Friendship Making," *Child Development* 48, no. 2 (1977): 495–506.

45. (F = 2.41, p < .006)

46. D. Olweus, *Aggression in the Schools: Bullies and Whipping Boys* (Oxford, England: Hemisphere, 1978), http://psycnet.apa.org/psycinfo/1979-32242-000.

47. University of New Hampshire, *Why Do Some Children Bully Others? Bullies and Their Victims*, Family Development Fact Sheet (University of New Hampshire Cooperative Extension, 2002), http://extension.unh.edu/family/parent/SApubs/bully.pdf. Federal law requires that all special needs students be on an IEP. Thus, the existence of an IEP is a good marker of a student with some kind of disability. It should be noted, however, that it's far from a perfect marker: it is very probable that some children's disabilities are not detected or are not severe enough to warrant their placement on an IEP; Englander, "Preliminary Report: Bullying and Cyberbullying in Massachusetts 2011–12."

48. Faris and Felmlee, "Social Networks and Aggression at the Wheatley School"; Jaffee and Gallop, "Social, Emotional, and Academic Competence Among Children Who Have Had Contact with Child Protective Services."

49. R. Slaby and N. Guerra, "Cognitive Mediators of Aggression in Adolescent Offenders: I. Assessment," *Developmental Psychology* 24, no. 4 (1988): 580–588.

50. Harris Interactive, *Teens and Cyberbullying Research Study.*

51. Englander, *Study of 21,000 Children in Grades 3–12 in Massachusetts*; Faris and Felmlee, "Social Networks and Aggression at the Wheatley School"; Helper, S., "Bullies and Cyberbullies," *PBS & NPR Forum Network: Cambridge Forum*, September 21, 2011, http://forum-network.org/lecture/bullies-and-cyberbullies#; P. Elmer-DeWitt, *Nielsen: U.S. Teens Exchange 7 Text Messages Per Waking Hour* (NielsenWire, December 15, 2011), http://tech.fortune.cnn.com/2011/12/15/nielsen-u-s-teens-exchange-7-text-messages-per-waking-hour/.

52. S. Coyne et al., "'Frenemies, Fraitors, and Mean-em-aitors': Priming Effects of Viewing Physical and Relational Aggression in the Media on Women," *Aggressive Behavior* (December 2011): n/a, doi:10.1002/ab.21410.

Chapter 3

1. D. Finkelhor, *The Internet, Youth Safety and the Problem of "Juvenoia"* (Durham, NH: Crimes Against Children Research Center, January 2011), http://www.unh.edu/ccrc/pdf/Juvenoia percent20paper.pdf.

2. D. Olweus, *Aggression in the Schools: Bullies and Whipping Boys* (Oxford, England: Hemisphere, 1978), http://psycnet.apa.org/psycinfo/1979-32242-000.

3. Ibid.

4. J. H. F. Chan, "Systemic Patterns in Bullying and Victimization," *School Psychology International* 27, no. 3 (July 1, 2006): 352–369, doi:10.1177/0143034306067289.

5. B. Stelter, "Young People Are Watching, but Less Often on TV," February 8, 2012, http://www.nytimes.com/2012/02/09/business/media/young-people-are-watching-but-less-often-on-tv.html?_r=2&hpw=&pagewanted=all.
6. E. Englander and A. Muldowney, "Just Turn the Darn Thing Off: Understanding Cyberbullying," in *Proceedings of Persistently Safe Schools: The 2007 National Conference on Safe Schools*, eds. D. L. White, B. C. Glenn, and A. Wimes (presented at the Hamilton Fish Institute, George Washington University, Washington, DC, 2007), 83–92.
7. "Daily Media Use Among Children and Teens Up Dramatically from Five Years Ago—Kaiser Family Foundation," Kaiser Family Foundation, January 20, 2010, http://www.kff.org/entmedia/entmedia012010nr.cfm.
8. R. Pea et al., "Media Use, Face-to-Face Communication, Media Multitasking, and Social Well-being Among 8- to 12-Year-Old Girls," *Developmental Psychology*, January 23, 2012, doi:10.1037/a0027030.
9. E. Mills, "Bullying on Prime Time TV Sitcoms, " unpublished manuscript (Bridgewater State University, Massachusetts: Massachusetts Aggression Reduction Center, 2009).
10. S. Coyne et al., "'Frenemies, Fraitors, and Mean-em-aitors': Priming Effects of Viewing Physical and Relational Aggression in the Media on Women," *Aggressive Behavior*, December 2011, doi:10.1002/ab.21410.
11. M. Rumfola, "Cyber-Bullying: Bullying in the 21st Century" (counselor education master's thesis, State University of New York, Brockport, 2008), http://digitalcommons.brockport.edu/cgi/viewcontent.cgi?article=1092&context=edc_theses.
12. E. Englander, *Freshman Study 2011: Bullying and Cyberbullying*, Research Reports from the Massachusetts Aggression Reduction Center (Bridgewater State University, June 2011), http://webhost.bridgew.edu/marc/research.html.
13. S. Fahlman, "Smiley Lore :-)," http://www.cs.cmu.edu/~sef/sefSmiley.htm.
14. E. Englander, "Cyberbullying in 8- to 10-Year Olds: Research on 12,000 Children" (presented at the International Bullying Prevention Association Annual Conference, Kansas City, MO, November 5, 2012).
15. T. Correa, A. Hinsley, and H. de Zúñiga, "Who Interacts on the Web?: The Intersection of Users' Personality and Social Media Use," *Computers in Human Behavior* 26, no. 2 (March 2010): 247–253, doi:10.1016/j.chb.2009.09.003.
16. R. M. Milteer et al., "The Importance of Play in Promoting Healthy Child Development and Maintaining Strong Parent-Child Bond: Focus on Children in Poverty," *Pediatrics* 129, no. 1 (December 26, 2011): e204–e213, doi:10.1542/peds.2011-2953.
17. Ibid.
18. J. Almon, "The Crisis in Early Education: A Research-Based Case for More Play and Less Pressure, " Alliance for Childhood, November 2011, http://www.allianceforchildhood.org/sites/allianceforchildhood.org/files/file/crisis_in_early_ed.pdf.
19. R. Henig, "Taking Play Seriously," *New York Times*, February 17, 2008, sec. Children and Youth, http://www.whywaldorfworks.org/03_NewsEvents/documents/TakingPlaySeriously.pdf.

20. Milteer et al., "The Importance of Play in Promoting Healthy Child Development and Maintaining Strong Parent-Child Bond."
21. Henig, "Taking Play Seriously."
22. E. V. Hodges et al., "The Power of Friendship: Protection Against an Escalating Cycle of Peer Victimization," *Developmental Psychology* 35, no. 1 (January 1999): 94–101.
23. S. E. Caplan, "A Social Skill Account of Problematic Internet Use," *Journal of Communication* 55, no. 4 (December 2005): 721–736; Milteer et al., "The Importance of Play in Promoting Healthy Child Development and Maintaining Strong Parent-Child Bond."
24. Pea et al., "Media Use, Face-to-Face Communication, Media Multitasking, and Social Well-being Among 8- to 12-year-old Girls"; S. Oden and S. R. Asher, "Coaching Children in Social Skills for Friendship Making," *Child Development* 48, no. 2 (1977): 495–506.
25. H. C. Foot, A. J. Chapman, and J. R. Smith, "Friendship and Social Responsiveness in Boys and Girls," *Journal of Personality and Social Psychology* 35, no. 6 (1977): 401–411; R. George and N. Browne, "'Are You in or Are You Out?' An Exploration of Girl Friendship Groups in the Primary Phase of Schooling," *International Journal of Inclusive Education* 4, no. 4 (November 2000): 289–300, doi:10.1080/13603110050168005.
26. E. Powers and G. Bultena, "Sex Differences in Intimate Friendships of Old Age," *Journal of Marriage and the Family* 38, no. 4 (November 1976): 739, doi:10.2307/350693.
27. 2010 Tracking Survey, *Internet & American Life Project* (Pew Research Center, September 13, 2010).
28. M. Shermer, "Patternicity: Finding Meaningful Patterns in Meaningless Noise," *Scientific American*, December 2008; S. Murphy, J. Monahan, and R. B. Zajonc, "Additivity of Nonconscious Affect: Combined Effects of Priming and Exposure," *Journal of Personality and Social Psychology* 69, no. 4 (1995): 589–602, doi:10.1037/0022-3514.69.4.589.
29. T. Vaillancourt, S. Hymel, and P. McDougall, "Bullying Is Power," *Journal of Applied School Psychology* 19, no. 2 (December 12, 2003): 157–176, doi:10.1300/J008v19n02_10.
30. M. Camodeca and F. Goossens, "Aggression, Social Cognitions, Anger and Sadness in Bullies and Victims," *Journal of Child Psychology and Psychiatry* 46, no. 2 (February 2005): 186–197, doi:10.1111/j.1469-7610.2004.00347.x.
31. D. G. Dutton et al., "Intimacy-Anger and Insecure Attachment as Precursors of Abuse in Intimate Relationships," *Journal of Applied Social Psychology* 24, no. 15 (August 1994): 1367–1386; D. DiLillo, G. C. Tremblay, and L. Peterson, "Linking Childhood Sexual Abuse and Abusive Parenting: The Mediating Role of Maternal Anger," *Child Abuse & Neglect* 24, no. 6 (June 2000): 767–779; C. Rodriguez and A. Green, "Parenting Stress and Anger Expression as Predictors of Child Abuse Potential," *Child Abuse & Neglect* 21, no. 4 (April 1997): 367–377, doi:10.1016/S0145-2134(96)00177-9.
32. F. W. K. Harper, "The Role of Shame, Anger, and Affect Regulation in Men's Perpetration of Psychological Abuse in Dating Relationships," *Journal of*

Interpersonal Violence 20, no. 12 (December 1, 2005): 1648–1662, doi:10.1177/0886260505278717.

33. P. Gradinger, D. Strohmeier, and C. Spiel, "Motives for Bullying Others in Cyberspace: A Study on Bullies and Bully-victims in Austria," in *Bullying in the Global Village: Research on Cyberbullying from an International Perspective*, eds. Q. Li, D. Cross, and P. Smith (Boston: Wiley Blackwell, 2012), http://www.pdfdownload.org/pdf2html/pdf2html.php?url=http%3A%2F%2Ficbtt.arizona.edu%2Fsites%2Fdefault%2Ffiles%2FCyberbullying_Motives_Gradinger_in_press.pdf&images=yes.

34. K. A. Dodge et al., "Peer Rejection and Social Information-Processing Factors in the Development of Aggressive Behavior Problems in Children," *Child Development* 74, no. 2 (March 2003): 374–393; N. R. Crick and K. A. Dodge, "'Superiority' Is in the Eye of the Beholder: A Comment on Sutton, Smith, and Swettenham," *Social Development* 8, no. 1 (December 25, 2001): 128–131; K. Dodge et al., "Hostile Attributional Biases in Severely Aggressive Adolescents.," *Journal of Abnormal Psychology* 99, no. 4 (1990): 385–392, doi:10.1037/0021-843X.99.4.385.

35. K. Dodge and J. Newman, "Biased Decision-Making Processes in Aggressive Boys," *Journal of Abnormal Psychology* 90, no. 4 (1981): 375–379, doi:10.1037/0021-843X.90.4.375.

36. E. Gondolf, "The Case Against Anger Control Treatment Programs for Batterers," *Response to the Victimization of Women & Children* 9, no. 3 (1986): 2–5.

37. D. Dietrich et al., "Some Factors Influencing Abusers' Justification of Their Child Abuse," *Child Abuse & Neglect* 14, no. 3 (January 1990): 337–345, doi:10.1016/0145-2134(90)90005-E.

38. O. Mammen, D. Kolko, and P. Pilkonis, "Negative Affect and Parental Aggression in Child Physical Abuse," *Child Abuse & Neglect* 26, no. 4 (April 2002): 407–424, doi:10.1016/S0145-2134(02)00316-2.

39. M. B. Eberly and R. Montemayor, "Adolescent Affection and Helpfulness Toward Parents:: A 2-Year Follow-Up," *Journal of Early Adolescence* 19, no. 2 (May 1, 1999): 226–248, doi:10.1177/0272431699019002005.

40. B. Barber, J. Olsen, and S. Shagle, "Associations Between Parental Psychological and Behavioral Control and Youth Internalized and Externalized Behaviors," *Child Development* 65, no. 4 (August 1994): 1120–1136, doi:10.1111/j.1467-8624.1994.tb00807.x.

Chapter 4

1. Respectme.com, 2008.

2. TheOnlineMom.com, 2010, http://www.theonlinemom.com/blog.asp?id=1462&print=true.

3. Cisco, Inc., *Cisco Connected: World Technology Report*, September 21, 2011, http://www.cisco.com/en/US/solutions/ns341/ns525/ns537/ns705/ns1120/CCWTR-Chapter1-Press-Deck.pdf.

4. E. Englander, "Preliminary Report: Bullying and Cyberbullying in Massachusetts 2011–12" (presented at the Workshop: PCP Interventions, Freehold, NJ, 2011).

5. E. Englander, *Study of 21,000 Children in Grades 3–12 in Massachusetts*, Research Reports from the Massachusetts Aggression Reduction Center (Bridgewater State University, June 2011), http://webhost.bridgew.edu/marc/research.html.

6. E. Englander, "Cyberbullying in 8- to 10-Year Olds: Research on 12,000 Children" (presented at the International Bullying Prevention Association Annual Conference, Kansas City, MO, November 5, 2012).

7. N. Willard, "Techno-Panic & 21st Century Education: Make Sure Internet Safety Messaging Does Not Undermine Education for the Future," May 27, 2009, http://my-ecoach.com/project.php?id=16414&project_step=69260.

8. M. Ybarra, M. Diener-West, and P. Leaf, "Examining the Overlap in Internet Harassment and School Bullying: Implications for School Intervention," *Journal of Adolescent Health* 41, no. 6 (December 2007): S42–S50, doi:10.1016/j.jadohealth .2007.09.004.

9. S. Hemphill et al., "Longitudinal Predictors of Cyber and Traditional Bullying Perpetration in Australian Secondary School Students," *Journal of Adolescent Health*, February 2012, doi:10.1016/j.jadohealth.2011.11.019.

10. L. Magid, "Time to Take the 'Cyber' Out of Cyberbullying," CNET News, February 3, 2011, http://news.cnet.com/8301-19518_3-20030511-238.html.

11. D. Olweus, *Aggression in the Schools: Bullies and Whipping Boys* (Oxford, England: Hemisphere, 1978), http://psycnet.apa.org/psycinfo/1979-32242-000.

12. J. Dooley, J. Pyżalski, and D. Cross, "Cyberbullying Versus Face-to-Face Bullying: A Theoretical and Conceptual Review," *Zeitschrift Für Psychologie/Journal of Psychology* 217, no. 4 (2009): 182–188, doi:10.1027/0044-3409.217.4.182.

13. E. Englander, *Freshman Study 2011: Bullying and Cyberbullying*, Research Reports from the Massachusetts Aggression Reduction Center (Bridgewater State University, June 2011), http://webhost.bridgew.edu/marc/research.html.

14. Z. Whittaker, "Nine Out of Ten Teenagers Experience Bullying and Cruelty on Facebook, Twitter," ZDnet, November 9, 2011, http://www.zdnet.com/blog/ igeneration/nine-out-of-ten-teenagers-experience-bullying-and-cruelty-on-facebook-twitter/13321?tag=content;siu-container.

15. Englander, *Study of 21,000 Children in Grades 3–12 in Massachusetts*.

16. C. Naquin, T. Kurtzberg, and L. Belkin, "The Finer Points of Lying Online: E-mail Versus Pen and Paper," *Journal of Applied Psychology* 95, no. 2 (2010): 387–394, doi:10.1037/a0018627.

17. Englander, *Freshman Study 2011*.

18. E. Stephenson, "Is This Exam Hazardous to Your Grandmother's Health?," *Atlantic Economic Journal* 31, no. 4 (December 2003): 384–384, doi:10.1007/ BF02298496.

19. B. Rule and G. Leger, "Pain Cues and Differing Functions of Aggression," *Canadian Journal of Behavioural Science* 8, no. 3 (1976): 213–223, doi:10.1037/h0081949.

20. E. Englander, "Bullying and Cyberbullying in Teens: Clinical Factors" (presented at the American Academy of Child and Adolescent Psychiatry, San Francisco, CA, October 22, 2012), https://aacap.confex.com/aacap/2012/webprogram/ Session8538.html.

21. R. Slaby and N. Guerra, "Cognitive Mediators of Aggression in Adolescent Offenders: I. Assessment," *Developmental Psychology* 24, no. 4 (1988): 580–588.

22. T. Ito, N. Miller, and V. Pollock, "Alcohol and Aggression: A Meta-analysis on the Moderating Effects of Inhibitory Cues, Triggering Events, and Self-focused Attention," *Psychological Bulletin* 120, no. 1 (1996): 60–82, doi:10.1037/0033-2909.120.1.60.

23. J. Blum, "The Digital Skeptic: Teens Are Web-Addicted, but Digital Illiterates," *CantonDailyLedger.com*, June 26, 2012, http://business-news.thestreet.com/cantondailyledger/story/the-digital-skeptic-teens-are-web-addicted-but-digital-illiterates/11596144; Englander, *Freshman Study 2011: Bullying and Cyberbullying*.

24. Englander, *Freshman Study 2011: Bullying and Cyberbullying*.

25. S. Murphy, J. Monahan, and R. B. Zajonc, "Additivity of Nonconscious Affect: Combined Effects of Priming and Exposure," *Journal of Personality and Social Psychology* 69, no. 4 (1995): 589–602, doi:10.1037/0022-3514.69.4.589.

26. Englander, "Bullying and Cyberbullying in Teens: Clinical Factors."

27. E. Englander, "New Findings in Bullying and Cyberbullying Research" (keynote presented at the Wellness Conference for Brevard County, Satellite Beach, FL, September 10, 2012).

28. 2010 Tracking Survey, *Internet & American Life Project* (Pew Research Center, September 13, 2010).

29. E. Englander and A. Muldowney, "Just Turn the Darn Thing Off: Understanding Cyberbullying," in *Proceedings of Persistently Safe Schools: The 2007 National Conference on Safe Schools*, eds. D. L. White, B. C. Glenn, and A. Wimes (presented at the Hamilton Fish Institute, George Washington University, Washington, DC, 2007), 83–92.

30. American Psychiatric Association, "Self-defeating Personality Disorder," *Diagnostic and Statistical Manual of Mental Disorders*, 4th ed. (Washington. DC: American Psychiatric Association, 2005).

31. D. Craven, *Sex Differences in Violent Victimization*, Bureau of Justice Statistics Special Report (Washington, DC: U.S. Department of Justice, 1997).

32. M. Busko, "Anxiety Linked with Increased Cell-Phone Dependence, Abuse" (presented at the Anxiety Disorders Association of America 28th Annual Meeting, Savannah, GA, 2007).

33. D. Trim, "Five Reasons Students Don't Report Cyberbullying," February 24, 2010, http://www.insidetheschool.com/articles/five-reasons-students-don%E2%80%99t-report-cyberbullying/.

34. R. Ortega et al., "The Emotional Impact on Victims of Traditional Bullying and Cyberbullying: A Study of Spanish Adolescents," *Zeitschrift Für Psychologie/Journal of Psychology* 217, no. 4 (2009): 197–204, doi:10.1027/0044-3409.217.4.197.

35. Englander, "Bullying and Cyberbullying in Teens: Clinical Factors."

36. B. Spears et al., "Behind the Scenes and Screens: Insights into the Human Dimension of Covert and Cyberbullying," *Zeitschrift Für Psychologie/Journal of Psychology* 217, no. 4 (2009): 189–196, doi:10.1027/0044-3409.217.4.189.

37. "66% of the Population Suffer from Nomophobia the Fear of Being Without Their Phone," *SecurEnvoy.com*, February 16, 2012, http://blog.securenvoy.com/2012/02/16/66-of-the-population-suffer-from-nomophobia-the-fear-of-being-without-their-phone/.

38. E. Brown, "Volkswagen Turns Off Email for BlackBerry Workers," ZDNet, December 28, 2011, http://www.zdnet.com/blog/feeds/volkswagen-turns-off-email-for-blackberry-workers/4467.

39. G. Butler, M. Fennell, and A. Hackmann, *Cognitive-Behavioral Therapy for Anxiety Disorders: Mastering Clinical Challenges* (New York: Guilford Press, 2010), http://books.google.com/books?hl=en&lr=&id=2QvoM5tBoN8C&oi=fnd&pg=PR1&dq=awareness+mastering+anxiety&ots=V1d9dmrueu&sig=7wMVmcYuk20buMO_uLTAYwwjZmg.
40. Blum, "The Digital Skeptic."
41. M. Shermer, "Patternicity: Finding Meaningful Patterns in Meaningless Noise," *Scientific American*, December 2008.
42. M. Lindeman and M. Saher, "Vitalism, Purpose and Superstition," *British Journal of Psychology* 98, no. 1 (February 2007): 33–44.

Chapter 5

1. "Survey Suggests 'Sexting' Rampant in College," *US News & World Report*, July 21, 2011.
2. "Few Teens Sexting Racy Photos, New Research Says," Associated Press, December 5, 2011.
3. G. Bergen, R. Shults, and R. Rudd, "Vital Signs: Alcohol-Impaired Driving Among Adults—United States, 2010," *Morbidity and Mortality Weekly Report (MMWR)* 69, no. 39 (October 7, 2011): 1351–1356.
4. L. Rainie, A. Lenhart, and A. Smith, "The Tone of Life on Social Networking Sites," *Pew Internet & American Life Project* (Pew Research Center, February 2012), http://pewinternet.org/Reports/2012/Social-networking-climate/Summary-of-findings/The-tone-of-life-on-social-networking-sites.aspx.
5. d. boyd, "Digital Self-Harm and Other Acts of Self-Harassment," *DMLcentral*, December 7, 2010, http://dmlcentral.net/blog/danah-boyd/digital-self-harm-and-other-acts-self-harassment.
6. C. Cuomo, C. Vlasto, and D. Dwyer, "Rep. Anthony Weiner: 'The Picture Was of Me and I Sent It,'" ABC News, *ABCNews.go.com*, June 6, 2011, http://abcnews.go.com/Politics/rep-anthony-weiner-picture/story?id=13774605.
7. E. Englander, "Cyberbullying—New Research and Findings" (paper presented at the 2012 National Cyber Crime Conference, Norwood, MA, 2012).
8. M. Jolicoeur and E. Zedlewski, *Much Ado About Sexting*, unpublished report (Washington, DC: U.S. Department of Justice, June 2010), https://www.ncjrs.gov/pdffiles1/nij/230795.pdf; L. Henderson, "Sexting and Sexual Relationships Among Teens and Young Adults," *McNair Scholars Research Journal* 7, no. 1 (2011): 9, M. Drouin and C. Landgraff, "Texting, Sexting, and Attachment in College Students' Romantic Relationships," *Computers in Human Behavior* 28, no. 2 (March 2012): 444–449.
9. K. J. Mitchell et al., "Prevalence and Characteristics of Youth Sexting: A National Study," *Pediatrics* 129, no. 1 (December 5, 2011): 13–20, doi:10.1542/peds.2011-1730.
10. J. Dake et al., "Prevalence and Correlates of Sexting Behavior in Adolescents," *American Journal of Sexuality Education* 7, no. 1 (January 2012): 1–15, doi:10.1080/15546128.2012.650959.
11. Englander, "Cyberbullying—New Research and Findings."

12. E. Englander, "Bullying and Cyberbullying in Teens: Clinical Factors" (presented at the American Academy of Child and Adolescent Psychiatry, San Francisco, CA, October 22, 2012), https://aacap.confex.com/aacap/2012/webprogram/Session8538.html.

13. J. Ringrose et al., *A Qualitative Study of Children, Young People and "Sexting"* (London: NSPCC, May 2012), http://www2.lse.ac.uk/media@lse/documents/MPP/Sexting-Report-NSPCC.pdf.

14. E. Englander, *Digital Self-harm: Frequency, Type, Motivations and Outcomes* (Bridgewater, MA: Bridgewater State University, June 2012), http://webhost.bridgew.edu/marc/DIGITAL%20SELF%20HARM %20report.pdf.

15. Jolicoeur and Zedlewski, *Much Ado About Sexting.*

16. Mitchell, "Prevalence and Characteristics of Youth Sexting."

17. J. Wolak, D. Finkelhor, and K. J. Mitchell, "How Often Are Teens Arrested for Sexting? Data From a National Sample of Police Cases," *Pediatrics* 129, no. 1 (December 5, 2011): 4–12, doi:10.1542/peds.2011-2242.

18. boyd, "Digital Self-harm and Other Acts of Self-Harassment."

19. L. Phelps, ed., *Health-Related Disorders in Children and Adolescents: A Guidebook for Understanding and Educating* (Washington , DC: American Psychological Association, 1998).

20. E. Englander, "Preliminary Report: Bullying and Cyberbullying in Massachusetts 2011–12" (presented at the Workshop: PCP Interventions, Freehold, NJ, 2011).

21. E. Englander, "Cyberbullying in 8- to 10-Year Olds: Research on 12,000 Children" (presented at the International Bullying Prevention Association Annual Conference, Kansas City, MO, November 5, 2012).

22. Q. Li, "Cyberbullying in Schools: An Examination of Preservice Teachers' Perception," *Canadian Journal of Learning and Technology* 34, no. 2 (2008).

23. "Teachers' Newest Online Worry: 'Cyberbaiting,'" *ESchoolNews*, November 27, 2011, http://www.eschoolnews.com/2011/11/27/teachers-newest-online-worry-cyberbaiting/.

24. Ibid.

25. I. Parker, "The Story of a Suicide," *NewYorker.com*, February 6, 2012, http://www.newyorker.com/reporting/2012/02/06/120206fa_fact_parker?currentPage=all.

26. Englander, "Cyberbullying—New Research and Findings."

27. B. Rochman, "Am I Pretty or Ugly? Why Teen Girls Are Asking YouTube for Validation," *Time.com*, March 7, 2012, http://healthland.time.com/2012/03/07/am-i-pretty-or-ugly-whats-behind-the-trend-of-girls-asking-youtube-for-validation/.

Chapter 6

1. G. L. Kelling and J. Q.Wilson, "Broken Windows: The Police and Neighborhood Safety," *The Atlantic*, March 1982, http://www.theatlantic.com/magazine/archive/1982/03/broken-windows/4465/.

2. J. Wang, R. Iannotti, and T. Nansel, "School Bullying Among Adolescents in the United States: Physical, Verbal, Relational, and Cyber," *Journal of Adolescent Health* 45, no. 4 (October 2009): 368–375, doi:10.1016/j.jadohealth.2009.03.021; R. Faris

and D. Felmlee, "Social Networks and Aggression at the Wheatley School" (Department of Sociology, University of California, Davis, 2011); E. Englander, *Study of 21,000 Children in Grades 3–12 in Massachusetts*, Research Reports from the Massachusetts Aggression Reduction Center (Bridgewater State University, June 2011), http://webhost.bridgew.edu/marc/research.html.

3. E. Englander, *Freshman Study 2011: Bullying and Cyberbullying*, Research Reports from the Massachusetts Aggression Reduction Center (Bridgewater State University, June 2011), http://webhost.bridgew.edu/marc/research.html.

4. M. Wright Edelman, "Zero Tolerance Discipline Policies: A Failing Idea," *Huffington Post*, August 5, 2011, http://www.huffingtonpost.com/marian-wright-edelman/zero-tolerance-discipline_b_919649.html?view=print&comm_ref=false.

5. "Study Shows Bullying Affects Both Bystanders and Target," Penn State News, October 11, 2011, http://live.psu.edu/story/55627.

6. G. Gini et al., "The Role of Bystanders in Students' Perception of Bullying and Sense of Safety," *Journal of School Psychology* 46, no. 6 (December 2008): 617–638, doi:10.1016/j.jsp.2008.02.001.

7. R. Casella, "The Benefits of Peer Mediation in the Context of Urban Conflict and Program Status," *Urban Education* 35, no. 3 (September 1, 2000): 324–355, doi:10.1177/0042085900353004.

8. N. Burrell, C. Zirbel, and M. Allen, "Evaluating Peer Mediation Outcomes in Educational Settings: A Meta-analytic Review," *Conflict Resolution Quarterly* 21, no. 1 (2003): 7–26, doi:10.1002/crq.46.

9. S. Theberge and O. Karan, "Six Factors Inhibiting the Use of Peer Mediation in a Junior High School," *Professional School Counseling* 7, no. 4 (2004): 283–291.

10. Ibid.; E. Delisio, "Making Peer Mediation a Part of Campus Life," *Education-World.com*, 2004, http://www.educationworld.com/a_admin/admin/admin348.shtml.

11. C. Morgan, "Student to Student: The Use of Peer Mediation to Stop Bullying," Voices.Yahoo.Com, June 1, 2010, http://voices.yahoo.com/student-student-peer-mediation-stop-6113012.html?cat=17.

12. R. J. Adams, "Bullying Basics for K–12 and the Workplace," Awesomelibrary.org, 2011, http://www.awesomelibrary.org/bullying.html.

13. U.S. Department of Education, "Bullying: Peer Abuse in Schools," *LD Online*, 1998, http://www.ldonline.org/article/6171/.

14. E. Englander, "When Should You Hesitate to Mediate?," *Models of Respecting Everyone* 1, no. 1 (2005): 2–3.

15. E. Englander, "Cyberbullying—New Research and Findings" (presented at the 2012 National Cyber Crime Conference, Norwood, Massachusetts, 2012).

16. U.S. Department of Justice, *Want to Resolve a Dispute? Try Mediation*, Youth In Action Bulletin (Washington, DC: National Crime Prevention Council, March 2000), https://www.ncjrs.gov/pdffiles1/ojjdp/178999.pdf.

17. H. Garinger, "Girls Who Bully: What Professionals Need to Ask," *Guidance and Counseling* 21, no. 4 (Summer 2006): 236–243, doi:Article.

18. "Teachers Tell Bullied Kids: Don't Be So Gay," *Echo*, November 2, 2011, http://www.echo-news.co.uk/news/local_news/9337363.Teachers_tell_bullied_kids__Don_t_be_so_gay/?action=complain&cid=9788420.

19. N. Willard, *Safe and Responsible Use of the Internet: A Guide for Educators* (Responsible Netizen Institute, Eugene, OR, 2002), http://responsiblenetizen.org.
20. Ibid.

Chapter 7

1. R. Atlas and D .Pepler, "Observations of Bullying in the Classroom," *Journal of Educational Research* 92, no. 2 (November 1998): 86–99, doi:10.1080/00220679809597580.
2. P. O'Connell, D. Pepler, and W. Craig, "Peer Involvement in Bullying: Insights and Challenges for Intervention," *Journal of Adolescence* 22, no. 4 (August 1999): 437–452, doi:10.1006/jado.1999.0238.
3. U.S. Department of Education, "Bullying: Peer Abuse in Schools," *LD Online*, 1998, http://www.ldonline.org/article/6171/; J. Trach et al., "Bystander Responses to School Bullying: A Cross-Sectional Investigation of Grade and Sex Differences," *Canadian Journal of School Psychology* 25, no. 1 (March 2, 2010): 114–130, doi:10.1177/0829573509357553.
4. S. Davis and C. Nixon, *The Youth Voice Project* (Penn State Erie, stopbullyingnow.com, March 2010), http://www.youthvoiceproject.com/.
5. E. Englander, "Cyberbullying—New Research and Findings" (presented at the 2012 National Cyber Crime Conference, Norwood, MA, 2012).
6. A. Lenhart et al., *Teens, Kindness and Cruelty on Social Network Sites* (Pew Internet and American Life Project, November 9, 2011).
7. D. Olweus, *Bullying at School: What We Know and What We Can Do* (Oxford , England: Blackwell, 1993).
8. C. Salmivalli, "Bullying and the Peer Group: A Review," *Aggression and Violent Behavior* 15, no. 2 (March 2010): 112–120, doi:10.1016/j.avb.2009.08.007.
9. K. Konstantina and S. Pilios-Dimitris, "School Characteristics as Predictors of Bullying and Victimization Among Greek Middle School Students," *International Journal of Violence and School* 11 (September 2010): 93–113.
10. O'Connell, Pepler, and Craig, "Peer Involvement in Bullying."
11. Ibid.
12. M. Langevin, "Helping Children Deal with Teasing and Bullying" (presented at the International Stuttering Awareness Day Online Conference, Minnesota State University, October 22, 2001), http://www.mnsu.edu/comdis/isad4/papers/langevin.html.
13. A. Rolider and M. Ochayon, "Bystander Behaviours Among Israeli Children Witnessing Bullying Behaviour in School Settings," *Pastoral Care in Education* 23, no. 2 (June 2005): 36–39, doi:10.1111/j.0264-3944.2005.00330.x.
14. U.S. Department of Education, "Bullying: Peer Abuse in Schools."
15. J. Carney, C. Jacob, and R. Hazler, "Exposure to School Bullying and the Social Capital of Sixth-Grade Students," *Journal of Humanistic Counseling* 50, no. 2 (September 2011): 238–253, doi:10.1002/j.2161-1939.2011.tb00122.x.
16. I. Rivers et al., "Observing Bullying at School: The Mental Health Implications of Witness Status," *School Psychology Quarterly* 24, no. 4 (2009): 211–223, doi:10.1037/a0018164.

17. R. Faris and D. Felmlee, "Social Networks and Aggression at the Wheatley School" (Department of Sociology, University of California, Davis, 2011); Davis and Nixon, *The Youth Voice Project*; Lenhart et al., *Teens, Kindness and Cruelty on Social Network Sites.*
18. E. Englander, *Study of 21,000 Children in Grades 3–12 in Massachusetts*, Research Reports from the Massachusetts Aggression Reduction Center (Bridgewater State University, June 2011), http://webhost.bridgew.edu/marc/research.html.
19. M. Fekkes, "Bullying: Who Does What, When and Where? Involvement of Children, Teachers and Parents in Bullying Behavior," *Health Education Research* 20, no. 1 (July 14, 2004): 81–91, doi:10.1093/her/cyg100.
20. L. Crothers, J. Kolbert, and W. Barker, "Middle School Students' Preferences for Anti-Bullying Interventions," *School Psychology International* 27, no. 4 (October 1, 2006): 475–487, doi:10.1177/0143034306070435.
21. K. Rigby and D. Bagshaw, "Prospects of Adolescent Students Collaborating with Teachers in Addressing Issues of Bullying and Conflict in Schools," *Educational Psychology* 23, no. 5 (December 2003): 535–546, doi:10.1080/0144341032000123787.
22. D. Pepler et al., "A School-based Anti-bullying Intervention: Preliminary Evaluation," *Understanding and Managing Bullying* (1993): 76–91.
23. C. Murphy and V. Baxter, "Motivating Batterers to Change in the Treatment Context," *Journal of Interpersonal Violence* 12, no. 4 (August 1, 1997): 607–619, doi:10.1177/088626097012004009.
24. M. Ando, "Psychosocial Influences on Physical, Verbal, and Indirect Bullying Among Japanese Early Adolescents," *Journal of Early Adolescence* 25, no. 3 (August 1, 2005): 268–297, doi:10.1177/0272431605276933.
25. M. Camodeca et al., "Links Between Social Information Processing in Middle Childhood and Involvement in Bullying," *Aggressive Behavior* 29, no. 2 (March 2003): 116–127, doi:10.1002/ab.10043.
26. W. M. Craig and D. J. Pepler, "Observations of Bullying and Victimization in the School Yard," *Canadian Journal of School Psychology* 13, no. 2 (January 1, 1998): 41–59, doi:10.1177/082957359801300205.
27. B. Stiller, M. S. Tomlanovich, and R. Nese, "Bully Prevention in Positive Behavior Support: K–8 Adaptations" (presented at the Northwest PBIS Conference, Oregon State University, 2011), http://www.pbisnetwork.org/wp-content/uploads/2011/02/Bully-Prevention-B-Stiller-1.4.pdf.
28. Crothers, Kolbert, and Barker, "Middle School Students' Preferences for Anti-Bullying Interventions."
29. Davis and Nixon, *The Youth Voice Project.*
30. L. Crothers, J. Field, and J. Kolbert, "Navigating Power, Control, and Being Nice: Aggression in Adolescent Girls' Friendships," *Journal of Counseling and Development* 83, no. 3 (July 2005): 349–354, doi:10.1002/j.1556-6678.2005.tb00354.x.
31. E. A. Stewart, C. J. Schreck, and R. L. Simons, "'I Ain't Gonna Let No One Disrespect Me': Does the Code of the Street Reduce or Increase Violent Victimization Among African American Adolescents?," *Journal of Research in Crime and Delinquency* 43, no. 4 (November 1, 2006): 427–458, doi:10.1177/0022427806292338.
32. U.S. Department of Education, "Bullying: Peer Abuse in Schools."

33. Davis and Nixon, *The Youth Voice Project*.
34. G. Sugai, R. Horner, and B. Algozzine, *Reducing the Effectiveness of Bullying Behavior in Schools* (OSEP Center on Positive Behavior Interventions and Supports, April 19, 2011).
35. O'Connell, Pepler, and Craig, "Peer Involvement in Bullying."
36. M. Demaray and C. Malecki, "Perceptions of the Frequency and Importance of Social Support by Students Classified as Victims, Bullies and Bully/Victims in an Urban Middle School," *School Psychology Review* 32, no. 3 (2003): 471–489.
37. E. Menesini et al., "Enhancing Children's Responsibility to Take Action Against Bullying: Evaluation of a Befriending Intervention in Italian Middle Schools," *Aggressive Behavior* 29, no. 1 (January 2003): 1–14, doi:10.1002/ab.80012.
38. Davis and Nixon, *The Youth Voice Project*, 18.

Chapter 8

1. E. Lawrence et al., "Is Psychological Aggression as Detrimental as Physical Aggression? The Independent Effects of Psychological Aggression on Depression and Anxiety Symptoms," *Violence and Victims* 24, no. 1 (February 1, 2009): 20–35.
2. E. Englander, "Cyberbullying—New Research and Findings" (presented at the 2012 National Cyber Crime Conference, Norwood, MA, 2012).
3. E. Englander, "That's Confidential," 2012, http://englanderdownloads.webs.com/thats%20confidential%202011%20small.pdf.
4. E. Englander, "Massachusetts Aggression Reduction Center," Massachusetts Aggression Reduction Center at Bridgewater State University, n.d., http://webhost.bridgew.edu/marc/.
5. N. Darling et al., "Predictors of Adolescents' Disclosure to Parents and Perceived Parental Knowledge: Between- and Within-Person Differences," *Journal of Youth and Adolescence* 35, no. 4 (June 6, 2006): 659–670.
6. *Character Counts! Programs: Ethics of American Youth Survey: Josephson Institute's Report Card*, The Ethics of American Youth: 2010 (Josephson Institute, February 10, 2011), http://charactercounts.org/programs/reportcard/2010/installment02_report-card_honesty-integrity.html.
7. A. Vrij, L. Akehurst, and S. Knight, "Police Officers', Social Workers', Teachers' and the General Public's Beliefs About Deception in Children, Adolescents and Adults," *Legal and Criminological Psychology* 11, no. 2 (September 2006): 297–312.
8. A. Lenhart et al., *Teens, Kindness and Cruelty on Social Network Sites* (Pew Internet and American Life Project, November 9, 2011).
9. Ibid.

Conclusion

1. K. R. Ginsburg, "The Importance of Play in Promoting Healthy Child Development and Maintaining Strong Parent-Child Bonds," *Pediatrics* 119, no. 1 (January 1, 2007): 182–191.
2. "Early Childhood Curriculum and Developmental Theory," in *International Encyclopedia of Education* (Oxford: Elsevier, 2010), 514–519, http://linkinghub.elsevier.com/retrieve/pii/B9780080448947000877.

Appendix B
1. B. Benard, "The Case for Peers," *The Peer Facilitator Quarterly* 8, no. 4 (June 1991): 20–27.
2. L. Camino, "Youth-Led Community Building: Promising Practices from Two Communities Using Community-Based Service-Learning," *Journal of Extension* 43, no. 1 (February 2005): 4–12.

Acknowledgments

My research and teaching is a source of great pleasure for me. I also greatly enjoy helping the tens of thousands of children whom we reach every year through the Massachusetts Aggression Reduction Center. Writing about all this, though, is more laborious and (since writing is essentially a lonely activity) much less interactive. My father once said to me, "Writing isn't nice. What's nice is *having written.*"

And so it is with this book, as it was with my first. I hope the book is helpful—that's how I'll derive my pleasure.

First kudos go to my family, who tolerated a July where they didn't see much of me, and where we didn't go on vacation. Especially my husband, who doesn't need instructions and so readily picks up any baton I lay down. My three wonderful, patient kids make good vetting sources, too.

And thanks to Meghan McCoy, Theresa Enos, Ellen Kelliher, and all the students in TeamMARC, who work so devotedly with educators and children in Massachusetts and beyond, and whose dedication gave me the brain-space I needed to conceptualize this book.

A third thanks to Caroline Chauncey and the others at Harvard Education Press, for being consistently encouraging but not pulling punches.

Mostly, though, this book is dedicated to teachers—I know how corny that sounds, and I know how many of you have suffered through pabulum speeches about how Little Timmy Was Saved By A Special Teacher. But I will tell you that in my heart of hearts, I truly believe that there is nothing more important than children. And the caregivers of children, for that reason, command a special respect and regard. Never let anyone convince you that you are simply teaching content. As Aristotle held, you are teaching children *how to live.*

About the Author

ELIZABETH KANDEL ENGLANDER is a professor of psychology and the founder and director of the Massachusetts Aggression Reduction Center (MARC) at Bridgewater State University. MARC delivers antiviolence and antibullying programs, resources, and research for the state of Massachusetts and nationwide. Dr. Englander is a nationally recognized researcher and expert in the area of bullying and cyberbullying; childhood causes of violence, aggression, and abuse; and child development. She has a particular interest in technological aggression and how it interacts with peer abusiveness in general. MARC is the only center in public higher education that provides no- or low-cost cutting-edge programs and research for hundreds of schools every year. Dr. Englander trains and supervises graduate and undergraduate students and collaborates with multiple agencies around Massachusetts and across the nation.

Dr. Englander writes for both academic audiences and the public. She was the special editor for the Cyberbullying issue of the *Journal of Social Sciences*, and has written nearly a hundred articles in academic journals and books. She is the author of *Understanding Violence*, a standard academic text in the field of child development, biological psychology, and violent criminal behavior, which was released in 2007 in its third edition. She has also written a variety of curricula and educational handouts for communities, all of which are offered to K–12 schools at no charge. Reflecting her interest in educating laypeople as well, Dr. Englander has answered questions in a column for the *New York Times* (online edition), and she writes the column *Bullying Bulletin Board*, which is syndicated by Gatehouse Media in hundreds of newspapers nationwide. She has appeared on National Public Radio, Public Broadcasting Service, CBS News, and other media outlets, and has been cited by the *New York Times*, the *Wall Street Journal*, the *Boston Globe*, and many other magazines and newspapers.

Additional resources for *Bullying and Cyberbullying* can be found at Dr. Englander's website, http://www.elizabethenglander.com.

Index

abuse behaviors, 7–8
aggression in children, 54, 67–68, 75
alcohol use and aggression, 75
American Academy of Pediatrics, 164
Association for Childhood Education, 164
attachment and parenting, 67
aware peers in bullying, 125. *See also* bystanders

bias-based harassment, 40
boys
  changes in the nature of friendships, 62–63
  frequency of self-bullying, 91
  preference for reporting bullying to friends, 132
  reports of being pressured or coerced to sext, 86
  sensitivity to escalation of emotions, 77
  social cues' impact on aggression levels, 75
  tolerance for online threats, 24, 28–29
  understanding of privacy online, 98–99
  video game playing and aggression levels, 54
  view of adult responses to bullying, 135
  vulnerability to bullying, 48

broken windows theory, 103
bully-friends, 125. *See also* bystanders
bullying
  abusive nature of the behavior, 7–8
  addressing risks associated with, 162–163
  basis of reducing, 161
  changes in the nature of, 161–162
  characteristics of, 15–16, 52, 70–71
  children's use of the term, 5–6
  child versus adult perspective regarding, 27–29
  commonality with cyberbullying, 33–37
  complications regarding eliminating, 27–30
  consequences of downplaying the seriousness of, 6–7, 29
  consistency of the adult response importance, 162
  defined, 5
  developmental issues in children and, 163–164
  digital revolution and (*see* digital communications)
  distinguishing from cyberbullying, 70–71, 77–78
  educational play and, 61–62, 164
  fundamental complexities of, 1–2